Excellence
in Leadership

Excellence
in Leadership

Frank Goble

THE PRESIDENTS ASSOCIATION

International standard book number: 0-8144-5306-6
Library of Congress catalog card number: 72-79880

First printing

To
Donald B. Milliken
Friend and Associate

Foreword

IN the coming years it may well be said that the seventies were those years in which management ceased to be a *craft* dedicated primarily to the creation of economic wealth. It may be said that management came into its own as a *state of the art* to be pursued and applied to the whole human condition—to all types of organizations and institutions.

This state of the art may and can be a product of a synthesis, a multidisciplinary melding of diverse theories, principles, and practices into effective results-compelling cybernetic systems. The needs of this planet ache for leaders—managers—who possess the macrocosmic vision to bring about new, efficient, and humane solutions to a myriad of microcosmic problems.

The author, out of a career rich in practical experience and scholarly research, has provided us with just such a book. Its contents enable the mind of the reader to soar while requiring that he keep his feet firmly rooted in daily reality.

One gets the feeling he is listening—and talking—with a wise, tested, and concerned anthologist.

One also gains the feeling that here is a book which illustrates a healthy humbleness—an awareness that no one philosophy, theory, discipline, or "school of thought" provides all answers. Rather, that there is much to be gained from all types of people, situations, and events.

It is admittedly committed to excellence, and I warmly commend it to all who persist in that elusive and exciting quest.

Joe D. Batten

Preface

NEVER before in history have there been such numbers and varieties of organizations as there are today.

It is obvious that as the number, size, and complexity of these organizations increase, so does the need for competent leaders.

Peter Drucker, a respected name in management circles, has written: "The emergence of management as an essential, a distinct and leading institution, is a pivotal event in social history. Rarely, if ever, has a brand new basic institution, a new leading group, emerged as fast as has management since the turn of this century. Rarely in human history has a new institution proven indispensable so quickly." [1]

Drucker's words emphasize the fact that while leadership may never become an exact science, it is at the same time rapidly attaining the status of a profession.

The days of the "self-made leader," the man who has grown up with a business, knows it intimately, and relies primarily on personal experience and trial and error methods are numbered. Organizations today require leaders whose personal experience is supplemented by a thorough understanding of theory based on broad research. This is not to minimize the importance of firsthand experience. On the contrary, leadership skills can only be developed through practice. But the secret is to know what to practice.

So I feel it is a fact that executives, administrators, managers, supervisors, and foremen, both neophytes and veterans, need all the help they can get.

And help there is. There has been an explosive increase in research into and understanding of leadership and organizational dynamics. The increase has been so rapid that the majority of Americans, even the majority of executives themselves, are not fully aware of the important

[1] *The Practice of Management*, Harper & Row, New York, 1954, p. 3.

new knowledge. Studies conducted by trade associations, universities, and industry itself have analyzed the success and failure of thousands of organizations and their leaders. Management consultants, leaders, and scholars who have kept abreast of the rapidly developing technology have a better understanding of leadership than ever before in world history.

There is no shortage of literature or advice about leadership. Busy executives are deluged with ideas from every quarter. To read it all is impossible. The solution is to separate the wheat from the chaff, which is precisely what I have attempted to do in this book. I have sought to identify fundamental concepts common to all sizes and types of organizations.

Although the vast majority of research studies and case histories cited in this book come from business and industry, it is important to remember that the principles developed are common to all organizations. There are profound differences between organizations. Some are small and struggling for existence, others are old and coasting on their past reputations. Objectives of public institutions such as varying levels of government, universities, schools, hospitals, churches, etc., are very different from those of industry. And yet when it comes to people, the basic problems are very similar. For the small organization, the best way to remain small is to believe that those "big company ideas don't apply to us." There is a growing body of knowledge about leadership and organizational dynamics which has broad cross-cultural application.

What I have done is to describe, as accurately as the present state of the profession permits, what leaders are and what they must know and do. The attempt to define leadership should be a continuing effort, and while the publishers might wish that I didn't say so, this book will already be a little obsolete before the ink is dry on the first printing. Nor will this book, or any book for that matter, complete the job. Its role will be approximately the same as a book entitled *How to Play Golf*. Everyone knows that reading a book on golf will only help if you then practice what you have read. So, too, with a book on leadership.

Naturally my ideas about leadership have been heavily influenced by my 25 years with D. B. Milliken Company, as well as previous experience with a variety of organizations including the U.S. Post Office, Lockheed Aircraft, and Diamond Match Company.

In addition, the book is based on the Thomas Jefferson Research Center's nine-year analysis of the behavioral sciences, with particular emphasis on the application of the research findings to leadership, education, and the solution of motivational problems of individuals, organizations, and society.

The Center's research has involved hundreds of executives, psychologists, psychiatrists, management consultants, and behavioral scientists. A unique feature of the research is its emphasis on the systems approach —a coordinated, multidisciplinary approach to behavioral problems.

An important aspect of the Research Center's activities has been the continuous attempt to communicate our findings in a meaningful way to a variety of audiences through lectures, seminars, publications, and consulting.

In the early sixties something happened that had a profound effect on my understanding of leadership.

At D. B. Milliken we began to discover that the most effective way to run an organization was by the use of goals, coordinated teams, and positive motivation. We had stumbled into a crude form of McGregor's Theory Y, combined with the use of objectives. What resulted was enthusiasm, high morale, increased productivity, and a period of rapid and profitable growth.

More than a decade has passed since Douglas McGregor captured the imagination of many thousands of leaders and scholars with his *Human Side of Enterprise*. It is becoming apparent to an increasing number of executives that people rather than technology determine the success or failure of organizations. It is, as management consultant M. Scott Myers says, "The challenge of increasing human effectiveness [that] is emerging as the remaining frontier offering competitive advantage to the organizations most successful in channeling human talent and energy into constructive outlets. The reservoir is vast and talent at all levels is poorly utilized." [2]

This book emphasizes the human aspects of leadership. This is the most important, the most misunderstood, the most controversial aspect of leadership.

Many individuals have contributed directly or indirectly to the book. The names of all the people and organizations whose ideas and research are cited appear throughout the text and in the references. I am indebted to the late Dr. Abraham Maslow, who through his many publications and in our personal conversations had a great influence on my thinking.

Others who have made personal contributions to my understanding of various aspects of psychology and leadership are Joe Batten, John

[2] *Every Employee a Manager*, McGraw-Hill, New York, 1970, p. xii.

Boyle, Lloyd Marquis, Jim Newman, Earl Nightingale, Dr. William Glasser, Hobart Mowrer, and Myron Allen.

I have drawn heavily on research conducted at Texas Instruments Inc. directed by Dr. M. Scott Myers. TI has pioneered in converting modern motivational theory into practice with impressive results. And I have referred frequently to research conducted at the University of Michigan's Institute for Social Research as reported by Rensis Likert, its former director, and Stanley Seashore, who presently holds that position. The Institute is one of the largest behavioral research centers in the nation, and has conducted extensive leadership research since 1947.

I am grateful for the assistance of Amelia Manning, Mary Smulo, and Helen Streit, who helped with the research and typing of the manuscript, and to Peggy Granger and Jim Yates for their editorial assistance.

Our American society desperately needs excellent leadership. World society as well needs people who not only know how to lead but where to lead. If this book contributes to the continuing attempt to define and develop excellent leadership, it will have served its purpose.

Frank Goble

Contents

1

The Men at the Top

*No organization is sounder than the men who run
it and delegate others to run it.*   Alfred P. Sloan, Jr.

IF there is one ingredient essential to the success of *any* organization, it
is leadership. Peter Drucker put it succinctly: "If an enterprise fails to
perform, we rightly hire not different workers, but a new president."
The importance of leadership may be obvious to experienced executives,
but if we observe the casual way in which many organizations select and
train their leaders we must conclude that the majority of people in
society are not fully aware of the importance of leadership, or have not
even thought about it.

For many years I thought manufacturing success was a quality
product, manufacturing competence and successful selling. Then one
day I walked into the lobby of an electronics manufacturing plant, one
we had done business with for years. I sensed that something had
changed. The plant was a division of a large corporation but had enjoyed
considerable autonomy, and attitudes from top to bottom were both
dynamic and cooperative, and production had gone steadily upward. Now
almost overnight people were less enthusiastic, less willing to make decisions, less cooperative among themselves and with suppliers. I learned
later that the parent corporation had been acquired by a still larger
organization and as a result a new plant manager had taken over this
division.

Almost from the day of the change in leadership the productivity of
the plant started downward. Within a few months some of the most
valuable people were gone—either fired or resigned. A year later I ob-

Note: Sources are cited in full at the end of the book.

served the same phenomenon in another concern. It is astonishing how quickly a change at the top can change attitudes and behavior throughout an organization.

The literature of management contains many examples of change, sometimes for the better, sometimes for the worse. One electronics corporation had grown rapidly for ten years, with gross sales reaching a level of $72 million and profits of $4 million in the tenth year. But suddenly, in the next year sales dropped to about $70 million and the company lost $3 million. A consulting firm called in by the board of directors to analyze the situation found that the organization had outgrown its leadership. At the consultants' advice, the directors brought in a new and experienced manager, and in the next year sales reached $84.1 million and profits $3.2 million.

During the prosperous sixties, Dun & Bradstreet reported an average of more than 13,000 business failures annually and their analysis showed that the lion's share of these casualties (approximately 92%) were due to managerial deficiencies.

McKinsey & Company made a study, in the early sixties, of the success and failure of a number of printing concerns.[1] The printing industry is unusual in several respects. There are few trade secrets or unique patented processes, and the same types of equipment, materials and methods are used throughout the industry. It is a highly competitive business and at the time of the study approximately 45,000 companies were competing for business in the United States, with an average of $200,000 to $250,000 annual sales. The largest concern in the industry, Time Inc., represented only 3% of the total market. McKinsey selected 50 companies, 25 with unusually high profits—averaging about 10% before taxes—and 25 firms with average profits below 2%. The profit range for the 50 companies was from plus 17% to minus 8% before taxes.

The study identified four key factors that separated the successful firms from the unsuccessful.

1. Management response to market changes.
2. Cost and price discipline.
3. Coordination of equipment with sales.
4. Skill in managing a business that had grown larger.

The major conclusion from the printing industry study was "the most common difference between high- and low-profit companies is management."

George Doriot is president of the American Research and Development Company, a firm which specializes in investing in very young companies. Doriot believes that the men at the helm of these companies are the most important consideration. Of course, he says, ideas are important too, but, "I'd rather have a grade A man and a grade B idea than a grade B man and a grade A idea."

Nor is the importance of leadership restricted to industrial organizations. Dr. Rensis Likert and his associates analyzed the performance of more than 100 chapters of the League of Women Voters. The study revealed a direct relationship between quality of leadership and organizational performance.

Arnold Toynbee, the distinguished historian, discovered the importance of leadership to the rise and fall of societies. He concluded that "creative minorities" are the successful leaders, more advanced than the majority and responsible for the growth of civilization. When the situation shifts to one where leaders hold their positions by force, or something other than ability, they become what he calls "dominant minorities," and their society ceases to grow.

Current events confirm Toynbee's analysis. Entire nations change direction, sometimes quite suddenly, when their leadership changes. A member of the staff of *U.S. News & World Report* has written about what happened in Syria when General Hafez al-Assad seized control of the country on November 13, 1970.

> Syria has undergone an almost startling transformation. Anti-American tirades have been muted. U.S. tourists are welcomed, and they can pick up visas on the Lebanese-Syrian border in just a few minutes. . . . There is less and less emphasis on Marxist solutions to domestic problems. In a modest way, the government is encouraging private investments. Import bans on dozens of foreign products have been removed and the bazaars are once more filled with raucous bargain hunters. . . . After the seemingly endless and often bloody coups of the past 20 years, there is a spreading sense of order, peace and even relative freedom. The mood of most people can best be described as one of serenity—a word that hasn't been applicable to Syrians since they gained independence from France in 1944.[2]

Salaries paid to men at the top are another indication of their value to society. Some of the highest salaries in the United States go to leaders of business, labor unions, government and other organizations. Richard Gerstenberg, chairman of the board of General Motors, receives salary and other benefits totaling approximately $750,000 a year. The salary-plus-bonus for Ford and Chrysler chief executives is over $600,000, and for Standard Oil of New Jersey, IBM, and Mobil Oil more than $400,000. Each year recently a group of General Motors stockholders has introduced a proposal to limit executive salaries and bonuses to a $350,000 maximum. Just as frequently, the proposal is voted down. And at a recent meeting, the "no" votes represented 92.8% of General Motors stock.

A memorandum from the Bonus and Salary Committee at General Motors to the GM Board of Directors, and printed in the Corporation's proxy statement in reply to the proposal to limit executive salaries, said, "The success of any business enterprise must be attributable in large part to the quality of its management; it is people and their leadership which constitute the fundamental difference between one enterprise and another."

Nor are the rewards of leadership merely financial. Men at the top receive respect, recognition, and a host of other benefits.

Are Leaders Born?

For centuries men endowed with the mysterious qualities of leadership have appeared in society. Popular opinion has held that such men were born, not made. Plato wrote, "There must be discovered to be some natures who want to study philosophy and be leaders in a state, and others who were not born to be philosophers, but who are meant to be followers."

Today, because of the vast amount of research that has been undertaken, this image of leadership has changed. Perhaps there are innate characteristics that make some more qualified than others, but there is little doubt that any reasonably intelligent individual can learn to be a competent leader.

Stanley Seashore, director of the Institute for Social Research, states, "Management involves skills and attitudes that can be defined, taught and learned, and these skills and attitudes need not be confined to high-rank staff; each member of the organization, at least in some limited degree, must learn to help manage his own work and that of others related to him." [3]

In *Future Shock*, Alvin Toffler talks about the accelerating rate of change. "In economic development alone," he writes, "there is a startling example of the United States going within a single lifetime from the dominancy of agriculture (the original basis of civilization) to industrialism, and then to the world's first service economy." He says most people are grotesquely unable to cope with the accelerating change.

Our ideas about leadership are changing too and very rapidly. As we have said, the days of the "self-made" leader are numbered. These men are being replaced by professionals who understand theory as well as practice—men who supplement personal experience with the accumulated experience of others.

Warren Bennis, who followed Douglas McGregor at MIT's School of Management, remarked that prior to World War II there were only a handful of training courses in the entire United States seeking to teach advanced management principles to business executives. And Lawrence Appley, past president of the American Management Association, says that even in the late forties professional management techniques were understood and used by only a few isolated managers. "It was not known what managers should know nor was there any organized attempt to see that they were taught. They learned through exposure, and their know-how was a great mass of unrelated unorganized information." Appley considers the development of management as a profession "the most dramatic development in our society during the past quarter of a century."

Today many thousands of supervisors, executives and administrators are enrolled in training programs in colleges and universities, as well as in their organizations, and with professional societies and management consultants. Perrin Stryker describes this educational explosion as "potentially a more beneficial lesson for mankind than all the wonders of scientific technology." He predicts that the "twentieth century might be recorded as the epoch in which men for the first time attempted to cultivate methodically and on a large scale a class of superior managers."

What Is a Professional Leader?

Each fall hundreds of thousands of Americans spend prime recreation hours on hard stadium seats or else glued to television sets watching "professional" football. Why are the players called professionals? Because they earn their living playing football—they are not amateurs. The term means more than this, however; it means they are the best at what they do; they get results. They are not called professionals because they have completed some prescribed course of instruction, or graduated from the right college, or had a specified number of years of experience. They are professionals for only one reason and that is their *ability to perform.*

It is customary to describe doctors, lawyers, engineers, architects, and others with similar vocations as professionals because they have met certain prescribed requirements of study and practice. It is *assumed* that individuals who meet these professional requirements have the ability to perform competently. Thus we have two similar but actually quite different meanings for the word "professional."

The professional leader, as I use the term, refers to one whose principal characteristic is not academic achievement or years of experience, but like the football professional, *excellent performance*. If our society would pick leaders with as much care and intelligence as the National Football League teams pick their quarterbacks, the benefits to our society might be much greater than most people imagine.

Leader in this book refers to one who guides or directs the activities of others. This includes such terms as *president, director, administrator, executive, manager, superintendent, supervisor, department head, foreman, dean,* and so forth. It is a broader term than manager, which has traditionally been most closely associated with industry.

How does the professional leader differ from the amateur, the average, the mediocre? This is the question to which I have addressed myself. I have sought to create a model of professional excellence for leaders and their organizations; a model which applies to large organizations and small of all types including government, universities and even churches. And because we are dealing with fundamentals, this model applies, for the most part, to every level of supervision within the organization as well.

Leadership knowledge and ability may be divided into three general categories:

1. Technical
2. Organizational
3. Psychological

The technical aspects of leadership vary considerably from organization to organization. Here we include all the specialized knowledge pertaining to the activities of each organization. The printing executive, for example, must have a general knowledge of papers, inks, printing processes, typography, etc.

In addition to a general understanding of things peculiar to his organization, each leader needs a working knowledge of technical functions pertinent to all organizations, such as accounting, law, in-plant maintenance. This knowledge is common to most organizations, and people who have it are readily transferable from industry to industry; their skills are primarily technical rather than social.

It is well known that specialists as such make poor executives. The effective executive is a generalist. Men in positions of leadership should be fully aware of this simple but important fact. They must be generally familiar with the various technical aspects of their organization, but must leave technical details to others. Alfred Marrow, Harwood Companies Inc. board chairman, writes:

> It could usually be assumed in the past that the supervisors or managers were the most broadly skilled or technically knowledge-able persons in the enterprise. This assumption is no longer safe. It is now common that employees are more technically skilled than their supervisors. Even at the highest management level, it is no longer unusual for a staff of Ph.D.'s in physics to be directed and coordinated by a company president who has only an elementary college science course. But this is no handicap, for a manager's specialty is management, not science.[4]

A discussion of the specifics of technical knowledge is beyond the scope of this book, nor would such a discussion even be in order. Professional leaders need a systematic plan to identify, obtain and renew general knowledge of the technical aspects of their organizations. This process should not be left to chance; it should be a specific personal goal.

Recognition that executives must be generalists should be an essential premise of leadership training programs. Leadership development programs should systematically seek to increase the trainee's knowledge of the entire business as he moves upward through various levels of supervision.

The organizational aspects of leadership include an understanding of the various social functions of the organization. Here we are dealing primarily with people rather than "things." This category of leadership knowledge includes such items as planning, problem-solving, organizing, staffing, communicating, training and research. These functions are discussed in Chapters 2 through 8.

The third important area is in the realm of psychology, having to do with the executive himself, his personality, attitudes, style, and understanding of self and others. Although psychology is a vital part of leadership, it is the subject most frequently neglected in traditional training courses.

It is here that recent breakthroughs in understanding offer exciting possibilities for rapid improvements in the performance of leaders. The psychological aspects of leadership are discussed in Chapters 9 through 14.

Directors or Trustees

The leadership of public organizations, as well as many private ones, is placed with a board of directors or trustees by law. These boards have the ultimate responsibility for the conduct of the organization in its dealings with employees, suppliers, customers, stockholders (or members) and society. The most important responsibility of the board is to assure quality of the active management. The board selects corporate officers and maintains general surveillance and evaluation of their effectiveness. The ideal board is composed of men who represent a variety of disciplines and can contribute useful knowledge to the organization. It is customary to include both insiders and outsiders on the board. Generally speaking, the outsiders should be in the majority. This enables the board to maintain a reasonable degree of objectivity and is especially important when determining the salaries of those at the top.

Directors normally establish broad objectives and policies and guidelines for the corporation, but leave day-to-day operating decisions to the corporate executives.

The law permits boards to be as small as three in number. But for practical purposes at least five directors are desirable. If the board becomes too large, it is unwieldy. There is no sacred number, but my choice is 9 as an ideal board size, and 11 or 15 as a maximum. Above that, there is a decided loss in effectiveness.

A slightly different situation obtains with colleges, hospitals, and other nonprofit organizations. Their governing body is most frequently called a board of trustees. It is not unusual for the number of trustees to be as high as 30 or more.

Trustees of nonprofit organizations have an important added function —assistance in the solicitation of funds for their organization. This justifies the large board. Such groups should designate a smaller executive committee, preferably 7 to 9, to perform duties similar to a corporate board. Herbert J. Taylor, who has served on many nonprofit boards, names the qualities of trustees as the three W's: Wealth, Wisdom, and Willingness.

In theory, boards of directors are elected by the organization's members or stockholders. In practice, boards tend to be self-perpetuating.

Self-perpetuating boards have a tendency to gradually lose the energy and creativity that companies need to remain dynamic. The problem of aging boards develops so gradually that the problem is seldom recognized until it is almost too late. The best solution is to establish, as early as possible, policies and procedures to maintain a proper balance between youth and experience on the board. Some organizations solve the problem of aging board members by creating honorary or emeritus board memberships.

Board effectiveness is closely related to the competence of the board chairman. He, like the chief executive officer, needs to have a good general knowledge of the organization. It is not unusual in small organizations that the chief executive officer is also chairman of the board. This practice is roughly equivalent to having the company accountant also serve as company auditor. It is common practice for presidents to move up to chairman. This is an excellent solution, provided that the organization has an adequate policy regarding age limitations.

If I were to start a new corporation, I would establish the following operating procedures. I would make the board nine in number, with at least five of them outsiders. I would establish three-year terms, with three directors elected each year, and place a limit of two terms on five directors. That is, at any point in time there would not be more than four directors who served two or more terms. I would also stipulate that not more than three directors should exceed 65 years of age, and not more than one over 75. I would also establish a policy that the directors represent at least five different disciplines, chosen, of course, to suit the needs of the organization.

Over the long run, because they choose the operating executives, boards of directors (or trustees) determine the success or failure of their organizations. They are really the men at the top.

2

Goal Seeking

Success is the progressive
realization of a worthy ideal!   Earl Nightingale

PAUL C. FISHER was president of the Fisher-Armour Manufacturing Company, a screw machine shop, in 1950. Business was terrible and screw machines were worth about 10 cents on the dollar. The company had lost a great deal of money, and less than one week before the beginning of the Korean war, sold out. Fisher lost everything he owned except his clothing, furniture, and an old car. He persuaded one of his former business associates to lend him $24,000 with which to start Fisher Pen Company. But by June of 1951, he had lost another $20,000 and, in addition, had drawn out of the business $6,000 for living expenses. He was on the verge of bankruptcy and expected the sheriff any day.

Tired and discouraged, Paul Fisher took his first vacation in six years. With time to think, it occurred to him that he had been working with tools and machinery for many years. He had learned that it is easy to fool people but impossible to fool a machine. He knew that if a machine is to run properly, it must be tuned and set up correctly.

It occurred to him that the same scientific technique could be applied to running his business. He drafted a set of rules to govern his own actions and a set of rules, written objectives, and policies to govern his business actions. His efforts paid off remarkably. In three months he had made back the $20,000 he had lost the year before, and in less than a year, had paid back the $24,000 loan. Paul Fisher had stumbled onto the most important aspect of professional leadership. This is the way Fisher describes his "Scientific Technique":

DESIRE to reach a DEFINITE OBJECTIVE.

ONE plausible, definite but flexible PLAN for reaching that objective.

FAITH in your ability to carry out the plan.

TRIAL AND ERROR.

ACCURACY of observations, thought, and analysis.[1]

Goal seeking (which can also be called planning, management by objectives, management for results, goal setting, performance standards, or cybernetics) is the starting point for achievement of results. I prefer to call it goal seeking in order to shift the emphasis from the *setting* of goals to the *achievement* of goals, and also to indicate that it is a dynamic process. An achieved goal has lost its usefulness; thus, a professional manager must continually modify his goals.

It is a truism in mechanical engineering that an hour on the drafting board is worth many hours in the shop. Every administrator and supervisor in America should accept and act on the idea that an hour of goal seeking will save hours of organizational effort. He should print the following advice in big letters and put it where he will see it daily.

GOAL SEEKING IS MY MOST IMPORTANT ACTIVITY. AN HOUR OF PLANNING WILL SAVE HOURS IN EXECUTION.

Leadership revolves around goals, and efforts to achieve them. There is nothing more important, more effective, more central. Again and again, men who have studied success have come to this conclusion. This is true not only for the organization but for the individual as well. Napoleon Hill, in his classic, *Think and Grow Rich*, tells about the lives of more than 500 highly successful individuals. He shows, as the name of his book indicates, that these men were thinkers as well as doers. Henry L. Doherty, a great industrialist from an earlier era, said, "I can hire men to do everything but two things: *think*, and *do things in the order of their importance.*"

Frank Bettger was another early advocate of goal seeking. His book, *How I Raised Myself From Failure to Success in Selling*, is still a basic text. Bettger says:

> I set aside Saturday morning and called it "self-organization day." Did this plan help me? Listen! Each Monday morning, when I started out, instead of having to drive myself to make calls, I walked in to see men with confidence and enthusiasm. I was eager and *anxious* to see them because I had thought about them, studied the situation, and had some ideas I believed might be of value to

them. At the end of the week, instead of feeling exhausted and discouraged, I actually felt exhilarated and on fire with the excitement that next week I could do even better.

After a few years, I was able to move my "self-organization day" up to Friday morning, then knock off the rest of the week, forgetting business entirely until Monday morning. It is surprising how much I can get done when I take enough time for planning, and it is perfectly amazing how little I get done without it. I prefer to work on a tight schedule four and a half days a week and get somewhere than to work all the time and never get anywhere.[2]

Earl Nightingale, like Bettger, was determined to succeed. Born in 1921, he was deeply affected by the depression of the 1930s. He was determined not to be poor like his parents, and turned to the public library as a source of ideas about success. He was a voracious reader but could not find the answer he sought. If the subject of goals existed in the literature of the thirties he did not find it. Finally, at the age of 30 he discovered that personal goals were the secret of success. Within five years, this discovery enabled him to succeed as a radio commentator and acquire enough money to retire. Nightingale describes the importance of personal goals in his recording, "The Strangest Secret," a message that every executive, supervisor, and salesman should hear.

Today every good book on management has a section on planning, goal setting, or management by objectives. Yet experienced consultants know that this aspect of management is still little understood and seldom sufficiently utilized. In 1966, Ernest C. Miller published the results of an extensive survey taken in more than 100 companies that were using management-by-objectives techniques. Miller wrote, "Performance standards for executives have been known and used for many years, but their value and potential are only now beginning to be fully realized." [3]

Why is it such a problem for people to plan? I have puzzled over this for years, and concluded that there are two major reasons. The first is that while planning is important it is never urgent. One can put it off easily because of daily emergencies. Of course, planning is the very thing that can keep these same emergencies to a minimum.

The second reason is that the typical executive is a man of action. He is impatient to get the job done. And because of this he has a constant tendency to get on with the job before he has adequately described and planned what he is trying to do.

I have found that executives overcome this when they set aside time on a regular basis for goal seeking. Reserve one-half hour every morning or at the end of the day or whatever time works best for you. Establish this on your calendar and honor it just as you would an appointment with an important customer. Discipline yourself to keep these dates and use them constructively. Once you have satisfied yourself of the tremendous importance of systematic planning, it will become easier.

Organizational planning should be handled in the same way. Meetings for planning are scheduled and held on a regular basis; their frequency depending on the size of the organization and the level of supervision. The higher the level of supervision, the more frequent should be the meetings. In organizations with 100 or more people, the highest management level should meet at least three times a week; preferably daily. The lower levels should meet weekly at least. Large organizations frequently have a corporate planning committee meeting at regular intervals.

Peter Drucker says, "Objectives are needed in every area where performance and results directly and vitally affect the survival and prosperity of the business."

Organizations sometimes establish specific objectives for production people but neglect indirect workers—stenographers, file clerks, tool crib attendants, shipping clerks, maintenance workers and the like. Even crude objectives are better than none.

Snowden Marshall was an industrial engineer working in a Douglas Aircraft plant shortly after World War II. His supervisor suggested that he see what could be done to increase the efficiency of stock room attendants. The factory had 10 stock rooms in the plant receiving and dispensing various raw materials and supplies. Approximately 300 workers were involved.

Marshall had this group make simple stopwatch studies of what they were doing. After a while they developed a list of typical stock room activities, descriptions of the procedures followed and approximate times involved. Then with the agreement of the supervisors involved, it was decided that any two stock room employees who agreed on a new method or procedure could try it to see if it was an improvement. If the new procedure was better then all the workers were encouraged to use it. At the end of the first year, Marshall's simple goal-seeking procedures had increased stock room efficiency by approximately 120%. Actually, Marshall had tapped an important motivational technique: worker involvement.

Goals must be specific and measurable. Vague goals such as "make a profit," "sell as many as possible," or "produce a quality product" won't do. An example of a specific goal for a furniture factory might be to increase gross sales in the next calendar year from $200,000 to $240,000.

This is a specific goal and enables the development of specific plans. This goal calls for average gross sales of $20,000 a month. If business is seasonal the sales should be specified month-by-month. All kinds of decisions stem from a specific goal. The requirements for labor, materials, space, and money can be established and acted upon.

Nonprofit organizations need specific goals, too. A church, for example, might plan for a specific increase in membership for the next 12 months. This is not as simple as it sounds, because many churches are not sure what their membership really is. If this goal is to be meaningful it will require a precise definition of what constitutes membership.

The term "management by objectives" has become popular in the United States and other industrial nations. Although definitions vary, the term generally refers to a systematic organizational effort to establish measurable objectives (goals) at each level in the organization. Supervisors at each level seek to identify key result areas and develop written goals for each of them. Goals at each level in the organization are reached by agreement between the supervisor and his immediate superior. The general practice is that each supervisor develops his own goals, and then presents them to his supervisor for approval. The individual's objectives at each level are integrated with the objectives of the organization as a whole. Some organizations extend the process to individual workers. Objectives at all levels are reviewed on a regular basis—monthly, quarterly, or yearly, and as a general rule, re-established each year.

Hewlett-Packard Company has used management by objectives since the late fifties. Founded in 1939 by David Packard and William Hewlett, the company has grown from its modest beginning into one of the world's largest manufacturers of electronic and analytical computing instrumentation with sales in excess of $350 million annually. In the Appendix we have reprinted the Hewlett-Packard Statement of Corporate Objectives as an example of professional goal seeking.

Goal seeking emphasizes that goals are more important than the methods used to achieve them. This does not mean that the end justifies the means; it means that the end should determine the means. The Dow Chemical Company's Statement of Objectives puts it this way: "We will let ethical ends triumph over means and prefer substance over form; we will keep the goals we set rather than being preoccupied with the method or technique or procedure for reaching them."

Some authorities make a distinction between objectives and goals. Objectives are broad long-range intentions and goals are short range, specific and measurable. Unfortunately there is no standard terminology, most managers use words such as plans, goals and objectives interchangeably. Robert Townsend, former president of Avis, says, "In the case of Avis, it took us six months to define one objective—which turned out to be: 'We want to become the fastest-growing company with the highest profit margin in the business of renting and leasing vehicles without drivers.' " [4]

L. A. Carey of Continental Can writes, "The best long-range plan is one which establishes a broad, flexible objective which can serve as a guideline for subordinate plans and which is not likely to become obsolete as a result of a rapidly changing technology. The classic example, of course, is the buggy-whip manufacturer who set his goal to become the supplier of transportation equipment." [5]

The establishment of broad, long-range objectives can be highly productive. Ed Mayo, founder of Unitek Corporation, manufacturer of miniature spotwelders and orthodontic hardware, told me what happened at his firm. Mayo learned about goal-setting procedures at a one-week seminar presented by the American Management Association. He returned to his Monrovia company determined to put his new knowledge to work. He and 20 of his executives held a weekend retreat at a quiet mountain resort. Ed asked each of those present to write down, in as few words as possible what he thought Unitek was trying to achieve. There were, he said, 20 answers, all of them different. It took long hours to reach agreement on the overall objectives of the organization. A specific byproduct of the conference was the decision to add a new cleaning compound to their line, a decision which more than repaid the cost of the entire weekend. It was Mayo, many years later, who convinced me of the importance of planning. No wonder he was enthusiastic about it; Unitek's sales had increased 700% in ten years.

Control (feedback, evaluation, and modification) is an essential part of the goal-seeking process. This means control of the process rather than control of the people.

In their *Principles of Management,* Koontz and O'Donnell give the following description:

> Control implies measurement of accomplishment against the standard and the correction of deviations to assure attainment of objectives according to plan. Control is understandably closely related to planning. Once a plan becomes operational, control is necessary to measure progress, to uncover deviations from plans, and to indicate corrective action. . . . The essential of control is some sort of feedback.[6]

An important step is to determine the existing situation. Historical records are the usual means to do this, but frequently such records are lacking. Snowden Marshall solved his problem with Douglas stock rooms by developing some crude but simple time standards.

After plans have been established it is necessary to establish a method to provide continuous feedback of information regarding progress toward the plan. Today this process has become almost synonymous with computers. For many organizations computers have made the control process feasible. At the same time many organizations, large and small, achieve highly successful goal-seeking and control procedures without using computers.

Feedback provides the basis for evaluation and modification of plans. If a plan is not working, a new approach may be indicated. In other cases it may be determined that the goal is unrealistically high or low. Goals and plans become more precise and more realistic when goal-seeking procedures are used. Objectives, sometimes vague in the begining, become specific and realistic as the process develops.

I have personally observed executives who have established goals but consistently fail to achieve them. If proper control procedures were followed these executives would become alert to the fact that either the goals were unrealistic or they had failed to plan creatively.

Organizations frequently compare their performance to others in their industry. This is an extremely valuable exercise when such information is available.

Professional leaders use and see that others use goal-seeking procedures at every level of operation—daily, weekly, monthly, yearly, and long range.

Some organizations plan 20 years ahead. Do these organizations actually think they can predict where they'll be in 20 years? No, but the planning process can be highly creative. It enables organizations to identify a problem ahead which requires time to overcome. The National Association of Accountants published an informative study entitled "Long-Range Profit Planning." The report states that it was difficult to find companies (in 1964) that had successful experience with this type of planning. The report states:

> The idea of tying a comprehensive plan of company operations to a definite long-range profit objective is relatively new for most companies. [The process is] a stimulant to management . . . a creative exercise on the part of management . . . planning forces consideration of what the future holds and what management could do about it . . . planning formalizes the managerial process . . . the major benefits of planning [are] to be derived as much from the actual process of making plans as from their implementation or enforcement.[7]

The NAA report stresses the idea that planning activities are just as important for small organizations as they are for large ones.

For use in seminars at the Research Center, we devised a chart that illustrates the goal-seeking process (Exhibit 1). There are also a number of books on the subject. The American Management Association has published several manuals covering objectives for various areas of management. Management consultants experienced in this important area can be extremely helpful to executives who do not know how to proceed.

Exhibit I. The goal-seeking process.

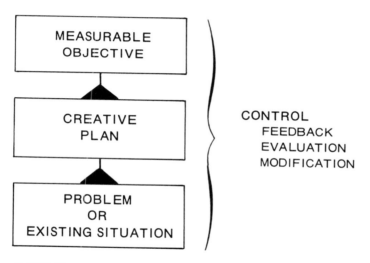

© 1970 Thomas Jefferson Research Center.

Here is a goal-seeking procedure that was devised for a small manufacturing company.

1. The estimated gross annual sales were projected for three years.
2. The total sales figure was converted to a specific quantity for each item in the product line.
3. Estimates were established from the sales projection regarding the required resources of workers, equipment, materials, and plant space.
4. Cash requirements were projected on the basis of estimated income, disbursements, and capital expenditures to obtain the projected sales.
5. The profit potential was determined by subtracting gross expenditures from gross sales.

This type of overall analysis will reveal some of the problems that may inhibit future growth—lack of factory space, machines, trained workers, supervisors, or cash.

Most people tend to act without sufficient planning. Occasionally in our seminars we discovered individuals with the opposite problem; people who tended to make plans but failed to implement them. Such individuals usually lack the courage that comes from experience and self-confidence. The solution lies in learning how to take risks and overcoming inertia. Part of the planning process is to make specific decisions regarding *who* is going to do *what* and *when*. Here is a useful goal-seeking checklist:

1. Recognize goal seeking as the most important activity of leadership.
2. Recognize that, although important, it is never urgent.
3. Set aside specific times for planning activities.
4. Establish specific, measurable goals in all areas of activity.
5. Involve others in planning in a creative way.
6. Establish a creative climate that is tolerant of occasional errors.
7. Train all levels of supervision in planning and see that they do it.
8. Bring in an outside consultant or consultants who understand goal seeking and can act as a catalyst.
9. Learn from the experience of others through studying management literature.
10. Create reminder cards and signs, and post them in prominent places.
11. Recognize goal seeking as a universal technique and apply it in all areas of activity.
12. Establish control—feedback and a system for constant evaluation of plans and objectives.
13. Place the emphasis on goals rather than methods to achieve them.
14. Always consider cost effectiveness.
15. Establish long- as well as short-range goals.
16. See that short-range goals are coordinated with long-range goals.

Professional leadership literally revolves around the establishment of goals and efforts to achieve them Goal seeking is the executive's most important activity.

3

Creative Problem Solving

The Edison Company offered me the general superintendency of the company, but only on condition that I would give up my gas engine and devote myself to something really useful.
Henry Ford, 1922

THE word "creativity" suggests the names and ideas of such men as Newton, Morse, Bell, Marconi, Edison, Fulton, or the Wright brothers. Mention industrial creativity to a group of executives and they will immediately suggest IBM, Xerox, Polaroid, and similar companies. No one can argue with these examples of creativity; they are notable examples of the great American success story. Creativity, however, is much more than the big breakthrough or the expensive research department. Creativity is something that successful people use every day. Edison's definition of creativity was, "There's a way to do it better—find it."

Excellent leadership is a creative process. The American Institute of Management's analysis of the success and failure of thousands of business executives concluded that creative dissatisfaction was one of the essential characteristics of excellence.

In 1953 Continental Can Company, long a major producer of metal containers, undertook a fundamental change in corporate strategy. Corporate executives decided to become suppliers of the best line of packaging products available anywhere in the world. General Lucius Clay, chairman of the board, established a five-year objective: one billion dollars annual gross sales. L. A. Carey, one of the executives, tells this story.

Since our sales the previous year had amounted to barely half that figure after 50 years of steady growth, the announcement of this goal was received with great skepticism. We soon learned, however, that the two objectives were based on a realistic plan and that both of them—diversification of our product line to encompass all forms of packaging and development of volume at an accelerated rate—would be pursued with an absolute single-mindedness of purpose.

The thinking of everyone in the organization had to go through a reeducation process, and in many cases a completely new approach to our business was dictated. We could no longer, as a company, approach every product with the question, "How can it be put in a can?" Instead we had to learn to ask, "How can we best package it?" This produced a mild case of corporate schizophrenia in some instances and required a firm adherence to the basic concept, on the part of top management, in the face of frequent conflicts among the burgeoning product divisions.

Little time was lost in setting the company out on the new course which had been charted for it. In what—in retrospect—seems like an astonishingly short time, we diversified into flexible packaging, glass containers, closures, paper packaging of all types, and, more recently, plastic bottles. Much of this was accomplished through mergers. But a broadening of product lines from within was also undertaken with considerable vigor to close the gaps between the operations which were being acquired. We soon learned that it was much easier to tell our top management why we should add a new product or enter a new market than it was to justify passing it by. If it was a package, it was our responsibility.

The two goals which were set for the company back in 1952 were met ahead of schedule. By 1957 we were major suppliers of virtually every type of package. And our sales passed the one billion mark in 1956—only four years after the decision to expand was made.[1]

The story of Continental Can is an excellent example of imaginative, creative leadership. Leaders limit the success of their organizations to the degree they lack imagination. For an organization to thrive, those at the top must understand creativity, what it is and how to increase it in themselves and at all levels in the organization. "Imagination," said Einstein, "is more important than knowledge." Goal seeking is the most important tool of leadership, but its success depends upon the creativity of those who are using it.

Research regarding human creativity has increased greatly in recent years and the evidence indicates that the vast majority of us are using only a tiny fraction of our creative potential. Years ago a group of university psychologists tested creativity in various age groups. They found that about 2% of 45-year-olds tested out as creative. When they tested a 44-year-old group the figure was the same, and so it was again for those 43 years of age and so on. But when they tested 7-year-old children the number that were highly creative jumped to 10%, and for their 5-year-old test group the figure was 90% creative. They concluded that nearly everyone is born creative but somehow this spark is lost in the growing-up process.

George Prince is the founder of Synectics, a corporation that helps executives rekindle their creative spark. He states, "It is remarkable that in spite of the way we are taught and in spite of all the obstacles, each of us, now and then when the need is great, can reach down and use that buried capacity to reach unusual achievement."

Sheldon Davis, TRW vice president, writes, "The capacity to exercise a relatively high degree of imagination, ingenuity, and creativity in the solution of organizational problems is widely, not narrowly, distributed in the population."

Earl Nightingale and Whitt Schultz collected their ideas about creativity and how to increase it in a tape cassette series entitled "Creative Thinking." They list 25 traits that are generally found in creative people. Not all creative people have all these traits, but they *do* have most of them.

1. *Drive*—a high degree of motivation.
2. *Courage*—tenacity and persistence.
3. *Goals*—a sense of direction.
4. *Knowledge*—and a thirst for it.
5. *Good health.*
6. *Honesty*—especially intellectual.
7. *Optimism.*
8. *Judgment.*
9. *Enthusiasm.*
10. *Chance taking*—the willingness to risk failure.
11. *Dynamism*—health and energy.
12. *Enterprise*—willing to tackle tough jobs.
13. *Persuasion*—ability to sell.
14. *Outgoingness*—friendly.
15. *Communication*—articulate.
16. *Receptive*—alert.
17. *Patient yet impatient*—patient with others yet impatient with the status quo.
18. *Adaptability*—capable of change.

19. *Perfectionism*—seek to achieve excellence.
20. *Humor*—ability to laugh at self and others.
21. *Versatility*—broad interests and skills.
22. *Curiosity*—interested in people and things.
23. *Individualism*—self-esteem and self-sufficiency.
24. *Realism-Idealism*—occupied by reality but guided by ideals.
25. *Imagination*—seeking new ideas, combinations and relationships.[2]

Contrary to the popular conception of genius, many of our famous creative people apparently were not born with unique genetic superiority. J. C. Penney observed, "Geniuses themselves don't talk about the gift of genius; they just talk about hard work and long hours." As Edison said: "Genius is 1% inspiration and 99% perspiration." Penney quoted other famous people who agreed with Edison.

MICHELANGELO: If people knew how hard I worked to get my mastery, it wouldn't seem so wonderful after all.

CARLYLE: Genius is the capacity for taking infinite pains.

PADEREWSKI: A genius? Perhaps, but before I was a genius I was a drudge.

ALEXANDER HAMILTON: All the genius I may have is merely the fruit of labor and thought.

Creative success involves much more than hard work, however. It involves the willingness to make mistakes, too. It is said that Thomas Edison tried ten thousand unsuccessful ways to create a filament for the electric light bulb. When Edison was asked if this didn't discourage him his answer was that these weren't really failures, they were merely the necessary elimination of ideas that wouldn't work.

Dr. Hideki Yukawa, Nobel Prize-winning physicist, said:

Creation is achieved through repeated failures. What, then, makes a person overcome this succession of failures? I feel it is his obsession. This sense of obsession is created in him by a kind of contradiction or conflict. It is important that he have a profound problem on his mind which he cannot get rid of. Should he come to resemble the sage who is untroubled by any such problem, his sense of obsession may vanish.[3]

A number of observers have concluded that the creative individual has the ability to go on despite failures because he has a high self-esteem. His persistence, in other words, is the result of unshakable faith in himself.

What can and should the professional leader do about creativity? First, he should be aware of its importance. Secondly, he should know what it is and how it can be encouraged. Thirdly, armed with this knowledge, he should seek to spark creativity—in himself—and in all those under his jurisdiction. How? There are at least three major possibilities. The first is to increase the amount of time devoted to creative activities. The second is to increase people's creativity through training and development programs. And the third is to develop a more creative climate in the organization.

The first idea may seem too obvious to be valuable but it frequently is overlooked. If an individual has a certain creative capacity, perhaps one idea an hour, and he spends one hour a week in creative thinking, his productivity will be one idea a week. If the same man spends two hours a week in creative thinking, his creative output will presumably double. Multiply this by ten, a hundred, or a thousand people in an organization, and one can see that merely increasing the time allocated to creative activities will increase the creativity of the organization.

L. C. Repucci and J. H. McPherson devoted considerable time and effort to creativity training at Dow Chemical Company, starting in 1954. They concluded that creativity training was useful, but that no single approach was a cure-all. Repucci wrote: "Each adherent of a particular system develops a reasonable rationale for his system and each adherent has some marvelous stories to tell indeed of the efficacy of his particular system. At the same time, each system has a corps of critics who say that the system does not work." [4]

Brainstorming is undoubtedly one of the best-known approaches to creativity. It was developed years ago by Alex Osborn shortly after he took over as executive vice president of Batten, Barton, Durstine and Osborn. In a business where new ideas are absolutely essential, Osborn noted that the majority of idea conferences were negative and nonproductive. He came up with brainstorming—a freewheeling, crazy-thinking approach which can be used by any number, from one to possibly a hundred.

In brainstorming, the leader gives the group some specific problem— the more specific the better. Everyone is encouraged to contribute as many ideas as possible and a secretary records it all. No value judgments or criticisms are permitted and participants are encouraged to hitchhike on other people's ideas. Wild ideas are encouraged because they stimulate the imagination. Osborn recommended a time limit. After the session is over, the secretary types the ideas into lists. Then, and only then, are the ideas criticized and evaluated by those responsible for solving the problem under discussion. Charles Clark, one of the country's leading exponents of brainstorming, says that experience shows at least 6% of the ideas are usable. Sometimes the percentage is much higher.

Proponents of brainstorming teach people to recognize and avoid "killer phrases." In his book, *Brainstorming,* Clark advocates the use of a bell at brainstorming sessions.[5] Whenever someone uses a killer phrase, whoever is nearest to the bell rings it. Here are some killer phrases:

We've never done it that way before.

It won't work.

We haven't the time.

We haven't the manpower.

It's not in the budget.

We've tried that before.

We're not ready for it yet.

All right in theory, but can you put it into practice?

Too modern.

Too old-fashioned.

We're too small for that.

We're too big for that.

Production won't accept it.

Myron Allen, director of the Creative Growth Center in Los Gatos, California, believes that brainstorming works best when all members of the group are of approximately equal rank in the organization and the problem is not too controversial. Otherwise, fear of embarrassment, lack of self-esteem, and fear of reprisal greatly limit the willingness of group members to contribute. Allen has developed an ingenious approach to quickly tap the creativity of people at all levels in an organization.

His method, called Morphological Synthesis, overcomes these limitations by giving each member of the group complete anonymity. He writes:

By the use of Morphological Synthesis, it is not only possible but highly desirable for an entire organization, from the president down to and including the lowest-ranking operator, to be working silently in the presence of all others. Each person stimulates and is stimulated by all others present in the work group.

The time required for each individual is cut to the barest possible minimum by the use of cards. In 20 minutes, . . . 50 men can easily submit one thousand ideas (or more) that cover all sides of a problem, giving a multilevel viewpoint that would require many hours of a verbal argument type of discussion, including some ideas that would never be given publicly.[6]

Participants are furnished a 2½″ x 3″ card (3″ x 5″ cards cut in half) and instructed to write their ideas quickly, briefly, and legibly on the cards. The small cards force people to be concise, and the size is convenient for sorting. Complete anonymity is guaranteed by Allen, who keeps the cards and later destroys them so that handwriting cannot be traced. The problem to be analyzed may be as broad as, "Why isn't our school more productive?" or narrow as, "How can we increase our sales of household vacuum cleaners?"

If overall organizational effectiveness is under analysis, two separate meetings are required. At the first meeting people are asked what problems are blocking achievement of the primary objectives of the organization. Then at a second meeting, two or three weeks later, and after an analysis of answers to the first question, the group is asked to suggest solutions to the problems they collectively identified at the first meeting. Once Allen has the completed cards, which frequently number several thousand, he sorts them, using his creative, intuitive process (which he teaches others to use, too). No matter how many ideas are submitted he eventually condenses them into seven major categories. Dr. Allen says that the rational human mind has difficulty in dealing with more than seven separate ideas simultaneously as a synthesized whole. The Morphological Synthesis approach is a remarkably quick way for leaders to find out not only what people at all levels think is wrong with the organization, but what they feel can be done about it.

Synectics, Inc. encourages new ways of looking at old problems: "To make the familiar strange is to distort, invert, or transpose the everyday ways of looking and responding which render the world a secure and familiar place. This pursuit of strangeness is not merely a search for the bizarre and out-of-the-way. It is a conscious attempt to achieve a new look at the same old world, people, ideas, feelings, and things."[7]

During World War II, air force engineers were urgently seeking the solution to a problem revealed at Pearl Harbor. The December 7 attack caught American fighter planes on the ground or in hangars and destroyed most of them before they were airborne. The problem was how to get fighter planes out of their hangars quickly. A fellow by the name of Mitchell solved the problem by turning it upside down. Instead of asking, "How can we get the planes out of the hangar?" he asked, "How can we get the hangar away from the planes?" The result was a two-piece hangar with each section mounted on wheels with sufficient power to move the two sections of the hangar away from each other at 35 miles an hour. This enabled the fighter planes to take off in all directions simultaneously.

Charles Kettering, the famous General Motors scientist, used a similar approach to solving the problem of lubricating airplane motors at arctic temperatures. After the proper solution had eluded Kettering's staff, and nothing else seemed to work, he suggested that they think of the worst possible lubricant to do the job. This topsy-turvy approach sparked new ideas that led to the solution of the problem.

Most approaches to creative problem solving use a formula similar to this:

1. Define the problem—decide what it is or what goal you want to achieve.
2. Assemble the known facts about the situation and list some of the possible solutions.
3. Decide what additional facts are necessary and work out a plan to assemble them.
4. With all available facts at hand, think intently about these facts and possible solutions.
5. Allow a period of incubation; that is, forget the problem for a while and turn your mind to other matters, but keep paper and pencil handy to jot down any ideas that may occur to you.
6. Reexamine the problem and reach a decision based on the ideas that have come to you during the period of incubation.

This formula can be used by individuals or by groups. Of course, it is primarily for difficult problems rather than simple ones. The solutions to many problems will be apparent by the time step 4 is completed.

Alfred Sloan, during his regime at General Motors, said, "An essential aspect of our management philosophy is the factual approach to business judgment. . . . Notwithstanding that we have the reputation of a fact-finding organization, we do not get the facts even now as completely as we should. We sit around and discuss things without facts. I think we should break ourselves of that." [8]

Most people are not nearly as creative as they could be because they don't understand how to utilize their subconscious minds. Evidence from a variety of sources indicates that the subconscious mind acts like a random access computer. The trick is to charge your subconscious mind with the facts and the problem and then stop thinking about the problem consciously and do something else. Mow the lawn, take a walk or take a drive. According to Maxwell Maltz, C. G. Suits, Chief of Research at General Electric, found that "nearly all the discoveries in research laboratories came as hunches during a period of relaxation, following a period of intensive thinking and fact-gathering." [9]

I have studied the explanations of creativity by a variety of people from many disciplines. Their words may differ, but the processes they describe are similar to the six steps listed above. Bertrand Russell said:

> I have found, for example, that, if I have to write upon some rather difficult topic, the best plan is to think about it with very great intensity—the greatest intensity of which I am capable—for a few hours or days, and at the end of that time give orders, so to speak, that the work is to proceed underground. After some months I return consciously to the topic and find that the work has been done. [10]

Busy executives stifle creativity by trying to solve problems too fast. When all the facts are in sight a quick decision may be proper, and at times there are decisions which simply have to be made immediately. But important, difficult and complex problems should not be solved too quickly—not if you want truly creative solutions.

The third major approach to increasing organizational creativity is through the development of a creative climate. Based on his research at Dow Chemical, Dr. Repucci considers this the most important area of all. Dow's supervisors are taught "climate training" as well as creativity training, and Repucci describes this as "the single most important variable in any creativity training program." He states, "Some climates allow for creativity and some do not. Where we find a climate which allows for creativity, there we find that any program will meet with at least moderate success. Where we find a climate which does not allow for creativity, there we find that any program will meet with little success." [11]

Dow considers creativity so important that the concept has been incorporated into Dow's overall corporate objectives:

We reaffirm that continuous innovation is the primary basis of our profit growth, whether it be accomplished through process improvement, through new products, or new uses for existing products, through new ways of marketing products, or through basic research. . . .

We will avoid settled ways of doing things, we will avoid loss of flexibility, loss of innovation; we will avoid too many written rules and precedents. We must recognize that unwanted, unwritten rules are the hardest to identify and avoid. . . .

We will tolerate some inconsistencies, some profusion of purposes and strategies, some conflict, some differing traditions, some diversity of intellectual positions.

We will tolerate revolutionaries who pursue their objectives with singleness of purpose, encourage a "loyal opposition," and listen carefully to critics who call attention to an area which requires renewal.[12]

Standard Oil (New Jersey) considers the supervisor's ability to encourage the creativity in others as one of the most important criteria for advancement. Supervisors at all levels are expected to be sensitive to change and to have the ability to obtain the enthusiastic participation of those reporting to them. A manager can, quite literally, turn workers on or off by the way he deals with them. A Standard Oil executive observes, "To hammer an organization into passive compliance requires little skill; to generate a climate in which people at every level feel free to suggest new ideas—to venture beyond the sure, the known, and the safe—is the mark of a true leader."

Edwin Land of Polaroid, whose creativity is certainly well recognized, believes that everyone, regardless of his formal education or rank in the organization, has tremendous undeveloped creative potential. At Polaroid they take people without scientific training from the production line and put them in as assistants to experienced research scientists. Land calls the results amazing.

I am simply reporting on what we seem to find as a fact; that is, that the incrustation will fall away and that the inhibition can be removed, and then you have them, like the rain in Spain; you have them, you are stuck with them, and you have to find out what to do with these awakened people. . . . It is like taking the tulip bulbs which have been in the cellar all winter and putting them in the spring soil—quite suddenly and amazingly they flower and they flourish. In about two years we find that these people, unless they are sick or somehow unhealthy, have become an almost Pygmalion problem; they have become creative.[13]

So a creative climate is one which provides opportunity, challenge, recognition, approval, and respect and concern for people; in short, a *positive motivational climate.* I will have more to say about this in the chapters to follow.

Obstacles to Creativity

The best way to kill creativity is to select suspicious, critical, insecure, defensive people as supervisors at every level. At their inception most ideas are delicate and fragile and require careful nurturing. This is the reason, of course, that men experienced in developing organizational creativity stress creative climate. Most new ideas challenge deeply entrenched ideas and those entrenched ideas have many friends. The new idea does not. The more important the idea—the greater its potential—the greater the initial resistance is apt to be.

Every major breakthrough makes the impossible suddenly possible. No wonder new ideas have always had such a struggle for believability. When Guglielmo Marconi told his friends that he had discovered a way to send messages through the air without wires or other physical means, they promptly had him taken into custody and committed to a psychiatric ward.

When Samuel Morse appeared before a session of the 27th Congress, seeking $30,000 to erect an experimental telegraph line between Washington, D.C., and Baltimore, he was the object of ridicule. One congressman moved that half of the appropriation be expended in experiments in Mesmerism and 20 congressmen supported his resolution. Another member moved that the money be spent for an experiment to construct a railroad to the moon.

Back in 1926, a young salesman called on the Hookless Fastener Company in Meadville, Pennsylvania. When asked how the company could increase the sale of their zippers, he thought for a moment and came up with the idea that they could be used on the front of men's pants in the place of buttons. Everyone was convulsed with laughter. They demanded to know what self-respecting man would wear pants like that? There would be accidents and the company could be destroyed by lawsuits. Years later executives of the company (now called Talon Manufacturing) realized the fantastic worth of an idea they had very nearly turned down.

One would assume that creative individuals are more receptive to new ideas than the average person. Perhaps, but even highly creative people have had difficulty seeing new ideas when someone else was the creator. Consider, for example, Thomas Edison's lack of enthusiasm for talking pictures in 1926, "Americans require a restful quiet in the moving picture theater, and for them talking . . . on the screen destroys the illusion. Devices for projecting the film actor's speech can be perfected, but the idea is not practical." And a few years earlier H. G. Wells said, "I do not think it at all probable that aeronautics will ever come into play as a serious modification of transport and communication. . . . Man is not an albatross."

All the foregoing examples help emphasize that creative people require courage and persistence, the willingness to withstand ridicule, and the ability to overcome the fear of failure.

The typical inventor makes a poor manager because the attitudes and conditions desirable for creativity are quite different from those required for efficient production. This contrast is illustrated in the following list.

THE CREATION–IMPLEMENTATION CONTRAST

Creation	Implementation
Irrational	Rational
Unstructured	Structured
Chaotic	Organized
Unscheduled	Scheduled
Relaxed	Concentrated
Haphazard	Logical
Undisciplined	Disciplined
Spontaneous	Planned
Intuitive	Judgmental
Unspecific	Specific
Nonjudgmental	Decisive
Leaderless	Coordinated
Antitraditional	Traditional
Impractical	Practical

Many behavioral scientists believe the solution is to abandon, or at least reduce, traditional managerial attitudes in creative organizations. I disagree. What is required is a balance between these various elements. Brainstorming achieves balance by separating the two functions. First, there is the wild, unrestrained creativity session, and second, the careful evaluation. The same separation of functions is necessary throughout the organization. People whose primary role is creative need a great deal of freedom. People whose primary job is production need to accept a reasonable amount of order and discipline. In the ideal organization, creative people would have their periods of self-imposed discipline, while production workers would have their periods of undisciplined creativity. It is not true that highly disciplined people can't learn to be creative, or that creative people can't learn to be disciplined.

4

The Organization

Moses chose able men out of all Israel, and made
them heads over the people, rulers of thousands,
of hundreds, of fifties, and of tens. Exodus 18:25

PRECISELY how to organize people is still one of the most controversial aspects of leadership, both in industry and government. Several distinguished behavioral scientists have suggested that the less organization the better. It is popular in academic circles to imply that too much organization inhibits growth, creativity, and flexibility and results in an undesirable authoritarian style of leadership. At the other extreme is the record of countless organizations which have failed through too little rather than too much structuring. To be effective, goal-seeking procedures must be developed within an organizational framework.

Nearly everyone agrees that to delegate is good. Is there apt to be more delegation in an organization which has no clear lines of responsibility and authority or in one that does? I am convinced that the latter choice is the correct one. W. F. Dowling writes that Frank W. Woolworth, of "dime store" fame, used to try to run everything himself. It took a nervous breakdown to convince him that he needed the help of others. While he was recovering, he reached an important conclusion. "I lost my conceit that nobody could do as well as I could," he said; "so long as I had the idea that I must attend personally to everything, large-scale operations were impossible. So, indeed, was large-scale success."

The way companies are organized is greatly affected by size, but the basic principle common to all organizations is to establish lines of authority and delegate responsibility.

Exodus 18 tells how Jethro came to his son-in-law, Moses, in the wilderness. He watched Moses work from dawn until dark, consulting with his followers, giving advice and settling disputes. Jethro counseled Moses as any experienced leadership consultant might: "You can't do it all yourself. You'll wear yourself out. You've got to organize." Jethro's advice was to "choose able men from all the people, such as fear God, men who are trustworthy and who hate a bribe; and place such men over the people as rulers of thousands, of hundreds, of fifties, and of tens."

Any goal, task or function which is not the specific responsibility of some one individual in the organization will almost certainly be neglected. The best way to clarify organizational structure is to make an organizational chart. The chart establishes the formal lines of responsibility and authority and serves as the starting point for planning and modification. Despite rumbles of discontent from behavioral scientists, the vast majority of organizations still establish levels of authority in a pyramid-shaped structure. Critics of organizational charts and the pyramid structure charge that they produce inflexibility, bureaucracy, and authoritarianism, and the inhibition of creativity, worker morale and effective communication.

The solution is not, as some have suggested, to throw out the organizational chart, however. It is instead to change the chart at regular intervals or whenever the organization changes. What is required is organization planning on a continual basis. This is a *must* for all organizations to remain healthy. I have found that the following explanation regarding flexibility makes sense to most executives: The comparison of organizational structure to automobile structure. Automobile design (if we except Volkswagen) is flexible because it changes every year. And yet, at any point in time, the design is inflexible. Who would want an automobile not put together in some systematic, organized way? Organizational structure should be rigid at each point in time, and yet should be changeable with time.

Organization planning is a particularly important part of planning. It takes time to select and train people for various responsibilities; sudden changes in organizations are difficult. In other words, manpower needs—especially supervisory needs—require a long lead time. Most small organizations and many large ones neglect this all-important area of planning.

New organizations are frequently started by one or two, or occasionally several people. In the beginning, particularly for business organizations, the problems are financing, production and sales. The founder wears all hats. Organization is not a serious problem. As the organization grows, however, the structure becomes increasingly important. Management methods that worked very well in the beginning rapidly become obsolete. The specialist turned entrepreneur is rarely aware of the situation. He finds it hard to understand why policies so effective in the past no longer seem to be working. He is so used to being personally involved in every detail of the operation that delegation of responsibilities, even if he thinks of it, seems too difficult to practice.

Scholars, at least in modern times, have a "thing" about authority. John Gardner, who should know, calls it the "anti-leadership vaccine."

> People who have never exercised power have all kinds of curious ideas about it. The popular notion of top leadership is a fantasy of capricious power: The top man presses a button and something remarkable happens; he gives an order as the whim strikes him, and it is obeyed. Actually, the capricious use of power is relatively rare except in large dictatorships, and some small family firms.

> It is my belief that we are immunizing a high proportion of our most gifted young people against any tendencies to leadership. . . . Very little in his experience encourages him to think that he might some day exercise a role of leadership.

> This unfocused discouragement is of little consequence compared with the expert dissuasion that the young person will encounter if he is sufficiently bright to attend a college or university. In those institutions today, the best students are carefully schooled to avoid leadership responsibility.[1]

The misuse of authority does not necessarily stem from the pyramidal form of organization. It stems instead from executives and supervisors who are not qualified for their jobs, either technically or psychologically. Anyone in an organization whose level is out of phase with his knowledge and ability will cause trouble. Resentment of legitimate authority is usually the result of worker immaturity. Criminals and delinquents who are at the extreme low end of the maturity scale nearly always exhibit strong resentment of authority.

Organizational structure need not limit worker creativity, although it frequently, perhaps even usually, does. Again, the solution is not to abandon organizational structure, but to increase worker participation.

Small organizations usually organize along functional lines. For example, a typical manufacturing company has for its major functions, research, engineering, finance and accounting, and production. When the number of employees exceeds 500, it usually becomes advantageous to decentralize. Decentralization usually is done by product, but it can also be done by territory or type of customer.

The concept of decentralization has almost universal acceptance. Frederick Kappel, former chairman of the board of American Telephone and Telegraph Company, sums it up, "Responsibility and authority must be decentralized, and the more the better. . . . Decentralizing not only provides opportunity, but helps people prepare themselves for more of it." Alfred P. Sloan, a staunch proponent of coordinated decentralization, said, "The General Motors type of organization, coordinated in policy and decentralized in administration, not only has worked well for us, but also has become standard practice in a large part of American industry."

James Ewell, Procter & Gamble executive, says that P&G has 14 operating divisions, each of which has the working advantage of a small company backed up by the strength and diversity of a large one.

Consultant Jack Joynt believes that the time to shift from a functional type of organization to a divisional type is when each division will be big enough to justify semi-autonomous management.

Grant Dove of Texas Instruments describes the TI organization thus:

> There are a total of 77 of these Product–Customer Centers, or PCCs as we call them. . . . Our PCCs operate like complete small business organizations, with their own profit responsibility. Each PCC manager has decentralized responsibility for the create, make, and market functions to serve a particular class of customers in specific product areas. The PCCs have contributed much to developing a responsiveness to customers, a spirit of innovation, and practical training of entrepreneurial managers. . . . What we are trying to do at TI is to preserve the environment of the decentralized Product–Customer Centers, but at the same time to knit them tightly together within an overall goal structure.[2]

All organizations should seek to minimize the number of levels of supervision in the organization. Decentralization is one way to do this. Chris Argyris of Yale says that General Motors "decentralized when the chief executive officers found that it took more than a year to receive a reply to a routine memo."

This objective is also achieved in the organization or division thereof, by flattening the pyramid. What this actually means is to devise an organizational structure which diagrams as a short, squat pyramid rather than a tall, thin one. This objective is achieved by maximizing the span of authority at each level in the organization. The term "span of authority" refers to the number of individuals reporting to one supervisor. It has been common to recommend a span of from five to fifteen people but the proper number depends on many variables. Today, with greater downward delegation of responsibility, there is a trend toward larger numbers reporting to one supervisor.

Some years ago, Sears, Roebuck and Company made a study of the span of authority and its effect on efficiency. According to a spokesman:

> In the course of this study, the operations of two groups of B stores (150 to 175 employees) in towns of approximately the same size were analyzed. In one group the managers had organized their stores with an assistant manager and some 30 merchandise managers in charge of departments. In the other group the stores were organized along more conventional lines, with an extra level of management between store managers and department heads. Analysis of sales volume, profit, morale, and lower-management competence all indicated that the stores with the "flat" type of organization were superior on all scores to those more conventionally organized.[3]

One area that need not be affected by organizational structure is communication. In an organization with a healthy motivational climate, communication should flow upward, downward, and laterally without excessive concern for formal lines of authority.

There are organizations, and aerospace companies are an example, where tasks are changing almost constantly. Organization in this case may revolve around projects and project managers. Sheldon Davis of TRW refers to it as "a part of the direction that thinking in organization structure area is taking—away from using one type of structure, namely, the pyramidal bureaucratic model, regardless of the problem, but rather toward the development of a theory of organization around tasks and missions."[4]

Line or Staff

Authorities do not agree on the use of line and staff functions. The distinction between them is that staff personnel advise, and line personnel perform. In other words, staff people make plans but are not responsible for their implementation. Military organizations have known and used the staff concept for centuries. Most governments and large organizations use it extensively. Early in the twentieth century, Frederick W. Taylor, frequently called the father of scientific management, gave impetus to the staff concept in industry. Taylor believed in specialization, and the separation of planning and performance was one way to increase specialization.

Today there is a growing realization that, whenever possible, plans are best made by the men who will be responsible for implementing them. This trend is consistent with the trend toward participative management discussed in Chapter 12. It is easier to maintain accountability in organizations where most decisions are made and performed by line executives.

"Changes introduced by an individual not responsible for performance on the job," says M. Scott Myers, "are not likely to gain the same commitment as changes generated through employee involvement."

Another problem in line and staff organizations is that many supervisors have two or more people telling them what to do. It is not unusual, for example, for a mid-level executive to be receiving his production orders from one supervisor, and his instructions about personnel from a second, and about training from a third. Still another disadvantage is the fact that staff departments are difficult to cut back when workloads diminish.

Some organizations try to minimize staff-line conflict by assigning staff personnel as assistants to line supervisors. Robert Townsend, former president of Avis, and a man generally opposed to large staff departments, says that this is a poor solution, too.

> In my book, anyone who has an assistant-to should be fined one hundred dollars a day until he eliminates the position. . . . You can't really blame the assistant-to. He wound up there because the boss got overworked and then followed his instincts. Instead of giving pieces of his job to another line officer or carving out a whole job, or giving it to someone to run with, he hired an assistant-to, and immediately became much less effective than he was when he was just overworked.[5]

Shigeru Kobayashi, a Sony executive, wrote:

> The major bottleneck in Japanese companies, especially in relatively large corporations, is their strong tendency toward bureaucracy. Staff departments are gigantic beyond any comparison with their Western counterparts. . . .
>
> I would like to suggest first of all that staff departments should be reduced. It is my feeling that personnel management, cost control, and production control should become chiefly line-oriented functions. . . .

> Professional knowledge and skills are more and more required in our business, and we believe that these should be disbursed throughout the line organization at various levels. . . . Thus we require no great number of staff people—and large staff organizations. . . . As for myself, I can't help thinking that the majority of staff departments in Japanese industrial firms are trying hard—and with the best of intentions—to destroy their companies.[6]

One excellent solution for small organizations, and even for large ones, is the use of outside consultants for specialized functions of an advisory nature such as training, personnel, legal matters, and advertising. Even though consultant fees seem high in comparison to wages, the company may well get more for each dollar expended. Carefully chosen consultants bring specialized knowledge of a caliber frequently higher than that of staff specialists who are willing to work for wages. Consultants bring the organization an objective, outside viewpoint, and experience gained from serving a variety of organizations. Management is more likely to evaluate the performance of an outside consultant, and his hours and fees can be quickly adjusted as the work load fluctuates.

The Systems Approach

When asked if his organization used the systems approach, the assistant director of a large federal agency replied, "Yes, of course, we've had a computer for years." This remark serves to emphasize that many executives have only a vague idea of what a system is or what the systems approach does. The systems concept is an important one, especially in seeking solutions to complex problems and organizing to achieve large tasks. Simon Ramo, TRW vice chairman, describes the systems approach as a reasoned and total rather than a fragmentary look at the problem. All the parts in any system are interrelated. What is a system? An automobile is a system. An airplane is a system. A human being, a corporation, a family, a state, a nation—all are systems.

Stafford Beer, an English industrial consultant, said:

> Anything that consists of parts connected together will be called a system. For instance, a game of snooker is a system, whereas a single snooker ball is not. A car, a pair of scissors, an economy, a language, an ear, and a quadratic equation, all of these things are systems. They can be pointed out as aggregates of bits and pieces, but they begin to be understood only when the connection between the bits and pieces, the dynamic interactions of the whole organism, are made the object of study.[7]

Take the automobile. The mechanic who views it as a system would recognize that you should not double the horsepower without considering the effect on transmission, brakes, wheels, tires, etc., and that you should not radically change the type of fuel used in the automobile without considering the effect on ignition, cylinder walls and lubrication.

Professional leaders realize that organizations are systems. They know that a decision made in one department usually affects other departments. Skillful executives learn not only how to recognize the impact of decisions on all parts of the organization but also what to do about it.

Failure to think in this way can be expensive. During the late 1950s the D. B. Milliken Company was expanding rapidly. Our line of high-speed cameras was getting worldwide recognition and the company was having difficulty meeting the demand. The engineering department was under the direction of an experienced aerospace engineer, but one who had been with the company less than two years. He recognized that our system of numbering engineering drawings had become obsolete. There were thousands of parts involved and some of them had been modified several times. When customers ordered parts for field repair, even though they gave us the serial number of the camera, we could not be sure which modification of the part they required. The chief engineer developed a new print-numbering system based on his experience in large aircraft companies. His decision involved changing the numbers on thousands of tracings, running new prints, and destroying the old ones. Just changing the numbers on all the prints required several weeks of a draftsman's time.

My first knowledge of the change came when our purchasing agent asked me how his department should handle the change. Should they issue a new purchase order to every vendor, with renumbered blueprints? If so, he said, where would he get the extra help to get the job done? The next complaint came from production control. They wanted to know if Engineering realized how many records would have to be changed and how many inventory cards revised. And did we realize that parts storage in the stockroom was numerical and would require a great deal of labor to change to the new system? A few days later our sales manager came to me in a state of near shock and wanted to know if I realized that all our instruction manuals were now obsolete.

And the crowning blow came from our office manager. Why hadn't Engineering, he exploded, checked with him before they changed the print numbers? His department had been working for months on a plan to handle inventory control on an NCR computer. Now this idea would have to be abandoned because the new part numbers had more digits than the NCR could handle.

Thus, a decision, which at first glance seemed to be the sole concern of the engineering department, had actually affected virtually every department in the organization, a good example of what can happen when executives are not trained to think of the organization as a system.

Coordination

Rensis Likert, in his *New Patterns of Management*, published in 1961, described the coordinated group style of organization.[8] Discussions with hundreds of leaders, however, have convinced me that most executives still are not aware of its possibilities. The overlapping group or coordinated team approach is a tremendously important leadership concept, and a vast improvement over the simple organizational structure described thousands of years ago to Moses. This concept is not only far more effective as a method of organization and coordination, but it taps powerful motivational forces as well. Exhibits 2, 3, and 4 are from *New Patterns of Management*.[8] In the traditional man-to-man pattern of organization (Exhibit 2), the president meets with his sales manager, and they make decisions relating to sales. Then the president meets with the chief engineer, and they make engineering decisions, etc. This is time-consuming and the procedure fails to recognize that the organization is a system. Exhibit 3 shows the team pattern of organization. Here the president and the heads of major departments meet together and work out major decisions as a team. Exhibit 4 illustrates how problem-solving teams at various levels in the organization overlap. In actual practice, the number of individuals at each team level would probably be more, utilizing the span-of-authority concept.

Under the coordinated team approach, problem-solving teams at each level meet on a regular basis. At D. B. Milliken the executive team met daily at a regular time for a period not to exceed one hour. Attendance was compulsory and no excuses were accepted. Nor were any interruptions allowed unless it was an emergency. Lower-level teams met on a weekly basis. Meetings at all levels were used to communicate among departments, to make important daily decisions, and to conduct goal-seeking activities.

The coordinated team approach has the following important advantages. It

1. Provides continuous coordination among all levels of management.
2. Uses group creativity.

Exhibit 2. The man-to-man pattern of organization.

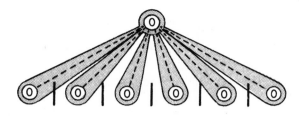

Exhibit 3. The group pattern of organization.

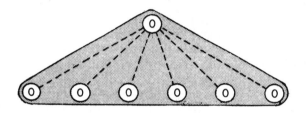

Exhibit 4. The overlapping group form of organization.

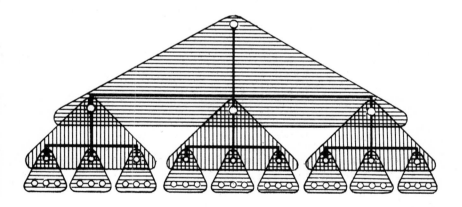

Work groups vary in size as circumstances require although shown here as consisting of four persons.

SOURCE: Rensis Likert, *New Patterns of Management,* McGraw-Hill, New York, 1961.

3. Develops generalists.
4. Increases the quality of decisions.
5. Provides a regular, "sacred" time for goal-seeking activities and makes these activities pleasant rather than drudgery.
6. Reduces interdepartmental warfare.
7. Increases the speed of communication and provides for upward as well as downward communication.
8. Develops greater commitment to company objectives (through involvement).
9. Fulfills people's psychological need to belong.

Under our present system of education most people are trained as specialists, tending to start in that capacity in an organization. When they become part of a team in the organization, they are involved with the problems and thinking of other specialists and learn to become generalists. At the presidential team level, for example, the vice president of sales becomes involved in engineering decisions, and the vice presidents of engineering and sales become directly involved in problems of corporate financing. Each executive learns (probably to his surprise) that he can contribute in a meaningful way to important decisions outside his own special area.

Important considerations in using coordinated teams:

1. The group size must be controlled. If it is too large, there will be problems in reaching specific decisions.
2. Team members must be qualified to participate—new people may be permitted to observe but not participate.
3. The leaders should lead, although there are some authorities who disagree. The leaders should be responsible for an agenda, keeping the meeting on the track, pressing for decisions, and assignment of responsibilities for implementation.
4. The climate must be positive, not critical.
5. Teams should meet at specific times and places, with a fixed meeting duration and protected from interruption.

The coordinated team approach is one of the most powerful techniques of professional management. "In business, as in sports," states J. C. Penney, "it takes teamwork to reach goals. And other people won't help us reach our goals unless we help them reach theirs."

5

Staffing for Results

It is not technology itself which succeeds; it is trained and motivated man who applies technology with judgment and creativity. It is man who must assume responsibility, plan new approaches, take risks, and make difficult decisions.
Paul Thayer, President, LTV Aerospace Corp.

A major contribution to the success of any organization is the time, effort, and creativity used in finding and placing its people. The ability to choose the right person for each job is clearly one of the most important characteristics of the excellent leader. Alfred Sloan, Jr., built General Motors into the world's largest manufacturing corporation. Harold Wolf, who studied the extraordinary growth of General Motors, concluded that an important reason for Sloan's success was his ability to hire and promote the right people.

During Sloan's reign the General Motors' Statement of Policies and Objectives listed the following as a primary management goal:

> The careful selection and placement of employees to make sure they are physically, mentally and temperamentally fitted to the jobs they are expected to do; to make sure that new employees can reasonably be expected to develop into desirable employees, and so that there will be a minimum number of square pegs in round holes.[1]

Saul Gellerman, authority on motivation, says:

The original decision to hire a man will largely determine not only the character of future leaders but the attitudes of the men they will lead as well. In fact, since neither hiring nor promotion changes the fundamental character of a man, it follows that the processes by which an organization acquires its people have a greater effect on motivation and productivity than any personnel actions it can take afterward.[2]

One of the worst mistakes an executive can make is to hire mediocre people. If a new employee is truly incompetent, it is soon obvious and he can be dismissed. But with the so-so employee, the tendency is to continue to hope he will improve. Every job filled by a mediocre person reduces the organization's effectiveness. My recommendation is to print this sign and place it where it will be seen.

HIRE IN HASTE, REPENT AT LEISURE!

A seldom-mentioned aspect of management is the executive's natural reluctance to fire people. Incompetent employees linger on month after month, sometimes year after year, because their supervisor doesn't have the guts to fire them. The president of one West Coast corporation insisted on having a hand in hiring people, but was never there when a final notice was given. When he wanted someone dismissed his practice was to leave the plant and call from a phone booth and instruct his general manager to wield the ax. He stayed away until the employee was gone.

An excellent policy is to place all new employees on probation—90 days is usually adequate. Their immediate supervisor's responsibility is to determine within the probationary period whether they are suitable for permanent employment. After the 90-day period, the employee is considered permanent and not subject to dismissal for incompetence, although he might be dismissed for gross negligence. This places the responsibility for proper selection and training where it belongs—on the supervisor—and gives employees the security that they deserve.

The American Management Association has made several attempts through surveys to determine the cost of hiring or replacing one worker. In one survey, for clerical workers the estimate varied from $50 to $2,000. An earlier survey revealed that the estimated cost of hiring one salesman was more than $6,000. And 33 out of the 136 companies responding estimated that the total cost of an unsatisfactory salesman who served a reasonable trial period was more than $10,000.

How to Select People

The first and perhaps most important step in this area is to decide to allocate enough time to do a thorough job. The next step is to clarify your objectives and your plan to achieve them. What precisely is the person you seek to accomplish? What will be the hours, pay, benefits, etc.? What criteria will be used for selection? What tests and screening procedures will be used? From what sources will applicants be sought?

As a general rule, especially when the employment market is tight, hiring strategy should be patterned after Israeli military strategy. Concentrate your efforts. Organizations prolonging the process will lose the best prospects to more efficient organizations that reach fast hiring decisions. It is far better, for example, to interview 90 prospects in one week than to interview 30 prospects a week for three weeks. Concentration of effort should not be confused with *hurried* effort. The hiring process should move quickly from the first announcement of an opening to the final decision as to who will fill it.

Successful staffing requires creative thought about all possible sources for applicants. After years of trial and error, and many costly mistakes, I have regretfully come to the conclusion that, generally speaking, *in normal times the people you want for skilled jobs are employed and probably satisfied with their present jobs.* In other words, if your primary source for people is from those unemployed, your chances of hiring outstanding people are diminished.

E. A. Butler, management consultant and head of E. A. Butler Associates, says, "The man who quits a job before he's got another one nailed down ought to have his head examined. The moment an executive is out of work his market value drops about 300%."

It is essential that organizations have a systematic procedure to consider all existing employees before going outside to fill a job. Many organizations consider "promoting from within" one of their most important personnel policies. Pacific Telephone, for example, has six levels of supervision, and rarely are outsiders hired for any position higher than first-level supervision. When there is an opening for a supervisor, a "Request for Candidates" is sent to the next higher level of supervisors in all nearby divisions. The request describes the opening, including personal qualifications and job knowledge required. Managers receiving the request are required to submit the names of all eligible candidates within two weeks.

Texas Instruments, whose corporate philosophy is to develop maximum individual responsibility throughout the work force, believes that it is a mistake to leave in-plant promotional activities solely up to managers. Their initial procedure was to post all job opportunities on bulletin boards throughout the plant. When problems ensued, a special task force representing all corporate levels studied the procedures thoroughly. The findings were that open job-opportunity posting had indeed created problems. Some individuals were submitting their names for several openings at the same time and cluttering up the system. Others were being permitted to transfer laterally and were taking jobs that would have created an opportunity for promotion from lower-job levels. Frequent job transfers weakened some departments, and some workers were transferring before they reached a sufficient degree of competence on their existing jobs. The revised TI internal staffing procedure overcame the defects in the initial program by limiting concurrent job bids per person to two, permitting lateral transfers only when progression on the present job was blocked, allowing placement of temporary "transfer-out moratoriums" for work groups which were presently understaffed, and requiring 6 months on the existing job for nonexempt personnel and 12 months for exempt personnel before bidding on new jobs.

It is the belief at Texas Instruments that hiring is primarily a line rather than a staff function. Myers gives the following explanation for this somewhat unorthodox policy.

> The larger the organization, the more likely the recruiting function is to be delegated to professional recruiters, who tend to select candidates whose values match their own, or match their perception of the requisitioning supervisor's personality. The line manager generally tends to be more goal- or achievement-oriented, but his recruiters and other personnel specialists tend to be more maintenance-oriented. Though the personnel man's maintenance orientation can be explained in terms of his forced preoccupation with maintenance problems unloaded by line managers, it does, nonetheless, color the strategy for attracting job candidates.

> For example, professional recruiters frequently advertise jobs as pleasant and easy, and as offering generous pay, supplemental benefits, and a congenial environment.[3]

Present workers are an excellent source of leads for new employees from outside the organization. As a general rule, the more people interviewed for a job, the better the chances of finding the right person.

H. Ross Perot, whose success as president of Electronic Data Systems (EDS) was so spectacular that *Fortune* dubbed him the fastest, richest Texan ever, says that the careful selection of employees is one of his major rules for success. EDS will sometimes interview 400 applicants to find one new employee.

Once applicants are uncovered, there are three major tools for screening and selection:

1. Written application
2. Personal interview
3. Testing procedures

Most organizations put applicants through a preliminary screening process to eliminate those obviously unsuitable.

Application forms, if they are to be effective, need to ask the right questions. St. Luke's Hospital, one of the largest in New York City, did a research study in order to improve their application form for several categories, including secretary, junior secretary, dietary aide, and male nursing attendant.[4] Their study analyzed the records of people who had quit. The employees were "short term" if they left within one year or less, and "long term" if they stayed three years or more. Then random samples of 30 short-term and 30 long-term employees for each job category were selected. The analysis showed that the following factors were the most significant in attempting to identify employees who would be most apt to stay:

Age. Employees of both sexes tended to be short term when under 25 years of age and long term when over 35.

Lived outside Manhattan. Workers whose residence was outside the city tended to be short term.

Too much education (college graduate). A college degree in the categories under investigation indicated the probability of short-term employment.

Years on last job. People who had been more than three years on their last job were much more likely to be long term.

Marital status. Married people provided a much higher number of long-term employees.

Years of experience. People with more than three years of previous job experience were consistently better risks for long-term employment.

The St. Luke's study provided the basis for an improved application form as well as some valuable criteria for evaluating those who completed the new form.

C. B. Buchanan, who has written several books about employment, says he tried 267 jobs and failed at every one of them before it occurred to him to analyze himself and find out what he was really suited for.[5] Now he teaches others what it took him so long to learn—how to find a job that fits the individual's capabilities.

His formula for employers is to get all the written facts they can about the applicant and then do enough checking to know that the facts are accurate. Most companies assign one or two lines to each of the individual's previous positions. Buchanan requires applicants to write one or more pages on each of their previous jobs. His method of checking applications is truly ingenious. He says that approximately 50% of job applicants falsify their past experience. And even the 50% who are honest tend to exaggerate past achievements. Buchanan's procedure is to go personally, if possible, or by phone if necessary, to one of the applicant's past employers and ask the previous employer the same questions that the applicant has already answered about himself. After Buchanan has obtained all the facts he can from the employer, he asks a question something like this, "Mr. Jones, we are considering your former employee, Harry Smith, for an important position." Then he describes the job and asks, "I would appreciate your personal opinion regarding Smith's suitability for this particular job." When asked in this way, most executives begin to qualify their previous remarks. They become more realistic about Smith's *real* qualifications.

Back in his office, Buchanan then compares the employer's story with that of his former employee. Fraudulent applications are quickly revealed.

Most organizations make only a superficial investigation of an applicant's performance on previous jobs and yet this is one of the most reliable ways to predict his value. One executive hired an experienced bookkeeper who was highly recommended by his previous employer. The man proved to be an alcoholic and was dismissed. Then the executive rechecked with the past employer and asked if the fact that the man was an alcoholic was known; the reply was, "Yes, we knew it, but you didn't ask us about that."

The oral interview is the second major approach to employee selection. Jack McQuaig, head of the McQuaig Institute of Executive Training, states, "Large corporations spend fortunes on psychological tests to do the job for them. However, I believe that you can do an outstanding job yourself, simply by sitting down in your office with a man for an hour of concentrated conversation—if you are armed with a few basic rules and techniques." [6]

McQuaig's starting premises are simple. People's basic personalities and characteristics are formed early in life. The most accurate way to predict a man's future performance is to study his past performance. *"If you need hard workers, choose men who are already hard workers. If you want strong leaders, choose men who are already strong leaders. A man's character is already formed by the time you hire him. Make sure that character fits the needs of your job from the day he starts to work, or both he and you will be in trouble."* He warns that it is almost impossible to evaluate a man's potential by observing his superficial characteristics: looks, dress, ability to communicate, and the like. The job can only be done by following careful interviewing procedures. These procedures are carefully described in McQuaig's book, *How to Pick Men.* He lists five traits that contribute to successful job performance.

1. *Positive attitudes.* The ability to say yes. To try. To expect success.
2. *Strong drives.* Top capacity for work. The ability to break down barriers.
3. *Steady persistence.* Determination. The will to never quit. To keep on trying when others give up.
4. *Mature personality.* Reliability. Realistic thinking. The ability to take hard knocks. Good judgment. Self-control.
5. *Marked aptitude for getting along with others.*

"Every one of these is an inner trait," says McQuaig. "None of them can be seen in a man's appearance, or learned from a casual conversation. They exhibit themselves only in action, and over long periods of time."

Tests are the third major method to evaluate job applicants. Tests are used to determine specific skills. For secretaries and stenographers, for example, a typing test is easy to give and essential. Other tests seek to determine aptitudes and general intelligence. The Wonderlic Tests are excellent for this purpose and do not require special skills to administer or evaluate.[7] Another testing area is personality traits. C. B. Buchanan has researched virtually every type of psychological test used by personnel departments and found them of low reliability. He can, he says, show the average job applicant how to reach satisfactory scores on most of these tests after 30 minutes of coaching. The testing program that Buchanan considers reasonably accurate, and impossible to deceive, is the battery of aptitude tests given by the Human Engineering Laboratories, founded and directed by Johnson O'Conner.[8]

One California machine shop devised an ingenious method for selecting machinists. When a machinist who seemed qualified applied for work, he was immediately put to work on a paid trial basis for four hours. They put him alone in a small but well-equipped shop and gave him the blueprint for a part which involved a variety of machine operations. Within four hours or less, they had an accurate idea of his ability and speed. Men who talked with great assurance about their abilities sometimes walked out without another word when asked to demonstrate their competence in this way.

Consultants and suppliers are an extension of organizational staff. Their selection requires the same careful systematic approach recommended for employees. Take sufficient time to do a thorough job. Obtain sufficient facts.

Performance Appraisals

Staffing does not end with the selection and placement of people. It also involves continued evaluation of their performance, leading to possible pay increases, transfers, promotions, or, conversely, dismissal. The performance appraisal is still a controversial aspect of leadership, although most consultants seem to believe it is an essential activity. A 1959 survey concluded that more than three-fourths of American companies have performance appraisal programs. But a number of consultants have questioned the effectiveness of traditional appraisal programs. Douglas McGregor wondered whether these regular reviews didn't do more harm than good. Peter Drucker says that most companies have them, but few supervisors use them, and the regular appraisal reviews "never take place." The problem with the typical formal review, in Drucker's opinion, is its emphasis on weaknesses rather than strengths. He refers to it as "the wrong tool, in the wrong situation, for the wrong purpose."

Professor Chris Argyris of Yale cites studies indicating that formal appraisals are frustrating to both supervisors and their employees. "At their best," says Argyris, "they do not provide positive influence for the growth of the subordinate being evaluated. At worst they magnify the subordinate's feelings of dependence and submissiveness and eventually destroy his desire for self-development while requiring increased conformity." [9]

There is increasing awareness that criticism, if it is to have any positive effect, must be acceptable by the person being criticized. Joe Batten, author of *Tough-Minded Management*, says the solution is to build on strengths rather than weaknesses. [10] Most appraisals do just the opposite. Other consultants stress the advantages of the management-by-objectives approach, which tends to shift the emphasis from evaluation of traits or personality to a discussion of results based on progress toward objectives that the employee had a hand in establishing. Shigeru Kobayashi, author of *Creative Management*, says, "The leader is required to review his people's performance and make pertinent comments about it. He should, of course, praise excellence of performance, and mention any poor results—but warmly."

6

Communication

Communication is the chain of understanding that integrates an organization from top to bottom, from bottom to top, and from side to side.
William Oncken, Jr., President, Oncken, Heydrick and Company

MOST of us take communication for granted. After all, we've communicated most of our lives. Effective communication, however, is anything but easy. There are important skills involved, and the average adult does not learn them through blind trial and error. Communication—written, verbal, and nonverbal—is the glue that holds organizations together.

The Human Engineering Laboratories, which specialize in testing people's skills and abilities, tested the qualifications for 52 occupational groups and found that company presidents were at the top in English vocabulary. This placed them higher than freelance writers, who were second, and college professors, editors, and lawyers in descending order. Of the 52 occupations tested, grocery clerks showed the lowest vocabulary.

Supervisory and management people from 100 industrial firms were interviewed in depth and were revealed to spend approximately 70% of their waking hours in communication activities. Of the time spent in communication, the breakdown was as follows:

Writing	9%
Reading	16%
Speaking	30%
Listening	45%

Although nearly everyone agrees that communication is essential, it is one of the most frequently neglected areas of organizational concern. It is an aspect of leadership that, like goal setting, is extremely important but seldom urgent.

Words mean different things to different people. Winston Churchill told about a serious misunderstanding at a meeting of the British and American chiefs of staff. The British delegation proposed to "table" an important resolution. To them this meant to discuss it immediately. To the Americans the phrase meant an indefinite postponement, and they insisted that the matter should not be tabled. Valuable time was wasted in heated argument before the committee realized that they all wanted the same thing.

Ted Pollock, author of *How to Listen*, says, "The 500 most commonly used English words have more than 2,500 dictionary meanings! Don't believe it? Look up the word 'fix' in a good dictionary."

Communication, as with nearly every other aspect of leadership, is most effective when goal-seeking procedures are used. In other words, know what you want to accomplish, have a plan or outline of what you're going to say, and get feedback.

There is more to communication than meets the ear. Nonverbal signals can be more important than the message itself. An example is the following "simple" exchange between a father and his 16-year-old daughter, who is leaving for her first date with a new beau. Father says, "Jane, I want you to be in this house no later than 12:00." Jane answers, "Yes, father," and she's out the door. The exchange at a mechanical level was clear, explicit, and almost impossible to misunderstand. But at a deeper level this simple exchange was loaded with emotional and nonverbal factors. The father's message was influenced by his impressions of his daughter's past performance and some of the frightening things he has heard and read about drugs, reckless driving, and promiscuity. Perhaps a glimpse of the new date was not overly reassuring. The daughter's response was influenced by her desire to be popular, her previous success or failure at getting that second date, and her impression, based on past experience, of what her father will do if she does not comply with his request. Jane's decision to comply or not to comply with his request will be the result of all of these factors, none of which was part of the exchange of words itself.

Communications between supervisors and employees are affected by factors outside the conversation, too. Perhaps the employee is unable to concentrate on the careful instructions of his supervisor because he has just had a fight with his wife, or when he opened his mail yesterday he had an unexpected tax bill. Or perhaps he is so fearful of losing his job that he cannot concentrate on the conversation.

When a supervisor meets emotional resistance, superior logic will not suffice. Jesse Nirenberg, communications consultant, says that emotional hang-ups *must* be cleared away before proceeding with the conversation. The solution is not to talk but to listen, drawing the person out by skillful questioning.

The more the experts study communication the more obvious it becomes that listening is frequently the key. J. C. Penney says, "The occupational disease of a poor executive is the inability to listen. . . . In handling grievances, let the employee tell his full story without interrupting. A kind word will help." Active listening, the kind of listening that successfully draws other people out, requires study and practice. The listener must learn how to ask the right kinds of questions.

Frank Bettger credits his skill as a listener for millions of dollars of insurance sales. Bettger kept a record of more than 5,000 interviews to find out why people did or did not buy. He was surprised to discover that 62% of the time the reason given by his client was not the real reason at all. This discovery puzzled him until he read something that J. Pierpont Morgan, Sr. once said: "A man generally has two reasons for a thing—one that sounds good, and a real one." Bettger discovered the right question would frequently uncover the potential customer's real objection. After a turn-down with a logical reason, he would ask, "In addition to that, isn't there something else in the back of your mind?"[1] Variations of this question, phrased to fit the situation, sometimes produced miraculous results. The real reason for the customer's refusal to buy his proposal was smoked out. Armed with this knowledge Bettger was in a position to make an acceptable proposal.

A Baptist minister taught me the importance of allowing time for ideas to soak in. He discovered that when he developed an idea for his church, walked in and presented his proposal cold to his board of trustees, it usually met with opposition and frequently was turned down. Then he found that when he took time to talk individually with his trustees about the idea well in advance of the meeting, they had time to accept the idea and would usually give it their approval.

Persuasion

Persuasion, especially sales persuasion, is the most difficult and the most important type of communication. Every individual and every organization, if they have a purpose at all, must be successful in persuasion. The fact that successful salesmen are always in short supply and command top pay even when times are bad is an indication how scarce and important this talent is.

The key to successful persuasion is getting the other person involved. Dr. Nirenberg says, "When one person presents an idea and the other person does not talk about it, there is no real penetration." He advises his students to think of selling ideas just as if they were selling a suit. The chance of selling a suit is not good until you can get the man to put it on. You can't get a man to accept your ideas until he, in a sense, tries them on himself. Harry Overstreet, the famous psychologist, stated, "The very essence of all power to influence lies in the ability to get the other person to participate. The mind that can do that has a powerful leverage on his human world."

Alfred Marrow, chairman, Harwood Companies Inc., gives an excellent example of persuasion through participation. During World War II Harwood was seeking to expand its workforce but had difficulty attracting qualified workers. Management felt the solution was to employ older people, but line supervisors were resistant, feeling that older workers would not be able to do the job. John French, Jr., director of personnel research for the company, tried to reason with the supervisors, mentioning scientific evidence that these people did have proper skills and aptitudes. But his arguments got nowhere. He could have insisted that they hire older workers, but he wanted their active support.

Dr. French finally accomplished his objective by involving the line supervisors in a research project. He suggested that if older workers were inefficient the company should investigate how bad the situation was so the company could decide whether they should release some of the older people already on the payroll. Responsibility for making the investigation was placed with the supervisor's own staff.

"The findings," says Marrow, "were in sharp contrast to staff's expectations. Not age, but other factors, determined success or failure on the job. But the analysis being their own, the staff trusted it. Thus being enabled to reexamine their beliefs through firsthand exploration, they were helped to new understanding. In the process, they 'unlearned' some of the beliefs they had been convinced were true and were now ready to affirm quite different ones." [2]

Feedback is essential to the process of persuasion. The skillful persuader knows how to draw out his listener with unstructured questions that won't take a yes or no answer. When the suit salesman asks whether you prefer silk or wool it is a structured question. But when he asks, "How do you feel about this material?" it is unstructured and is more likely to produce a useful answer.

Years ago salesmen were trained to make logical, rational, and well-organized sales presentations. Today there is much greater emphasis on listening, involvement, and getting the other person to do much of the talking. The new approach places the emphasis on the benefits rather than the product. In the advertising business the phrase is: "Don't tell me about your grass seed, tell me about my green lawn."

A few years ago the Panther Oil Company, in Fort Worth, told salesmen how to sell PANCO lubricant: "Tell the customer: 'Here's how PANCO products protect your valuable machinery, Mr. Jones. See how easily it is handled? Proper lubrication relieves you of all your worries about maintenance.' Don't say: 'Our lubricants are made from the finest ingredients known to science. They are the best on the market today.' " [3]

Dan MacDougald, an Atlanta attorney who has developed a dramatic new technique to change the attitudes and behavior of hardened criminals, says it is very difficult to get people to change their behavior by direct criticism. This is especially true for criminals and delinquents who have developed a thick protective shell against any form of criticism. But it is true, to a lesser degree, for nearly everyone. People hate criticism. It damages their ego, and their natural tendency is to reject it. The solution for rehabilitating criminals is through indirection. Criminals are not told how to change. They are asked questions—in the Socratic manner—which lead them to reach the right conclusions on their own.

William Glasser, the psychiatrist whose Reality Therapy technique is changing the direction of psychiatry, made a similar discovery. The best way to get delinquent girls to change is to ask them questions. Direct criticism accomplished little or nothing.

Perception

Perception is an important and frequently neglected aspect of communication. Nearly all of us are guilty of what Dr. Nirenberg calls "wishful hearing." We tend to decide what we will and will not hear. We laugh at the ostrich because he buries his head in the sand when trouble comes, but most of us do the same thing. Hating criticism, we welcome outrageous flattery because we want it to be true. Toward the end of World War II, Hitler became less and less objective. Military officers were afraid to tell him the truth because he became so emotional. An officer could jeopardize his career by telling the Führer bad news. The situation became so serious that because of his "wishful hearing" Hitler was no longer able to make sound military decisions.

In 1961 Jerome Bruner, a Harvard psychologist, described the new knowledge of selective listening to a congressional committee. In one experiment he recorded the brainwaves of a cat listening to a buzzer sounding at regular intervals. Electrodes attached to the cat's brain showed that he was perceiving the buzzer signals. Then a glass bell jar containing three white mice was placed before the cat. Immediately he stopped hearing the buzzer sound. His mind simply tuned it out in order to concentrate on something more important.

Bruner explains that the five senses deliver approximately 10,000 units of information to the mind at any moment in time, but the mind can only receive about 7 items of information at once—the normal range is from 5 to 9. Thus the mind filters the information presented. This inhibitory system, as it is called, is similar to the operation of an ordinary radio. Many signals are picked up by the radio antennae and forwarded to the radio, but the radio operator tunes out all but the one he wants.

MacDougald put this new understanding of perception to practical use in his technique for changing the behavior of criminals. He and his associates found that goals and attitudes have a major influence on perception—what people actually hear, believe, and retain. Because of their extremely negative and hostile attitude toward themselves and others, criminals filter out the very ideas essential to their own well-being. MacDougald's group developed methods to prove the self-destructive results of their faulty perception to criminals. When they discovered how to establish constructive goals and change their attitudes accordingly, their perception changed too.

An understanding of perception and the mind's inhibitory system is significant to students of communication for at least two reasons. The first is that familiarity with the mind's operation makes you a better perceiver. You become aware of your own tendency to filter out various types of information. You can detect your tendency to biased hearing in such controversial areas as politics and religion. Men who listen realistically tend to be more creative and make better judgments.

The second reason for understanding perception is to gain effectiveness in communicating with others. When you become aware of others' goals and attitudes you can predict what information they will reject.

For years the D. B. Milliken Company was concerned primarily with the design and manufacture of mechanical devices. Both Milliken and I were mechanical engineers. As time went by, however, our firm became more and more involved with electromechanical manufacturing. I left the electronics to others, consistently tuning out technical discussions about it. In contrast, Milliken listened to the electronics engineers with an open mind and eventually acquired an excellent working knowledge of electronics. I admit it. My lack of electronic perception restricted my technical education.

Organizations need effective communication to succeed. "Only when communication is direct and simple and continuous between all branches of the company," says Polaroid's President Edwin Land, "can people work together to make sure that they are producing the best product in the simplest way." Because communication is the most frequently neglected aspect of leadership development, the possibilities for rapid improvement are excellent. Leaders should establish communication objectives, goals, plans, and policies for themselves and for their organizations. Communication skills can be improved by reading, attending seminars, in-house training, and the use of communication consultants. A practical understanding of communication is closely related to an understanding of psychology and motivation—subject to be discussed in later chapters.

7

Training and Development

No training, uninspired by leadership, can produce more than technical competence. No leadership, however inspiring, which does not issue in a comprehensive system of training, can produce more than enthusiasm unsupported by skill.
Lyndall Urwick, *Leadership in the 20th Century*

FRIGIDMEATS, Incorporated, in Chicago, processes cut steaks, roasts, and hamburger patties for restaurants and hotels. One of the first operations is to trim fat and bone from the meat to be processed. Sidney Jaffe, company president, says that trimming is a precise art requiring careful training. A careless trimmer can cost the company as much as $300 a day. In a situation like this it is easy to see that worker training is an economic necessity.

There are thousands of operations in tens of thousands of organizations with people functioning in ways which must be right if the organization is to flourish.

Organizational training practices vary from incredible neglect to massive programs requiring significant investments of time and money. No one knows exactly how much American industry is spending on training and development. Estimates vary from $5 billion to as high as $20 billion a year. Georgia State's Professor Robert Fulmer says, "American management may soon be spending more to train and educate employees than U.S. public schools and colleges spend to educate its youth."

Some organizations, especially small ones, seek to avoid training expenses by hiring competent people who know their jobs. This "economical" approach has, however, several serious limitations. No matter how well individuals may know their specialties, they certainly do not know the policies and procedures of their new employer. And what does the organization do when the quality of specialists from outside sources is inadequate? Does the average secretary, machinist, typesetter, etc. know his job as well as he should? How does the organization considering training "too expensive" make sure that secretaries as well as other employees develop new skills as methods, machines, and procedures change?

Organizational leaders must give these questions serious consideration. In nearly every case the realistic conclusion will be that systematic training programs are essential in any organization seeking to maximize worker effectiveness.

Texas Instruments discovered that orientation procedures for new and transferred workers had a tremendous effect on performance, at the beginning and for many months thereafter. Their study revealed that nearly all new workers have considerable anxiety.[1] New-job nervousness reduced the worker's ability to learn his job, reduced quantity and quality of production, and increased new-worker turnover. TI, as most companies do, left worker training to department foremen. The typical supervisor, even though he knew better, tended to hurry the training process, and usually found it difficult to appreciate how strange everything was to the new employee.

Earl Gomersall decided to run an experiment to see if there was a better way to get new workers off to a good start. His department at TI manufactured integrated circuits, and included more than 1,400 women operators performing approximately 1,850 different operations, working on three shifts. In addition to several experimental training groups, Gomersall established several control groups. The control groups followed the normal procedure, which began with a two-hour briefing by the personnel department on hours worked, insurance, parking, work rules, employee services, and the like. The briefing sessions included warnings about the consequences of worker failure and, although it was not the intention, increased rather than decreased worker anxiety. After the two-hour orientation by Personnel, the workers were turned over to their "friendly but very busy supervisor," who gave them specific job instructions and put them to work on the assembly line.

The experimental groups started with the conventional two-hour orientation by Personnel. But at the end of that session they were sent in groups to a conference room, where they were told that they would not do any production work the first day. They were encouraged to relax and take this opportunity to become better acquainted with the company and each other and ask questions. The orientation guide emphasized four ideas designed to reduce worker anxiety.

1. *Your opportunity to succeed is very good.* Employees were told that better than 99% of all people hired or transferred were successful. They were also told that it would take time for them to learn to do their new job and the company was prepared to give them this time.

2. *Disregard "hall talk."* The neophytes were told about some of the hazing practices they might receive from older workers, the type of exaggerated talk that experienced employees seem to enjoy.

3. *Take the initiative in communication.* Trainees were taught to ask questions when in doubt. It was explained that, unless they asked questions, supervisors would assume they understood.

4. *Get to know your supervisor.* The experimental groups were encouraged to seek a friendly relationship with their supervisors and were given information about the supervisors' characteristics, hobbies, and idiosyncrasies to help break the ice. At the end of the one-day orientation session, members of the experimental groups were introduced to their supervisors, and their regular job assignment followed.

The differences in attitudes and job performance between the two groups were remarkable. The experimental group learned faster, reached higher rates of production, and had lower rates of absenteeism. Scott Myers, who helped direct the experiment, reports the following gains.

- Training time was shortened by one-half.
- Training costs were lowered to one-third of their previous levels.
- Absenteeism and tardiness dropped to one-half of the previous normal rate.
- Waste and rejects were reduced to one-fifth of their previous levels.
- Costs were cut as much as 15 to 30%.

Organizations need specific procedures, not only for the orientation of new workers to their jobs, but also to improve performance on existing jobs, and to prepare workers for different jobs and job advancement.

The first obvious decision leaders must make is that training is essential. The second and more difficult decision is how, what, where, and by whom is the training to be done. As with any other aspect of professional management, a successful training program requires objectives, plans, feedback, and evaluation. Some courses stress the advantage of "stranger groups"—groups of individuals from different companies. The American Management Association has found that seminar participants value the opportunity to meet men doing jobs similar to theirs but from different organizations. At the other extreme is the "family" group seminar, which involves people from the same organization who work together on a day-to-day basis.

Many organizations rely primarily on in-house training facilities. Others utilize outside consultants or attend seminars presented by universities, trade associations, or consulting firms. Each of these training approaches has its unique advantage. Experienced leaders use a variety of approaches in order to achieve the best results. Different people respond to different types of training experiences.

Some authorities believe that workers should take the responsibility for their own training. Scott Myers says, "If individuals are to experience sustained growth and maturity, their training must result from their own initiative." Sheldon Davis writes, "The company cannot develop employees; employees must develop themselves with the proper support from the company." I do not question the validity of these suggestions as indications of the ideal situation, especially when the training and development are related to job advancement. But most organizations make training for the proper performance of an existing job compulsory. Of course, this type of training is normally done during working hours and at company expense. Incidentally, the distinction between training and development is that training is the transmission of knowledge; development refers to changes in attitudes and behavior.

Probably the greatest job-training effort in history occurred during World War II. American industry was faced with the task of hiring and training hundreds of thousands of unskilled people. To help industry accomplish this monumental task, the U.S. War Manpower Commission created the Training Within Industry Service. This agency developed a number of excellent training programs and techniques, some of which were so well thought out and basic that they are still being used with excellent results. The Training Within Industry Job Instruction Training Course is still one of the best for teaching manual skills. Here is its outline.

How to Get Ready to Instruct

Have a Timetable
    How much skill do you expect the trainee to have, by what date?
Break Down the Job
    List important steps.
    Pick out the key points. (Safety is always a key point.)
Have Everything Ready
    The right equipment, materials, and supplies.
Have the Workplace Properly Arranged
    Just as the worker will be expected to keep it.

How to Instruct

Step 1. Prepare the Worker
Put him at ease.
State the job and find out what he already knows about it.
Get him interested in learning the job.
Place him in the correct position.
Step 2. Present the Operation
Tell, show, and illustrate one IMPORTANT STEP at a time.
Stress each KEY POINT.
Instruct clearly, completely, and patiently, but no more than he can master.
Step 3. Try Out Performance
Have him do the job; correct errors.
Have him explain each KEY POINT to you as he does the job again.
Make sure he understands.
Continue until YOU know he knows.
Step 4. Follow Up
Put him on his own. Designate to whom he goes for help.
Check frequently. Encourage questions.
Taper off extra coaching and the close follow-up.

IF THE WORKER HASN'T LEARNED, THE INSTRUCTOR HASN'T TAUGHT.

Closed-circuit television is gaining popularity as a training device. The initial investment is relatively low and individual programs can be created faster and cheaper than traditional motion picture techniques. Some organizations use television as an adjunct to the orientation of new employees, who are given an opportunity to see, and hear remarks by, various top officials of the company. Such programs can be quickly changed as top management changes.

E. B. Burnap, Personnel Division vice president for Metropolitan Life Insurance, likes video tape recording because of the low cost and reusability. He says, "In developing executive skills through role playing, our managers are able to see themselves perform, an advantage not possible in 'live' training sessions. Also since our role-playing situations are taped first and then played back before a classroom full of managers, there are no tendencies on the part of the players to ham up their performances."

Another company uses closed-circuit television in training its salesmen. Salesmen practice their approach before the TV camera with a co-worker acting as the buyer. One salesman who viewed his performance on the screen was astonished to discover that during his sales pitch he reached down to pull up his socks six times in 10 minutes, a practice of which he had been totally unaware.

Rockford Motors imports sewing machines and wholesales them to Montgomery Ward. Under the sales arrangement Rockford is responsible for training Ward's personnel, who must in turn train people to sell and service the machines. Rockford's training program had to be revised with each new sewing machine model. The problem was solved by creating video tapes covering all aspects of sales and service. These video tapes were then duplicated and mailed to Rockford's six field representatives, who used them to train Montgomery Ward personnel.

Programmed learning is another important training technique. The University of Michigan has established a center for programmed learning for business. The technique offers the advantage that students can proceed on their own without an instructor, and they can proceed at their own speed. This type of individualized, self-help instruction has proved highly effective in a variety of teaching situations.

Management consultant Eugene Benge believes that individualized instruction can greatly increase the efficiency of training programs. He made a study [2] of a group of 30 key employees sent to a company's home office for three weeks of intensive training. His survey showed that—

Two trainees knew more than the typical instructor.

Five could have conducted certain sessions as well as the assigned instructors, but benefited from the remaining sessions.

Sixteen were properly in the group.

Seven had such inadequate education or experiential background that they got little from the training.

Benge made the following recommendations to correct the inefficiencies revealed by the survey.

1. Hold qualifying tests in the field. These would have revealed the two men who didn't need the training and the seven who couldn't profit by it.

2. Analyze the gaps in the knowledge of the remaining 21.

3. Prepare a "training prescription" for each man to fill out his knowledge or skill. Preferably this step should be done by individual discussion with the trainee.

4. Conduct group training for some subjects and some persons, preferably using the conference training method.

5. Schedule individual training with present experts and, later on the job, for the remainder.

Peter Drucker believes that American executives can learn a great deal from the Japanese approach to industrial training, which he says is continuous.

> This means, first, that every employee, very often up to and including top managers, keeps on training as a regular part of his job until he retires. This is in sharp contrast to our usual Western practice of training a man only when he has to acquire a new skill or move to a new position. Our training is promotion-focused; the Japanese training is performance-focused.
>
> Second, the Japanese employee is, for the most part, trained not only in his job but in all the jobs at his job level, however low or high that level is. . . . This system . . . is just about 50 years old.[3]

Many training efforts fail or fall far short of their potential because they do not carry through into the "DO IT" phase. Lectures, role playing, buzz sessions, movies, and so on are all important training devices. In the final analysis, however, the man has learned very little until he actually DOES IT in the real-life situation. There is a simple formula that fits most teaching situations: The student should HEAR, SEE, DO, and REVIEW. This is one important advantage of on-the-job training, and one of the reasons that the World War II Training Within Industry program was so successful. It carried through to the actual job. On-the-job training has an important economic advantage because when workers are trained by coping with real on-the-job problems the results have immediate utility.

F. A. Powell, IBM's director of education, said in an interview:

> In talking about executive development, I should like to underscore one important point: the importance of on-the-job development. It is very easy, when talking about executive education, to concentrate on the formal programs that you have established, but this can be very misleading. I must emphasize the fact that a man's actual personal growth takes place on the job as a result of relationships among him, his manager, and the other managers whom he encounters in carrying out his ongoing responsibilities. Important as the classroom operations are, you should recognize that 80 to 90% of all development takes place on the job. I think the best teacher of a manager is his own manager, not some management development staff member in a classroom.[4]

Small organizations have difficulty with training because of limited resources. The best solution can be the use of training facilities offered by universities, trade associations, and the like. The American Management Association has been a leader in this area. In Los Angeles the Merchants and Manufacturers Association offers a number of excellent training programs. These outside programs, however, do not eliminate the need for in-plant training and orientation programs.

Spring Realty Corporation in California solved the problem by creating its own training workbook. Their manual incorporates all the essential facts about company policies and procedures and valuable ideas about personal motivation from Maxwell Maltz, James Newman, Earl Nightingale, and others. Each new employee is required to read the manual and complete the accompanying written exercise. Employees also attend regular monthly training meetings to review and update their knowledge. The average salesman starting with Spring had been earning about $7,000 or $8,000 a year. After a year of training and experience, the average salesman earns $15,000 annually. In a relatively few years Spring Realty has grown into one of the most successful realty firms in California.

Evaluation of Training Programs

Training programs need the same constant, tough, and impartial evaluation of results as most other organizational activities, and preferably by someone other than the training director or his associates. This applies to in-house training programs as well as outside ones. The quality of programs available to organizations in the open market varies from worthless to extremely helpful. This variation is much greater than inexperienced leaders might suspect. Evaluation of training efforts is difficult, but almost any appraisal is better than none.

Texas Instruments did the job in a professional way by establishing control groups, as described earlier. The task was made easier by the fact that workers were being trained for specific tasks where productivity was easily measured. Many training seminars try to obtain an evaluation from seminar participants through the use of written questionnaires. A still better approach is before-and-after tests. These take more time, but the results are more objective and they can become part of the learning process. If a second test is given a month after completion of the training course, it will reveal the staying power of the program.

When training is a staff function, some organizations make the training department a cost center. Under this system, other department heads "buy" training services; the cost of training is charged to their department as a budget item. This approach places the training department under the constant cost effectiveness evaluation of its in-company consumers.

Several years ago, President George Keck of United Airlines appointed a five-man executive committee to review the company's training programs for stewardesses, ticket agents, maintenance personnel, and cargo and ramp personnel. At that time the company was spending approximately $14 million annually on this part of its training program. The committee was composed of executives not personally involved in training programs. A full-time staff was assigned to gather facts. In addition an outside consultant was employed to assist in the investigation, which involved a variety of techniques: questionnaires to instructors, personal interviews with instructors and students, and a number of conferences with trainers and trainees. This in-depth study of the strengths and weaknesses of United Airlines' training programs resulted in nearly 80 recommendations and a major revision of training and development policies and procedures.

Leadership Development

Leadership development is at once the most important and perhaps the most difficult aspect of organizational training. As we discussed at length in Chapter 2, it is the men at the top who, in the final analysis, determine the success or failure of the organization. Thus the quickest and most effective way to change the performance of an organization is to change the performance of its leaders. One way to do this is to change leaders. The other way, and the one most practicing leaders naturally prefer, is to change the performance of existing leaders through training and development. There are still many die-hards who remain convinced that not training, but continuous on-the-job trial and error, is the only way to produce leaders. Adherents to this point of view must disregard a great deal of evidence to the contrary.

A number of authorities have criticized our universities for their lack of success in training leaders.

Lawrence Appley, when president of the American Management Association, said, "They don't teach management in our academic institutions today. They teach the functions of management—finance, bookkeeping, marketing, traffic, transportation, labor relations."

Robert Townsend quotes Peter Drucker, who wrote, "The business schools in the United States, set up less than a century ago, have been preparing well-trained clerks." To which Townsend adds, "Peter, who is a good guy and shouldn't be judged by his pupils, ought to know. He teaches at NYU's business school." Townsend's advice is, "Don't hire Harvard Business School graduates. . . . This elite, in my opinion, is missing some pretty fundamental requirements for success: humility; respect for people on the firing line; deep understanding of the nature of the business and the kind of people who can enjoy themselves making it prosper; respect from way down the line; a demonstrated record of guts, industry, loyalty down, judgment, fairness, and honesty under pressure." [5] It should be evident that academic leadership training programs usually fail to carry through into what I have termed on-the-job DO IT.

The starting point for any successful leadership training effort is the knowledge of what excellent leadership is. Then, leadership training programs must start at the very top. When responsibility for organizational development is placed with a training director at the vice-presidential level or lower, the emphasis is almost invariably directed downward from that position. Rarely will the organization's vice-presidents be involved and almost never the president, chairman of the board, or directors. The ultimate responsibility for the success of an organization lies with its directors. They choose and evaluate its executive officers and determine major policies. Yet directors are rarely involved in any effort to improve their understanding of leadership.

An important study prepared by the American Institute for Research entitled "Top Management Development and Succession" was released in 1968. The study was sponsored by the Committee for Economic Development, an organization composed of 200 businessmen and educators, most of whom are presidents or board chairmen. This report states:

> Central to the success of any development program is the involvement of the chief executive, which needs to be visible, continuous, and administratively effective; that is to say, the president will ensure the adequate performance of the developmental responsibilities that he has delegated. . . . The chief executive is the prime mover who energizes the entire developmental system.[6]

My recommendation goes further. I recommend that the chief executive and his directors (or trustees) must, themselves, be participants (as students) in leadership development activities. To a large degree the growth of supervisors, and the organization itself, will be limited by the personal growth and development of those at the very top.

It is an important part of an executive's job at every level to develop the supervisory capacities of those who report to him. William Oncken, Jr., New York consultant, stresses the concept of replaceability. He considers corporate organization planning as

> . . . the key top management activity in its perpetual war on management obsolescence. Obsolescence of the organization and its key members is the fountainhead of all other forms of obsolescence—obsolescent products, processes, and management techniques. . . . Every manager, from foreman to president, is involved in achieving this aim by (a) seeing to it that he can be immediately replaced by an immediate subordinate at least as capable as he, and (b) seeing to it that all his subordinate managers do the same.[7]

He quotes from an early publication of the American Management Association (1927): "When management prepares for executive vacancies with the same resourcefulness that it now uses for planning for production, purchasing, accounting, and financing, the supply of good executive material will exceed the demand."

Many organizations consider job rotation an important aspect of their leadership development program. Executives are shifted from job to job both geographically and functionally in order to broaden their experience. President Frieda Libaw of Cognitive Systems, Incorporated, advocates job rotation not only as a training device but as a means to spark creativity. She writes:

> For one or two hours every week, each one of us works at the tasks of another department, doing whatever happens to be needed at the time. . . . This "exchange program" has brought us some of the most valuable ideas for product improvement, for marketing, and for efficiencies in routine tasks by taking people out of their routines and asking them to put on their thinking caps and cast a fresh glance at the tasks of others. It has also had a salutary effect on the way people think about their own work by making them anticipate the reactions of others to it.[8]

Organizational Development (OD) is another approach to the development of leaders. Consultant Marvin Weisbord writes: "Generally speaking, it refers to systematic, planned activities, usually managed from the top, that are designed to help people within the company use *all* available resources—including the style and behavior of management itself—in more effective ways." OD practitioners are usually trained behavioral scientists, many of them associated with the National Training Laboratories, originators of sensitivity training. The OD approach stresses that all organizations are systems.

Warren Bennis, who followed McGregor at MIT, says:

> Organization development is a response to change, a complex education in strategy intended to change the beliefs, attitudes, values, and structure of organizations so that they can better adapt to new technologies, market, and challenge, with [a] dizzying rate of change. . . . [It] is an educational strategy [used] to bring about planned organizational changes. . . . The change agent is almost always a professional behavioral scientist. . . . Organizational development, for the most part, takes as its focus of convenience *The Human Side of Enterprise.* . . . [And] emphasizes experienced behavior. . . . Feedback, sensitivity training, the consultation meetings, and other experience-based methods are widely used to generate publicly shared data.[9]

Sheldon Davis stresses the idea that OD is not a luxury item but is useful in bad times, too. He feels that one of the most useful OD concepts is team building, which he defines as

> The notion that the members of the group will spend some time together where their agenda is "How Might We Improve Our Effectiveness as a Team?" . . . where they step back from actually doing the job and take a look at it in a behavioral sense. Things like how they're organized, how they make decisions, how they resolve conflicts, the quality of their staff meetings, interpersonal problems that might exist, issues they have with other teams, hidden agendas (for example, you go into a meeting ostensibly to discuss the design of a new control system, but your real goal is to knife those so-and-so circuit designers), and so on.[10]

He defines a team as any organizational element whose members have a common supervisor.

At one time TRW decided to use team building at the beginning of a new engineering project. The idea met with a great deal of skepticism from team members, who wanted to get on with the job rather than sit around and talk about how they were going to work together. In spite of the opposition, the group did spend three days in team building before starting the actual project. In evaluating the experience several months later, one of the group members summed up the experience: "I think it was time well spent, because after the three days we spent in the team-building process, we then, on the fourth day, began to work together as if we had been doing so for six months. And that was just money in the bank, so far as we were concerned." [11]

What to Do About Training

An executive must convince himself that training and development are vital aspects of organizational success. He must approach it as a major objective, requiring creative goal-seeking procedures on a continual basis. Training and development are too important to delegate to a lower level and then ignore. Our discussion of the subject is far from complete. We have only attempted to indicate some of the things that organizations have found worthwhile. Leaders should consider the following training criteria.

1. Well-defined training objectives.
2. Continuous top-level concern and support.
3. Continuous top-level evaluation (accountability).
4. Involvement of organization leaders as trainees.
5. Involvement of board of directors as trainees.
6. Well-planned lesson material.
7. Use of both in-house and outside sources for training.
8. Careful evaluation of outside sources.
9. Instructors who know their subject.
10. Proper balance between lecture, discussion, and practice.
11. Instruction follows through to on-the-job DO IT.
12. Line supervisor involvement as trainers.
13. Supervisors trained to be effective instructors.
14. Provisions to maximize feedback.
15. New-employee orientation adequate.
16. Training aids such as programmed instruction, closed-circuit television, filmstrips utilized.
17. Employees encouraged to take the initiative in self-improvement.
18. Periodic review courses for trainees.

8

Research and Development

There is nothing more difficult to take in hand,
more perilous to conduct, or more uncertain in its
success, than to take the lead in the introduction
of a new order of things. Niccolò Machiavelli

THE scientific approach and the systematic research that stems from
it have come a long way since 1600. That was the year Giordano Bruno
was burned at the stake in Rome because he advocated the Copernican
theory of astronomy, which placed the sun at the center of our solar
system. Perhaps this is part of the reason that it was well into the
eighteenth century before men began to speak openly about the idea
of progress through science (observation, experimentation, and measurement).

Industrial research in the United States did not gain momentum
until 1900. At first most research activities were carried on by independent inventors like Fulton, Bell, Marconi and the Wright brothers—
men who worked alone, frequently in kitchens or barns. Thomas Edison
was unique in this respect. His private laboratory included a machine
shop, model shop, and an impressive reference library. Approximately
70 men worked there under Edison's direction.

The idea of organized industrial research similar to that pioneered
by Edison gained rapid popularity and today new developments come,
for the most part, from the efforts of scientists, engineers, and others
working cooperatively together. Recognition of this phenomenon caused
J. A. Schumpeter, the Harvard economist, to conclude in 1928 that
"industrial growth is dependent on innovation." From our present
vantage point it is important to add that the growth and vitality of

virtually all organizations, profit and nonprofit alike, are dependent on research and innovation.

Charles F. Kettering, who contributed so much himself, labeled research as an "organized method of finding out what you are going to do when you can't keep on doing what you are doing now."

Research may be classified as either basic or applied. In basic research the investigator is concerned primarily with gaining fuller knowledge or understanding of the subject under study. In applied research the investigator is primarily interested in a practical use of the knowledge or understanding for the purpose of meeting a recognized need.

Development, according to the National Science Foundation, is "knowledge directed towards the production of useful material, devices, systems, or methods, including design and development of prototypes and processes. It represents the application of the findings of research to meet practical problems." [1]

Obviously, our technical research has paid off in terms of a staggering array of new and better products ranging from new cars, supersonic airplanes, and astonishing space vehicles, to such items as color television, dishwashers, and electric toothbrushes. Bell & Howell recently estimated that more than 80% of its present sales are from products that were not in existence five years ago. And Sol Polk, mass merchandiser with a reputation for tough realism, said: "In the next 10 years, you will see as many innovations as in the past 50. Half of what I am going to be selling in 10 years is not even being produced; it is in the planning stage."

Nearly everyone agrees that there is a direct relationship between U.S. technical superiority and the quantity and quality of our technical research. But our leadership in R&D is rapidly dwindling. In August 1971 Department of Commerce Secretary Maurice Stans told a congressional committee: "Western Europe and Japan are narrowing the technology gap. . . . They have increased R&D expenditures substantially and their increases in productivity over the last few years have outpaced ours. The result is that American producers are finding it hard to hold their own against foreign manufacturers at home and abroad." Stans told the congressmen that Department of Commerce figures for 1968 showed that business-oriented research took 1.6% of our Gross National Product, while the corresponding figure was 3.6% for West Germany and 3% for Japan.

Research costs money. Leaders must evaluate the cost effectiveness of research activities just as they must every other organizational activity. John Lobb, president of John Lobb Associates, has a simple approach, which he recommends for small and medium-size organizations: "We go back five years and find out how much we have spent on R&D. . . .

Then we ask ourselves: What sales did we generate through this R&D effort? What percentage of sales in 1970 came from products developed since 1965 by our research department?" In some cases the question must include consideration of research directed toward cutting operating costs as well.

Research departments need leadership, too. This means the person in charge has to be more than a good technician. Since research affects other departments, particularly marketing and production (at least in profit corporations), it is essential that the activities of this department be coordinated with those of other departments. "Product development and product marketing," says Herbert Bissell, vice president of marketing for Honeywell, Incorporated, "must move together hand in hand." The necessary coordination can be provided by utilizing the coordinated team approach recommended in Chapter 4.

Bissell cites an example of research failure which stemmed from insufficient foresight at high levels. "Electronic tube manufacturers," he writes, "were not interested in developing new ways of controlling the flow of electricity. They were interested in making more and better electronic tubes. Someone else developed the transistor and took the business." [2]

Shortly after World War II the D. B. Milliken Company had a contract with one of California's largest producers of orange juice to develop a device to refrigerate, store, and dispense fresh orange juice in restaurants. We dealt directly with the president of the orange juice company. After many months and many thousands of dollars of research, we had a working model with a number of patentable features. Modeled to some extent after the Sparkletts water dispenser, our machine required that orange juice be delivered to restaurants in two-gallon bottles, which were then placed directly in the dispensing unit. Our client was delighted and arranged a demonstration so that his company executives and several from Sunkist could see the juice dispenser. Then the roof caved in. When his factory men saw what was involved they were horrified. They told their boss it would probably cost more than a million dollars to modify their machines and procedures to put fresh orange juice in two-gallon bottles and deliver it to restaurants. The production and distribution problems proved to be so difficult that this entire design concept was abandoned.

This example shows how the systems approach is almost essential in solving today's complex research problems. Dow Chemical executive Stephen Jenks writes, "The only way the major complex problems, both technical and social, are going to get solved is through combinations of specialists; that is, through the use of teams. No one alone has enough knowledge to solve today's problems, and individual specializations are so narrow that there is a need for the creation of teams to bridge from one specialization to another." [3]

The computer has had a tremendous impact in many areas of research, technical and behavioral. Computer simulation is a technique to test the soundness of various design concepts without actually making physical models.

Computer expert Robert Vichnevetsky said:

> Today almost all aircraft or aerospace vehicles designed are being simulated in every feasible type of environment before the first test flights take place. . . . Although the aerospace industry is still the largest user of simulation, the concept has spread very quickly to other industrial and university users. Relatively speaking, non-aerospace industrial and university users of computer simulation are much more important today than they were a few years ago. [4]

Vichnevetsky tells the story of the early days of aircraft simulation. A programmer was given the mathematical model of a high-speed aircraft and asked to simulate its performance over a range of speed and altitudes. Some time later he reported to his superior that the computer was having trouble simulating performance at certain combinations of high speed and high altitude. According to the story, his boss said, "I know." They had just lost a couple of planes at high altitude and were trying to discover why.

Arthur D. Little, Incorporated did an extensive study of innovation for the National Science Foundation. The conclusions were released in 1963 in a report entitled "Patterns and Problems of Innovation in American Industry." The three industries studied were textiles, machine tools, and building. The report challenged a widely held concept of technical change, which was:

> Within any given industry new technology comes primarily from the research and development efforts of firms established in the industry. The rate of technological change in the industry is therefore primarily a function of research and development investment by those firms and their skill in commercializing research results. [5]

The study revealed that there were few major technical innovations contributed by well-established companies in the industries studied. Instead, the report stated:

> Major innovations have come primarily from outside the traditional industry. They have come . . . from foreign technology, from

independent inventors, from the startup of new small firms, from the invasion of the traditional area by technically advanced, established firms in other industries. . . . The principal source of major technical change in mature industry, in spite of common-sense views of the matter, is innovation by invasion. . . .

Innovation through the work of independent inventors and through the entrepreneuring of new small firms has been traditional in American industry. But the present study indicates that it is by no means limited to the distant past.[6]

This pattern of innovation was not found to be true in all industries. Some, such as aircraft, space, and chemicals, have research-oriented organizations that encourage innovation. According to the report:

They are science-based; their research and development activity is not an appendage to other functions of the firm but is an integral part of it—the capital resources are considerable. . . . They established, at their own beginnings, a style of research-oriented, entrepreneurial activities which is still unfamiliar to most companies.[7]

Professional leaders need to consider all possible sources of innovation. Independent research centers may be able to do the job more economically than in-house research facilities. New products may be purchased from independent inventors on a royalty basis. Small organizations should systematically scan the research of others. Some organizations (Polaroid is outstanding in this respect) systematically encourage ideas for new products and improvements to existing products from production workers.

"Technology transfer" refers to the utilization of an idea developed in an entirely different field. For example, materials and techniques developed in our space program now are being used for a number of nonspace applications. Schools, churches, and hospitals have not yet taken full advantage of the tremendous possibilities for leadership technology transfer from industry.

Some firms have established a special R&D section systematically seeking transfer possibilities. Richard Foster, director of technology management for Abt Associates, states, "A well-developed technology transfer program can substantially increase the playback potential of the R&D effort in large and small organizations alike."

Professionally managed industrial firms make their sales department a major adjunct to research efforts. Their sales representatives are trained to find out customers' needs.

Market research (efforts to discover what customers want or how they might respond to a proposed product) is an increasingly important area. It also provides data for manufacturing, scheduling, and price determination.

Louis Cheskin is president of Louis Cheskin and Associates, which tests marketability of products, trademarks, and methods of packaging. Cheskin says that much market research fails because researchers confuse what people say they will do with what they will actually do. This happens because people are not fully conscious of their own motivations. Cheskin's organization seeks to overcome this through test procedures which uncover these unconscious motivations.

In spite of their theoretical conviction that much motivation is unconscious, behavioral researchers make the same error—confusing what people say they will do with what they actually will do.

I have emphasized research to the extent that I have because there are still too many organizations, particularly in the nonprofit sector—schools, colleges, hospitals, churches, and even government itself—that do little or no research to improve their own activities. Perhaps this is because our emphasis on technological and product research has tended to divert attention from other important kinds of research regarding methods, procedures, policies, markets, and services.

The American Institute of Management has devised the "Management Audit," a procedure for systematically examining, analyzing, and appraising the performance of *any* administrative body. "Research and development," according to Audit instructions, "is often thought of as primarily scientific and technological, but A.I.M. comprehends in this category all areas, including basic research if any, market research, and product and process development. Research, properly regarded, also includes the investigation of such areas as organization, communications, systems, and executive development."

The A.I.M. management auditors are taught to seek answers to the following questions:

> Does management restrict R&D to product and process development, or is provision made for basic research as well? How are the results of R&D coordinated with other functional departments, especially with Production and Sales? How are R&D functions organized? How are R&D personnel recruited, assigned, supervised, and promoted? What are management's policies governing the allocation of R&D budgets? What are the methods of direction and control of R&D? Is R&D essentially market-oriented from a long-, short-, and medium-range point of view?

The attitude of top management is critically significant in determining the quality and scope of company R&D.[8]

Procedural Research

Too many people think of research in terms of products. Procedural research is just as important, and the need for it applies to all organizations almost without exception. It involves a continuous, systematic examination of how the organization does things—its methods, policies, and procedures in all areas, especially organization, communication, staffing, training, motivation, and the like.

I had been managing the D. B. Milliken Company for about 20 years before it struck me that most of the problems that we were meeting for the first time had already been met and solved by other managers. The thing to do to improve my own leadership skills, I decided, was to learn from the experience of others. Why not, I thought, write to the managers of a few successful companies and find out what they were doing that I was not? Since IBM was one of the fastest growing companies in the country, I wrote to Thomas Watson, Jr. Accompanying his letter in response to mine was a copy of his book, *A Business and Its Beliefs*, in which Watson explained the IBM philosophy. He had underlined in ink some of the paragraphs that answered my questions. These are some of the underlined sentences:

> This, then, is my thesis: I firmly believe that any organization, in order to survive and achieve success, must have a sound set of beliefs on which it premises all its policies and actions.
>
> Next, I believe that the most important single factor in corporate success is faithful adherence to those beliefs.
>
> And finally, I believe that if an organization is to meet the challenges of a changing world, it must be prepared to change everything about itself except those beliefs as it moves through corporate life.[8]

The way that IBM and other successful organizations "change everything about themselves except their basic beliefs" is through systematic procedural research. Whether this is carried on by a research staff, or as a part of the job of line supervisors, it is a necessary function for all organizations.

Procedural improvement programs travel under a variety of labels—methods improvement, work simplification, systems analysis, problem analysis, value engineering, or value analysis. But whatever the label, it is, or should be, a creative goal-seeking activity. Is methods improvement a line or staff function? The present trend, and I am convinced it is a correct one, is toward line rather than staff responsibility. But this approach creates problems, too. Are line supervisors at all levels trained for methods improvement? Will they give it attention when competing with the demands of daily activities? Will they take time to do an adequate research job? All too frequently the answer is no. Procedural improvements, important though they are, generally tend to take a back seat to daily crises. The solution is a continuous effort, starting at the very top, to see that procedural improvements are not neglected.

Polymer Company, Ltd., a Canadian firm, launched a work simplification program to counter a problem of rising costs and diminishing profits. C. A. McKensie, manager of manufacturing, says, "It was usually thought in this company that improvement ideas would have to come from the engineers. We changed that when we gave our nontechnical supervisors the opportunity to participate in work improvement." The program, directed by an outside consultant, started with orientation seminars for top management. Two hundred and forty supervisors, foremen, and technical people in groups of 16 to 20 completed a workshop, meeting 2 hours each week for 12 weeks. Supervisors were taught the team approach and how to obtain worker participation in the identification, analysis, and improvement of various company activities. Each seminar participant was required to develop one improvement proposal for his work area. The work improvement program became a regular part of company activity on a continuing basis and resulted in substantial dollar savings.

All the indications are that the twentieth century, which may go down in history as the century in which technical innovation came into its own, may also be recognized as the century during which procedural innovation caught fire, too. This second aspect is only now beginning to gain momentum.

9

Psychology:
The New Frontier

*To be worthy of management responsibility today,
a man must have insight into the human heart, for
unless he has an awareness of human problems, a
sensitivity toward the hopes and aspirations of
those whom he supervises, and the capacity for
analysis of the emotional forces that motivate their
conduct, the project entrusted to him will not get
ahead*—no matter how often wages are raised.[1]
Clarence D. Randall, former Chairman, Inland
Steel Company

THERE seems to be general agreement in management circles that
skill with people is a vital aspect of leadership, but qualified observers
also agree that for the majority of organizations there is a significant
gap between what is known and what is practiced. Consultant Joe
Batten writes, "American business is currently overlooking its greatest
ace in the hole. . . . Literally millions of people are leaving their jobs
every evening with much of their energy and productivity still unused.
They throw themselves into bowling, little league baseball, and other
activities with a kind of enthusiasm and identification that management
has not even tapped." [2]

The purpose of the next six chapters is to examine the gap between
psychological theory and practice, and what leaders can do to minimize
it. An important aspect of the problem is the communication gap
between psychologists, who understand psychology but not manage-

ment, and executives, who understand management but not psychology. Precisely because they are not psychologists, most executives are not aware of the fact that modern motivational theory is a minority position among psychologists, psychiatrists, and behavioral scientists. Psychological concepts taken for granted in well-informed management circles are still unknown by the majority of social and behavioral scientists. The number of qualified experts in motivational psychology may be much smaller than most executives realize.

Another difficulty in both research and practice is the intimate relationship between motivation and other aspects of management. Almost every management decision has a motivational aspect. It is difficult if not impossible to isolate motivational activities or create a separate department of motivation—executives at every level are both motivated and motivators. McGregor said, "Behind every managerial decision or action are assumptions about human nature and human behavior. . . . They are implicit in most of the literature of organization and in much current managerial policy and practice." [3]

Decisions which seem purely technical frequently are not. Most executives, for example, have experienced frustration when new machinery or office equipment, purchased after the most careful technical evaluation, falls short of performance expectations because those who use the equipment are not enthusiastic about it.

At the time of the Korean war, the D. B. Milliken Company took a contract to make a threaded part for a major manufacturer of military rockets. We got the order because we made the lowest cost bid, and we were low bid because we planned to make the part on a specially designed machine instead of using conventional turning equipment, which would have been much slower. The contract was for hundreds of thousands of parts, and the delivery rate was 1,000 a day. We built the special turning and threading machine and it performed just as we thought it would. But when we went into production, everything went wrong. Every hour or two the threading tools broke down, and we were spending more time repairing the machine than making parts.

We tried every conceivable combination of speeds, feeds, cutting tools, cutting oils, and different tooling materials, but nothing seemed to work. We were falling behind on our production schedule and losing money, too. Then the operator who was running the machine became sick, and we put another man on the job. That was the end of our trouble. The machine ran for three days without a tooling breakdown. Our problem had not been technical at all. It was human. A careless operator was causing our trouble.

Milestones in Development of Motivational Theory

Most students of industrial motivation trace modern theory to the work of Elton Mayo, Harvard psychologist, and his observations at the Hawthorne Works of Western Electric Corporation between 1927 and 1932. Actually Mayo's interest in worker motivation started in 1923 and 1924, when he studied the reasons for excessive turnover in a department of a Philadelphia textile mill.

Experiments at Hawthorne started when company engineers tried changing the illumination to increase the productivity of women electrical assemblers. The engineers were astonished to find that when the lighting was increased, decreased, or held constant, production went up in each of the assembly departments where the experiment was conducted. At this point Mayo and his associates were called in. They continued the experiment by varying rest periods and the length of the working day. Again output went up regardless of what they did.

The researchers had accidentally uncovered a powerful principle of motivation, which Mayo described: "The major experimental change was introduced when those in charge sought to hold the situation humanly steady . . . by getting the cooperation of the workers. But what actually happened was that six individuals became a team and the team gave itself wholeheartedly and spontaneously to cooperation in the experiment." [4]

Years later the University of Michigan's Institute for Social Research became an important source of motivational research. Since 1947 the Institute, under the direction of Rensis Likert, conducted extensive leadership research covering a wide variety of organizations.

The research, which involved many thousands of employees and their supervisors, disclosed significant differences between highly productive managers and low producers. The high producers were found to be what Likert described as "employee-centered," while the less productive managers were what he called "job-centered." He states, "Those supervisors whose units have a relatively poor production record tend to concentrate on keeping their subordinates busily engaged in going through a specific work cycle in a prescribed way and at a satisfactory rate as determined by time standards." [5]

The job-centered supervisor does not really understand his employees or how to motivate them. Employee-centered supervisors are those skilled in building morale, enthusiasm, and cooperation among their workers. Thus Likert established a significant relationship between style of supervision and worker motivation and productivity.

It has been the ideas of the late Douglas McGregor, more than those of any other one person, that have captured the imagination of executives and consultants. When the Conference Board surveyed the impact of behavioral sciences on a cross section of 302 North American companies in 21 product and service categories, McGregor was most frequently mentioned as the most influential individual. The others mentioned in descending order were Frederick Herzberg, Rensis Likert, Chris Argyris, Abraham Maslow, and Robert Blake and Jane Mouton (authors of *The Managerial Grid*).

McGregor, past president of Antioch College and then professor of management at the Massachusetts Institute of Technology, published his classic, *The Human Side of Enterprise*, in 1960. It was McGregor's contention that the majority of business organizations were operating on the wrong assumptions about human motivation. He called the incorrect approach Theory X and proposed that management could achieve greatly increased productivity and better worker morale when it understood and dealt with human motivation.

He called the new approach Theory Y management—a philosophy of management which gave workers more freedom but at the same time more responsibility. "The central principle of organization which derives from Theory X," said McGregor, "is that of direction and control through the exercise of authority. . . . The central principle which derives from Theory Y is that of integration, the creation of conditions such that the members of the organization can achieve their own goals *best* by directing their efforts toward the success of the enterprise." [6]

Although McGregor translated a general theory of human motivation into a theory for business and management, it was Abraham Maslow, a clinical psychologist, who provided the foundation for McGregor's work. Maslow, not McGregor, is the father of modern motivational theory. His hierarchy of psychological needs is the starting point for virtually all the modern proponents of industrial motivation.

Maslow's *Motivation and Personality*, published in 1954, was a reaction to the overemphasis on pathology and statistical averages that had dominated psychology and the behavioral sciences for many years. Maslow advocated an approach to man based on the study of the finest psychological specimens. The new approach revealed man as more capable, rational, and self-reliant than previous theories had found. It is a return in many respects to the optimistic viewpoint espoused by William James early in the twentieth century. James, like Maslow, believed that the average individual was using only a fraction of his potential.

From his study of outstanding individuals, which he called self-actualized people, Maslow developed his theory of specieswide, apparently unchanging, psychological needs. "This is not an improvement of something," wrote Maslow, "it is a real change in direction altogether. It is as if we were going north and are now going south instead."

Chris Argyris, professor of administrative sciences at Yale University, has studied the success and failure of many hundreds of organizations and their executives. "It is the study of relatively healthy individuals," states Argyris, "that resulted in the new emphasis on man's responsibilities and commitments. . . . There is an increasing number of psychologists who believe that self-esteem, self-acceptance, and psychological success are some of the most central factors that constitute individual mental health in our cultured people." [7]

The president of an electronics manufacturing company challenged Dr. Argyris to prove his contention that the average worker was giving the company only about one-third of his full capacity. Argyris set up a 12-month experiment in which twelve women electronic assemblers were given individual responsibility for assembling an entire electronic unit. Instead of being told how to do the job by efficiency experts, the assemblers were given the freedom to develop their own methods. Each woman was to inspect the finished product, sign her name to the product, and then handle related correspondence and complaints from customers.

In the first month of the experiment productivity dropped 30% below that of the traditional assembly line method, and worker morale dropped too. But by the end of the eighth week production started up; in 15 weeks production was higher than ever before and overhead costs of inspection, packing, engineering, and supervision went way down. Rework costs dropped 94% and customer complaints dropped from 75% a year to only 3%. When the 12 women were returned to the routine assembly line 3 of them were relieved by the decrease of responsibility. The others found it hard to adjust to the old routine; they missed the challenge of greater freedom with greater responsibility.

Argyris stresses the importance of "psychological energy," both for workers and supervisors, especially for their supervisors. He recommends greater decentralization of responsibility and such motivating factors as high but realistic expectations, meaningful work, freedom to act, accountability, and goal-oriented team action.

Harvard psychologist David McClelland concentrated upon one motive—achievement. McClelland's massive research, started in 1950, revealed that children's books were an excellent indicator of where a society was going. The study involved children's literature of 40 contemporary nations and ancient Greece and India.

The researchers found a significant correlation between the achieve-

ment orientation of children's books and the rate of economic growth
for that nation for the next 20 years. McClelland said:

> Children's stories appear to be revealing, with remarkable validity,
> the motives and aspirations of the people who give them to their
> children to read. . . . In one country a story about children build-
> ing a boat would emphasize the construction of the boat, how to
> make it so it wouldn't sink or tip over—achievement motive. In
> another country, the same story would tell about how much fun
> the children had working together on the boat and sailing it—the
> value of affiliation. And a third country would center the story
> on the power need, maybe by making a hero out of a boy who led
> the other children into the job and told them what to do.[8]

The significance of McClelland's work to executives is in the
discovery that achievement (drive, motivation, energy, ambition) seems
to be far more the result of education and culture rather than genetic
inheritance. In later research McClelland demonstrated that the need
for achievement could be developed and increased even with adults.

People with high need for achievement tend to make excellent
executives. McClelland says of such people:

> I find them bores. They are not artistically sensitive. They are
> entrepreneurs, kind of driven—always trying to improve them-
> selves and find a shorter route to the office or a faster way of read-
> ing their mail. . . . It's an efficiency kind of thing, but it also
> includes taking personal responsibility to solve problems and
> achieve moderate goals at calculated risks—in situations that pro-
> vide real feedback. . . . People with a high need for achievement
> are not gamblers; they are challenged to win by personal effort, not
> by luck.[9]

McClelland finds that contrary to the opinion of Karl Marx, who
believed that capitalists were motivated by greed, successful executives
tend to be motivated more by the challenge of the job and the resulting
feeling of achievement. The money is important, however; like chips
in a poker game, it is a measure of the degree of achievement.

Frederick Herzberg of Case Western Reserve University is distinguished for his emphasis on the difference between motivational factors
and what he calls hygienic factors. Hygienic factors include such things
as fringe benefits, pay, job security, working conditions, and particularly
fair treatment. Herzberg finds these factors prerequisites for effective
motivation but not motivators in themselves. The motivating factors
needed to increase productivity include personal growth, achievement,

recognition, responsibility, advancement, and interesting work. He calls the motivators "satisfiers" and the hygienic factors "dissatisfiers." [10]

Herzberg based his conclusions in part on a 1959 study of some 200 engineers and accountants working for 11 different companies in the Pittsburgh area.

In 1961, Texas Instruments started a six-year study of supervisory style and worker motivation. A full description of its motivational activities may be found in the book, *Every Employee a Manager*, by M. Scott Myers, who for ten years was the organization's director of management research.

Myers advocates a combination of three management concepts: management by objectives, the systems approach, and skillful human relations. He considered these three aspects of management interdependent and essential for organizational effectiveness at all levels. If corporate growth is the measure of success, TI's use of motivational concepts has been highly successful. Since the end of World War II the company's sales have grown at an average compound rate of 25% each year, reaching $764 million by the end of 1971. Profits have also grown at an average compound rate of 25% each year over the same period.

In 1971, not a good year for many electronics firms, the price of TI stock rose 56%, putting it near the head of the list for blue chip stock gains in that year.

Texas Instruments set out to determine what motivated workers. The research involved more than 2,000 managers and workers. Trained as a psychologist, Myers was greatly influenced by the work of Maslow, Herzberg, McGregor, and other behavioral scientists. He found that women assemblers seemed to require more recognition and approval from their immediate supervisors than did scientists and engineers, who tended to stress the excitement and challenge of their job, and greater freedom to pursue it. Myers' conclusion was that employees are motivated to work effectively when they have a "challenging job which allows them the feeling of achievement, responsibility, growth, advancement, enjoyment of work itself, and earned recognition." Workers become dissatisfied when they do not have opportunities for meaningful achievement. Then they begin to complain about peripheral issues such as work rules, lighting, coffee breaks, titles, wages, or fringe benefits.

Texas Instruments puts great stress on worker participation and job enlargement. Workers at every level are systematically involved in many of the functions previously reserved for management. Experiment after experiment revealed that, when workers had the opportunity to participate in the goal-setting process, morale and productivity were greatly enhanced. "The leadership style," says Myers, "determines whether primary groups are united in support of, or in rebellion against, the formal organization. . . . The supervisory style of the goal-oriented manager is characterized by balanced concern for the needs of the organization and its members." [11]

Management by Participation, a well-documented case history of Weldon Manufacturing Corporation and how it changed from Theory X to Theory Y management, should be high on the list of required reading for executives.[12] In the early 1940s Weldon was one of the fastest growing manufacturers of quality pajamas in the country, growing steadily until 1955, with about 3,500 people. But the two men who managed Weldon continued to operate the company exactly as they had in the beginning.

They were ambitious, self-made men who made their own decisions and seldom consulted others. As a result of this inflexibility, Weldon began losing momentum. It dropped to 1,000 employees and in 1962 was acquired by its leading competitor, Harwood Manufacturing Corporation.

The two organizations were similar in many respects. They both were manufacturing pajamas, although for different customers. Both employed about 1,000 employees and used similar machinery and methods. But Harwood was using the most advanced methods of professional leadership—participative management—and the corporation was making 17% on its capital investment, while Weldon was losing 15%.

The new owners found the workers at Weldon indifferent, hostile, and suspicious. Turnover and absenteeism were extremely high and performance was low in quality and quantity. Under the direction of Harwood's chairman, Alfred J. Marrow, himself a behavioral scientist, Harwood executives launched a program to change the management philosophy of Weldon. They engaged Drs. Bowers and Seashore from the Institute for Social Research, and several other management consultants, to cooperate in the changeover and evaluation of results.

At first, the employee attitudes in the two companies were quite different. Nearly half the employees at Weldon were thinking of quitting, while at Harwood the figure was 17%. Average monthly turnover at Weldon was 10%, 14 times higher than Harwood's, and the monthly rate of absenteeism, 6%, was double that at Harwood.

The major changes at Weldon were completed in two years. The results, recorded by the University of Michigan scientists, were highly impressive. Return on invested capital, which had been minus 15%

at the beginning, was now a healthy plus 17%. Production efficiency, measured by industrywide standards, went from 89% of standard to 114%. The improvement in worker morale was demonstrated by the decrease in monthly turnover from the original 10% to approximately 4%, and absenteeism diminished to half the previous rate. Manufacturing rejects and scrap loss, which had been very high at Weldon, were reduced 39% by the change program, and customer rejects dropped 57%.

In mid-1969, four and a half years after completion of the organizational change program at Weldon, Bowers and Seashore made a follow-up study to see if early benefits had continued. Their report states: "The Weldon organization, far from reverting to its prior condition, has during recent years made additional progress towards the organizational growth envisioned by the owners and managers in 1962." [13]

Dow Chemical Company is another corporation which has pioneered in testing the Maslow-McGregor motivational theories.

Herbert Doan became president of Dow in 1962 and early the next year, with encouragement of corporate chairman Carl Gerstacker, introduced a new concept of management to the company. Doan referred to Dow as an organization that emphasizes people, not organization. In a speech to Dow employees at Midland, Michigan, on August 14, 1968, he said, "Abraham Maslow of Brandeis University has developed a scale of individual motivation that is well known, and it seems to me sound. It is my belief that we could do the most—achieve almost anything—if we could reach the objective of releasing the ability of each and all of our individuals."

An examination of Dow's statement of corporate objectives reveals the company's emphasis on such concepts as freedom, justice, integrity, creativity, optimism, opportunity, respect for the individual, decentralization, and individual responsibility. The results since 1962 are most impressive. Dow was awarded the 1968 Kirkpatrick award for outstanding management achievement in the chemicals industry. One of the judges who made the award stated, "During the period 1963 through 1967 Dow has absorbed a 22% increase in the cost of wages, salaries, and benefits; has reduced its selling price 13% and yet has been able to achieve an increase of 80% in earnings per share on a 49% rise in sales."

By the end of 1971 Dow's corporate earnings per share were 111% higher than 1962. For that same period the corporate earnings of their four major competitors in the chemical industry had increased by 9%. Dow executives are somewhat reluctant to attribute their success entirely to Theory Y management, pointing out that success or failure in the chemicals industry depends on many complex factors.

Not so reticent is Robert Townsend, past president of Avis. Townsend says:

Since 1952 I've been stumbling around building and running primitive Theory Y departments, divisions, and finally one whole Theory Y company: Avis. In 1962, after 13 years, Avis had never made a profit. Three years later the company had grown internally (not by acquisition) from $30 million sales to $75 million sales, and had made successive annual profits of $1 million, $3 million, and $5 million. If I had anything to do with this, I ascribe it all to my application of Theory Y. And a faltering, stumbling, groping, mistake-ridden application it was.[14]

The Managerial Grid ® concept, the brainchild of Robert Blake and Jane Mouton, has also had a significant impact on motivational theory.[15] The authors define managerial effectiveness in relation to a grid (Exhibit 5) on which the vertical axis is concern for people and the horizontal

Exhibit 5. The Managerial Grid®.

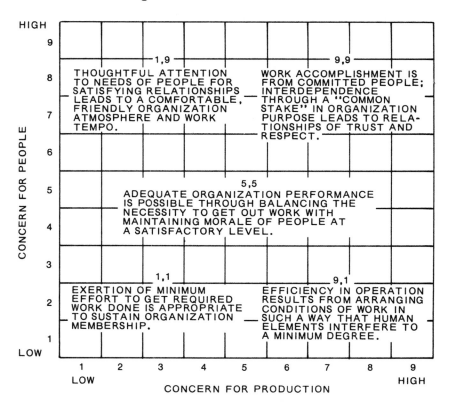

axis concern for production. Each axis is rated on a nine-point scale of concern, with 1 representing minimum and 9 maximum concern. A 1,9 manager gives more consideration to people than production. He assumes that demands for high production will be injurious to the organization, and emphasizes harmonious human relations. At the other extreme is the 9,1 executive. He too assumes an unavoidable conflict between the desires of people and the needs of high production. He feels his responsibilities are to plan, direct, and control the actions of his subordinates in whatever way is necessary to reach the production objectives of the enterprise. The boss plans, subordinates execute.

A 1,1 manager is the least effective. He has little concern for people or production. His motto is "Don't make waves" and his style is conformity, neutrality, and indecision. The 9,9 manager combines a high concern with production with a high concern for people. This is the ideal, based on the assumption that there is not an inherent conflict between the needs for high production and the needs of people. The objective of 9,9 leadership is to maximize productivity through utilization of creativity, team action, and high morale.

Shigeru Kobayashi was manager of Sony's Atsugi plant from 1961 to 1969. The majority of Japanese executives, he says, have tended to copy Western technology, both in the physical sciences and in managerial techniques. He describes the typical Japanese corporation as too concerned with structure, power, and authority and not sufficiently concerned about people.

> Traditional authoritarian organizations, in contrast to their creative counterparts, are pitifully troubled with arteriosclerosis; they are in danger of becoming immobile in the effort to maintain order. For, in such organizations, order disintegrates when people try to move in directions which are not provided for by their rule books. . . .
>
> Mere workers are seldom given credit for caring about their companies or their jobs in the slightest degree, much less loving them. Hence the justification for managers using their subordinates as tools—as slaves who must perform in exactly the way they are told to perform. This rationalization is virtually accepted as an axiom of organization and is reflected in invincible power-consciousness.[16]

Kobayashi sought to test the idea that given the proper people-oriented industrial climate, workers had vast potential and that all of them, consciously or unconsciously, were seeking worthwhile work that was enjoyable and exciting. He calls it people-oriented management based on the principle of perpetual search for perfection and growth.

The Atsugi plant manufactures transistors. Eighty-five percent of its workforce were girls graduated from junior high schools. They were recruited in groups from rural areas and lived in company dormitories. Although they were young, the Sony workers were not always docile. They had staged a strike on Sony's fifteenth anniversary, and they had a poor reputation with townspeople surrounding the plant. Kobayashi was determined to create a positive new relationship between executives and workers. He was familiar with American research at the University of Michigan and Texas Instruments and by Herzberg and others, and set out to give Theory Y the ultimate test. He wanted, he said, to "establish a system which will make people work voluntarily and make them feel worthy of living."

The entire plant was loosely organized into interlocking teams similar to the organizational concept developed by Likert. Responsibility was shifted downward in the organization. Time clocks were abandoned. Company surveillance in worker dormitories and the cafeteria was replaced by worker responsibility. Employees at all levels were involved in planning their own jobs. They were responsible not only for planning and performance but for checking results too. Workers were held accountable for producing results. But it was a positive rather than a negative process. Says Kobayashi:

> Under the principle of trust in human beings the checking that takes place is not meant to be surveillance. It is and can only be intended as encouragement—a fact that can never be overemphasized. Should we check for the purposes of surveillance even slightly, our trust in human beings would become mere lip service, and we would then be contradicting ourselves.

> Indeed, the trust we have come to place in our people in many such ways, the confidence growing out of their efforts to live up to this trust, and the universal satisfaction that has resulted comprise the backbone of the employer-employee relationship in our plant.[17]

He contrasts the approach at the Atsugi plant to more traditional management.

> Managers tend to place the job to be done ahead of people and to think of people as tools for doing that job. This makes them look chiefly for shortcomings in workers. . . . Overcoming this tendency requires, therefore, that managers think of the workers first and the job to be done second, as a means by which the worker supports himself. Only as managers assume this kind of attitude will they begin to know their workers' strength better.[18]

Did it work? Sony's Atsugi plant became an outstanding demonstration of professional people-oriented leadership. Mr. Kobayashi says:

> I myself have never entertained any thought that people could be so capable. My surprise, like that of my fellow managers, truly testifies to the fact that industrial companies have been utilizing only the "cogwheel" portions of their human resources, and that they have failed to make use of those qualities in human beings which determine their true nature. If each and every employee were to behave like a president, we would be able to mobilize a tremendous amount of energy from them. What could be more exciting and fantastic? . . .
>
> Sometimes this performance exceeds the wildest limits of the imagination; the aggregate abilities of people comprising a little team can produce results that defy expectations. . . . Management will make full use of the potential capacity of its human resources only when each person in an organization is a member of one or more effectively functioning work groups that have a high degree of group loyalty, effective skills of interaction, and high performance goals.[19]

The examples cited in this chapter indicate the direction and growing momentum of modern motivational thought. The list is far from complete. Many other companies, consultants, and research projects could be mentioned, but our conclusion would not change. Executive concern for the human element is increasing both in quantity and in quality. It is, as Myers says, "the remaining frontier offering competitive advantage to the organizations most successful in channeling human talent and energy into constructive outlets."

10

Motivational Theory

I believe the real difference between success and failure in a corporation can very often be traced to the question of how well the organization brings out the great energies and talents of its people.
                                     Thomas J. Watson, Jr.

EXECUTIVES who want to increase their effectiveness with people need to understand theory as well as practice. Kurt Lewin, himself a pioneer in motivational research, liked to say, "There is nothing more practical than a good theory."

The theoretical approach is so basic in the physical sciences that we take it for granted. The conquest of outer space is an excellent example of the practical application of theory. As a result of theoretical knowledge, scientists who had never been in space devised the program that placed men on the moon.

The aircraft industry pays designers for spending tens of thousands of hours designing a new aircraft. Then additional resources are expended in producing a working model. When the plane is done, and preliminary ground testing complete, a test pilot confidently climbs aboard and takes off. Blind trial and error? Not on his life! Each new design is based on a solid theoretical understanding of the dynamics of flight.

Technical progress is seldom the result of blind trial and error, but is for the most part the result of research and testing, and a growing understanding of the laws of the physical universe. Occasionally there is a breakthrough, a new insight which changes man's perception about chemistry or physics or astronomy or some other aspect of nature. A breakthrough that makes the impossible suddenly possible.

For centuries tuberculosis caused more deaths than any other disease. Doctors believed the disease to be hereditary and incurable. It took a young doctor, Edward Trudeau, who contracted tuberculosis soon after his graduation from medical school in 1871, to overturn the erroneous theory. He discovered that rest and diet were the secret to recovery. Because he made a theoretical breakthrough, a destructive disease once considered incurable is under control. As long as doctors clung to the incorrect theory, they could not cure TB, and did not even try.

The importance of theory is a basic premise of modern education. We do not teach students merely how to solve geometric problems, we also teach them how the formula is developed. In other words, we teach *why* as well as *how*. An understanding of motivational theory has the following advantages to executives.

1. Executives who understand theory—*why* as well as *how*—usually have a better understanding of *how*.
2. Theorists are usually ahead of pragmatists. The individual who follows theory is in a position to hear about new ideas first.
3. An understanding of theory is an invaluable aid to teaching motivational ideas to neophytes.
4. Most scientific progress is a result of theoretical breakthroughs rather than blind trial and error.
5. Motivational theory has both a broader factual base and a broader field of application than just the management of organizations (for example, child training, marriage, education, economics and political science).

The executive lacking an adequate understanding of human behavior does not know how to improve his own effectiveness with people. And even though he may have intuitively developed effective people-handling techniques, he finds it difficult to teach these skills to younger executives. He cannot project his work-acquired knowledge of people to other important areas of his personal, social, and civic life.

In discussions with hundreds of executives, I have found that the majority, if they are familiar with motivational concepts at all, know about McGregor's "X" and "Y" management but only a very small percentage know anything about the work of Abraham Maslow, which was the source of McGregor's ideas about motivation.

Maslow's motivational research had a broad multidisciplinary base. The general soundness of the theory has now been tested not only in management but in other areas of human behavior as well (education, child training, psychiatry, rehabilitation, clinical psychology) and has consistently proved its ability to produce excellent results.[1] Maslow was critical of some aspects of McGregor's work, but unfortunately his criticisms have not been well publicized in management literature.

He was disturbed by what he considered McGregor's naive assumption that everyone in industry is fairly well adjusted. Maslow said:

> A certain proportion of the population cannot take responsibility well and are frightened by freedom, which tends to throw them into anxiety, etc. This has been noticed often enough by the clinicians, but the management people apparently are not used to thinking in this way yet. . . . The healthy organization will need a steady supply of fairly well-matured and well-educated personalities (it cannot use delinquents, criminals, cynical kids, spoiled and indulged kids, hostile people, war mongers, destroyers, vandals, and so on).[2]

Maslow warned that workers used to tough, authoritarian leadership were apt to take advantage of what they considered weak managers. Maslow knew this from firsthand experience with students who did not respond well to a permissive educational environment.

> The correct thing to do with authoritarians is to take them realistically for the bastards they are and then behave towards them as if they were bastards. If one smiles at them, and assumes that trusting them and giving them the key to the pantry is going to reform them suddenly, then all that will happen is that the silver will get stolen.[3]

One of the distinctive features of Maslow's work was his emphasis on the study of the finest psychological specimens available. He compared this approach to that of the athlete who, seeking to improve his performance, always studied the best rather than the average performer. Maslow called his outstanding individuals self-actualizers— describing them as those who were achieving the full use and exploitation of talents, capacities, potentiality, etc. Such people, he said, seemed to be fulfilling themselves and doing the best that they were capable of doing.

Maslow believed that these outstanding individuals established a model of excellence for the entire human race. Maslow criticized other psychological theories for their emphasis on the study of the psychologically ill, animals, and statistical averages. He pointed out that the orthodox theories neither fit the existing facts, nor were they productive in solving society's mounting human problems.

He called his position the Third Force to distinguish it from Freudianism and Behaviorism, the two theories which have almost monopolized psychiatry, psychology and the social sciences. His book, *Motivation and Personality*, published in 1954, was a reaction to these pathology-centered theories which he knew so well.

His central concept was that the entire human species has common and apparently unchanging psychological needs (weak instincts). These needs, at least the more basic ones, form a hierarchy of urgency or importance, starting with the physiological needs for air, water, food, shelter, sex, and so forth. Man seeks, often unconsciously, to satisfy his needs, placing emphasis first on the most urgent; and, as these are satisfied, another need is felt in its place.

Shortly before his death in 1970, Dr. Maslow prepared an updated chart of psychological needs (Exhibit 6) for inclusion in my book *The Third Force*.

Dr. Maslow made a distinction between the basic needs, which he called "deficiency needs," and the "growth needs," or "higher needs." He believed that the higher nature of man required the lower nature as a foundation and, without this foundation, the higher nature collapsed. "The major emphasis in humanistic psychology," he stated, "rests on the assumptions regarding 'higher needs.' They are seen as biologically based, part of the human essence."

People who achieve a higher degree of self-actualization behave in a different way than the majority. Rather than struggling with life, these actualized people are more spontaneous, expressive, natural, and free, almost as if they have gotten to the top of the hill and are now coasting down the other side. The higher needs are not in a hierarchy. All are of equal value and are interrelated. Maslow estimated that only a tiny percentage, certainly less than 2% of the human race, ever achieved self-actualization. Self-actualized people, Maslow found, have the following characteristics.

1. *Purposeful.* Without exception, self-actualized people seem to be dedicated to some important work, project, or vocation. They work hard because they enjoy it, and the usual distinction between work and play tends to become blurred. Maslow concluded that commitment to an important task is a primary requirement for growth, self-actualization, and happiness.

2. *Realistic.* These people see life clearly as it is rather than as they wish it to be. They are less emotional and more objective about their observations of self and others. They are far above average in their ability to judge people and see through phonies. They are more accurate

Exhibit 6. Abraham Maslow's hierarchy of needs.

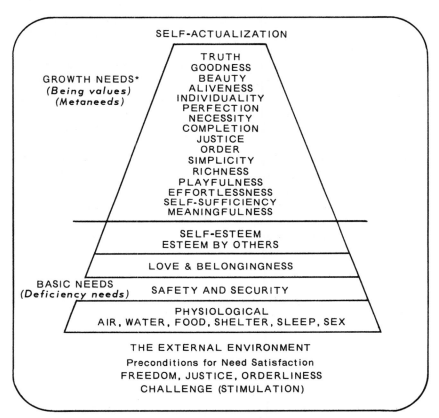

SELF-ACTUALIZATION

GROWTH NEEDS*
(Being values)
(Metaneeds)

TRUTH
GOODNESS
BEAUTY
ALIVENESS
INDIVIDUALITY
PERFECTION
NECESSITY
COMPLETION
JUSTICE
ORDER
SIMPLICITY
RICHNESS
PLAYFULNESS
EFFORTLESSNESS
SELF-SUFFICIENCY
MEANINGFULNESS

SELF-ESTEEM
ESTEEM BY OTHERS

LOVE & BELONGINGNESS

BASIC NEEDS
(Deficiency needs)   SAFETY AND SECURITY

PHYSIOLOGICAL
AIR, WATER, FOOD, SHELTER, SLEEP, SEX

THE EXTERNAL ENVIRONMENT
Preconditions for Need Satisfaction
FREEDOM, JUSTICE, ORDERLINESS
CHALLENGE (STIMULATION)

* Growth needs are all of equal importance (not hierarchical)

SOURCE: Frank Goble, *The Third Force* © 1970 Thomas Jefferson Research Center.

in their prediction of future events and tend to have a well-defined notion of what is right and wrong.

3. *Creative.* Creativity was another universal characteristic of all the outstanding people Maslow studied. He found creativity almost synonymous with health and self-actualization. The characteristics he found associated with creativity were flexibility, courage, spontaneity, willingness to make mistakes, openness, and humility.

4. *Humble.* They have the ability to listen to others and readily admit that they don't know everything and that they are not always

right. Because they are self-confident, they are not always defending themselves.

5. *Considerate.* They are able to understand other people's positions, even when they don't agree with them. Thus they are willing and able to consider other people's needs and feelings.

6. *Ethical.* "Trust, goodness, and beauty are in the average person in our culture only fairly correlated with each other, and in the neurotic person, even less so. It is only in the evolved and mature human being, in the self-actualizing, fully functioning person, that they are so highly correlated that for all practical purposes they may be said to fuse into a unity." [4] This discovery, Maslow said, is in contradiction to a basic axiom guiding most modern scientific thought—the axiom that the more objective, factual, and scientific perception becomes, the more removed it is from ethics and morality. Modern intellectuals, he said, have come to believe that facts and values are in contradiction to each other. Maslow's study of superior individuals seemed to refute this cornerstone of modern "scientific" faith.

7. *Spontaneous.* Spontaneity is almost synonymous with creativity. It refers to the quality of being natural, expressive, simple, and open.

8. *Courageous.* "Every one of our great creators . . . has testified to the element of courage that is needed in the lonely moment of creation, affirming something new (contradictory to the old). This is a kind of daring, a going out in front all alone, a defiance, a challenge. The moment of fright is quite understandable, but must nevertheless be overcome if creation is to be possible." [5]

9. *Self-disciplined.* These individuals find self-discipline relatively easy because what they desire to do conforms with what they believe is right. Their values are self-developed, rather than imposed by others. They live within a system of stable values and not in a robot world of no values at all. They are responsible because they believe responsibility is rewarding.

10. *Self-confident.* These people have a healthy respect for themselves, based on the knowledge that they are competent and decisive. They have a feeling of power stemming from a feeling of self-control.

11. *Integrated.* Because they have a purpose in life and well-developed ideas about right and wrong, self-actualized people have little self-conflict. They are not at war with themselves. Their personality is integrated. This gives them more energy for productive purposes.

Maslow's theoretical work, and its projection into industry by Douglas McGregor and by Maslow himself in *Eupsychian Management*, has had a tremendous influence on ideas about leadership and organization. The Hierarchy of Needs is quoted and reprinted again and again as if it were engraved on stone tablets. Yet Maslow himself was the first to admit that this was only a theoretical point of departure. He recommended further research, investigation, and clarification, evidencing the same humility that he found in other self-actualized individuals.

A vast amount of research has occurred since the publication of *Motivation and Personality* in 1954. It is more than enough, in my opinion (and in Maslow's too), to substantiate the general validity of his theory. At the same time, it indicates the need for reexamination of some of the details. Are people's psychological needs in a rigid hierarchy, as McGregor and many others have implied? Does a person fully satisfy his need for security before he seeks love, affection, and self-esteem? Are any of the needs ever fully satisfied? Do most people, even mature people, ever really satisfy their need for security? For example, does an individual who suffered hardship during the Great Depression of the 1930s ever feel entirely secure, no matter how prosperous he is today?

McGregor stated that only unsatisfied needs are motivators. My observation is that many people who have suffered basic need deprivation in the past are still motivated by that need, even though it seems to be satisfied at the moment. For example, individuals who were deprived of love in their childhood seem to need more love than those who grew up in a loving environment.

Is it logical to put sexual needs in the same category with physical survival needs? Survival needs are necessary for the individual to exist. The propagational needs, strong as they are, are not necessary for the existence of the individual. They are necessary for the survival of the species.

What are the basic needs? Did Maslow identify them correctly? Industrial research seems to indicate that achievement is a basic need. People have a need to achieve, which is slightly different from Maslow's need to grow or self-actualize. Maslow himself found that people need purpose. All his self-actualized people had it. Isn't it logical to assume that purpose is a basic need?

Victor Frankl has stressed this weakness in Maslow's work. Frankl believes that purpose is the prime motivator in life. He points out that purpose, or the lack of it, was the difference between life and death in German concentration camps. People with a purpose for living seemed to be able to withstand incredible hardships. The same phenomenon was revealed in the study of the behavior of American soldiers captured in Korea. Many of them simply lost their will to survive. It was almost as if they died of purposelessness.

Is self-actualization the overall motivational force? Or is it, as some of the greatest philosophers in history have contended, happiness? Happiness which results from self-actualization?

Is Maslow's distinction between basic needs and higher needs scientifically valid? Isn't there a great deal of evidence to indicate that freedom, justice, order, and challenge are just as necessary for psychological health as self-esteem and approval from others?

Does Maslow give an adequate explanation of why people fail to actualize their potential? I had a number of conversations with him on this point. In fact, the addition of the word "challenge" (he preferred to call it "stimulation") among the environmental factors necessary for self-actualization was a result of our conversations. Our discussions revolved around the point that a number of outstanding economists, particularly Adam Smith and Henry George, had concluded that the human species tended to conserve energy and that effort required some challenge or motivating force. Toynbee reached a similar conclusion from his study of the rise and fall of civilizations. Maslow was unfamiliar with the literature of economics. The evidence that impressed him was the work of George Kingsley Zipf, the Harvard scientist who developed an empirical basis for the concept of human conservation of energy. Zipf published his findings in 1949 in a book entitled *Human Behavior and the Principle of Least Effort*.

In our seminars we have found that experienced executives take it for granted that people must be motivated. That is, people won't work unless there is some reason for it. The idea that all humans have a psychological need to conserve energy confirms this pragmatic observation. It helps explain a contradiction in Maslow's original theory. He found it difficult to explain why, if growth toward self-actualization is normal and healthy, such a small percentage ever achieve self-actualization. The concept of human economy of effort suggests that the failure is because few people learn how to overcome their natural tendency toward inertia. This concept is very significant in the field of economics, where it represents a fundamental difference of opinion between advocates of socialism and those who believe in capitalism.

McGregor, Herzberg, Myers, and others have suggested that workers want responsibility. Yet most executives are frustrated by the fact that workers seem to avoid responsibility. This is true not only in the industrial situation but perhaps even more so in churches and civic organizations. Do people really seek responsibility? Or do people accept additional responsibility because they have learned that it has a payoff in greater freedom, achievement, and job advancement?

Exhibit 7. A revised hierarchy of needs.

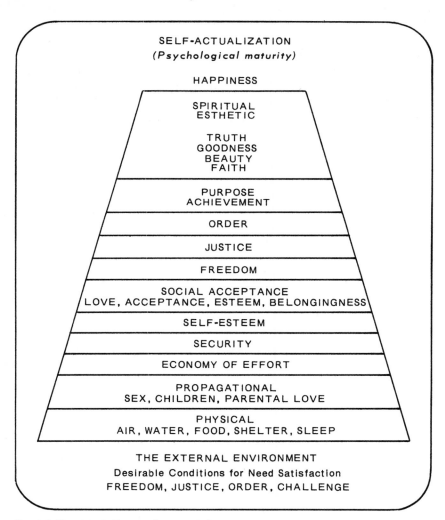

SELF-ACTUALIZATION
(Psychological maturity)

HAPPINESS

SPIRITUAL
ESTHETIC

TRUTH
GOODNESS
BEAUTY
FAITH

PURPOSE
ACHIEVEMENT

ORDER

JUSTICE

FREEDOM

SOCIAL ACCEPTANCE
LOVE, ACCEPTANCE, ESTEEM, BELONGINGNESS

SELF-ESTEEM

SECURITY

ECONOMY OF EFFORT

PROPAGATIONAL
SEX, CHILDREN, PARENTAL LOVE

PHYSICAL
AIR, WATER, FOOD, SHELTER, SLEEP

THE EXTERNAL ENVIRONMENT
Desirable Conditions for Need Satisfaction
FREEDOM, JUSTICE, ORDER, CHALLENGE

Exhibit 7 is my suggestion for a revised hierarchy of needs. It minimizes the distinction between basic needs and growth needs, and adds economy of effort and purpose to the list of needs. The revised theory suggests that the hierarchy is less rigid than previous theorists have maintained. It further suggests that the hierarchy varies from individual to individual, on the basis of each person's previous experience. Some place freedom above security, some emphasize purpose (achievement), and so forth. Both security and the need to economize effort are considered to be all-pervasive. A typical individual does not merely seek physical security but seeks it at every level and for every need.

Executives and consultants who fully understand both motivational theory and practice are still few. The majority of psychologists, psychiatrists, and behavioral scientists still cling to the older pathology-centered theories of which Maslow was so critical.

11

Motivational Techniques

*People are the principal asset of any company,
whether it makes things to sell, sells things made
by other people, or supplies intangible services.*
Nothing moves until your people can make it
move.   J. C. Penney

WHAT should leaders know and do about motivation? Briefly stated,
the recommendation is—they should do more. What follows is a more
detailed discussion of methods to motivate people. Motivation is not
yet a science, but from the study of people, both in industry and
elsewhere, there is a growing fund of useful knowledge about human
motivation.

Goal Setting

The establishment of challenging, measurable goals is probably one
of the most powerful motivating techniques of modern management.
Inexperienced supervisors frequently fail to motivate workers because
they are afraid to demand enough. Even experienced managers do not
realize that the establishment of goals has a strong psychological com-
ponent. It is a motivating device.

Astronaut Neil Armstrong was recently asked what the technological
effort of landing Americans on the moon proved about the American
spirit. His answer was:

The Apollo program demonstrated how really dedicated the American can be after he has accepted the challenge.

The entire project team would absolutely not stop working. Every-where you looked people were working late at night and across the weekends, usually without pay, as if their life, or more importantly, the life of their country, depended on it.

They believed in their goal, and they knew every man had to give more than his share to make that goal a reality. I only hope we can agree as well on other goals and see that kind of "American spirit" more often.[1]

Maxwell Maltz, whose *Psycho-Cybernetics* has become a bestseller, says:

Man is by nature a goal-striving being. And because man is "built that way" he is not happy unless he is functioning as he was made to function—as a goal-striver. Thus true success and true happiness not only go together but each enhances the other.[2]

Nor is goal setting restricted to group (organized) activity. It is the secret of personal success too. Every executive needs to apply it in his own life before he can successfully motivate others. Maslow found high purpose an indispensable ingredient for self-actualization.

Establishing challenging goals is only part of the process. If goals are to be truly motivational, they require worker commitment, not merely the leader's desire to achieve them. Goal-seeking procedures must be coupled with other positive motivational techniques described in the pages that follow.

Recognition and Approval

Years ago Andrew Carnegie paid Charles Schwab a million dollars a year. What made Schwab so valuable? "Charlie has a positive genius for handling men," said Carnegie. How did Schwab explain it? "I consider my ability to arouse enthusiasm among men the greatest asset I possess, and the way to develop the best that is in a man is by appreciation and encouragement."

Psychologist Herbert Otto, founder and director of the National Center for the Exploration of Human Potential, gives the following advice to executives:

Your first task is to sensitize yourself, to train yourself to become aware of accomplishments by others. You can be sure that right now you are mostly trained to be sensitive to their deficiencies, slips, and mistakes. Tone down and diminish this tendency you have acquired, this searching awareness of people's problems, their inadequacies and shortcomings. Begin to look for capacities, abilities, and accomplishments of others, their sound qualities, and their latent strengths or potential.[3]

Executives frequently ask at seminars, "But how do we criticize a man when he is wrong?" Criticism, if it is to be successful, needs to come from a supervisor who has first established a climate of respect and acceptance. Self-criticism is more acceptable than criticism by others. Criticism can frequently be avoided by placing the emphasis on problems rather than individuals.

Paul Meyer, president of Success Motivation Institute, recommends that executives

> turn an employee's self-criticism into a stimulus. When you give a man a chance to talk about himself and his work, ask him to tell you where he would like to improve. Chances are you'll get an honest answer, one that is based on honest insight. Then, if he knows you sincerely want to help him improve, he will try his darndest to improve himself.[4]

The inability to accept constructive criticism is a characteristic of emotional immaturity. Unaccepted criticism has no value—in fact it frequently has negative value, as it diminishes the self-respect of the immature person. So the executive's success as a critic depends on his understanding of the other person.

There are dozens of ways creative executives can give recognition and approval—achievement awards, safety awards, departmental awards for cleanliness, 5-, 10-, 15-, 25-year pins, production charts on the wall, mention in the company newsletter, press releases to the newspaper, suggestion awards. Unger Electric Tool Company in Hawthorne devised a "Suzie the Solderer" program to honor outstanding women solderers. Western Electric has a similar recognition program, the "100,000 Perfect Solder Club." Delta Airlines gives every employee down to the baggage clerk an opportunity to discuss his job with a top executive at least once a year.

Opportunity and Security

Workers need a feeling of security. It is a basic psychological need. The best way to provide it is through a policy of organizational growth.

Growth and sound procedures for promotion from within provide the necessary opportunity. "The chance to get ahead is essential to a good working climate," said Frederick R. Kappel, former AT&T board chairman.

"Fear exerts a heavy price upon the institution and upon the people within the institution," states William Crockett, vice president of Saga Corporation. "It reduces the freedom people feel to innovate, to be creative, to change and be responsive. It results in a rigidity of attitude, of structure and response and, worst of all, it strips us of some of our humanness." [5]

It is unrealistic to expect employees to increase their efficiency or output if the result is decreased job security. Here is an illustration.

At D. B. Milliken Company it was an unquestioned assumption that there was a three-month lag between receipt of an order for high-speed cameras and the effect of that order on our assembly department. Thus it was assumed that, if orders received peaked in January, activity in our assembly department would reach its peak three months later. Almost by accident, one of our supervisors superimposed a chart of camera backlog dollars on a chart of assembly department productivity. He was amazed to discover that at a time when sales backlogs were slim, productivity per worker was correspondingly low, but productivity increased at once when new orders increased the backlog. His analysis showed rather conclusively that as soon as the assemblers realized their future was secure, they increased their rate of production.

Organizations must establish a policy of continuous growth and opportunity and communicate this policy to employees at all levels.

Achievement

How can executives give people a feeling of achievement? The answer is challenging goals, worker involvement, plans that succeed, and feedback regarding task accomplishment. The consensus of qualified authorities is that achievement even without recognition is a motivator. Recognition may increase the effect but achievement is, so to speak, its own reward.

However, the research at Texas Instruments confirmed Herzberg's discovery that some people are "maintenance seekers"—people who "realize little satisfaction from accomplishment and express cynicism regarding the positive virtue of work and life in general." In contrast, "motivation seekers" are more inner-directed and self-sufficient and enjoy work and achievement.

Mitchell Fein, who bases his observations on many years of consulting to companies with "mass production" employees (those with large numbers of people in routine tasks requiring little skill), believes that for the nation as a whole achievement-oriented workers may be as low as 15 to 20% of the workforce.[6] But Robert Ford, author of *Motivation Through the Work Itself*, believes at least 85 to 90% of workers can be motivated through their work.

Kobayashi's experience at Sony would seem to indicate that when the motivational climate is sufficiently positive, nearly all workers feel satisfaction from achievement. It's true that Kobayashi's workers were mostly young girls and from a different culture.

Consultant Warren Bowles suggests that the fault is more frequently with the work situation than with the worker.

> To be strongly motivated, the employee needs to feel that his job is important and meaningful, and that his contribution to doing it has real value. Achievement can be gratifying even if there is no formal recognition of it. It is achievement for achievement's sake, a pride in workmanship and an identification of the value of oneself with the value of work.[7]

Mary Parker Follett, a respected and perceptive observer of the industrial scene during the 1920s, anticipated many of the motivational concepts we advocate today:

> We often tend to think that the executive wishes to maintain standards, wishes to reach a certain quality of production, and that the worker has to be goaded in some way to do this. Again and again we forget that the worker is often, usually, I think, equally interested, that his greatest pleasure in his work comes from the satisfaction of worthwhile accomplishment, of having done the best of which he is capable.[8]

Accountability

Almost two hundred years ago Adam Smith wrote:

> In every profession, the exertion of the greater part of those who exercise it is always in proportion to the necessity they are under in making the exertion. . . . Exertion is always in proportion to its necessity. . . . The endowments of schools and colleges have necessarily diminished more or less the necessity of application in

their teachers. Their subsistence, so far as it arises from their
salaries, is evidently derived from a fund altogether independent
of their success and reputation in their particular profession.[9]

Smith went on to predict that in universities where pay was unrelated
to performance the quality of performance would sink.

Unfortunately leadership terminology is not precise. Words like
"responsibility," "measurement," "controls," "feedback," "audit," and
"accountability" are frequently used interchangeably. Joe Batten defines
"control" as "information provided to measure the performance of
men, money, materials, time, and space in achieving predetermined
objectives." "Accountability" is a closely related word but it implies
more. Perhaps the simplest explanation is that people in an organization
are given responsibility for a task and then held accountable for its
accomplishment. Controls are various methods of measuring accountability. Accountability, then, in the sense I am using it, implies
measurement of results, but it also implies, and this is the important
distinguishing feature, that some other individual or group of individuals
is observing the measurement. When a man is held accountable for
something, he is not permitted to pass the buck.

Edward Glaser, West Coast consulting psychologist, offers an example of how accountability motivates executives.[10] One of his client firms
had a manufacturing division that was doing poorly. Operating costs
were high, but productivity was low and the division was losing money.
On Glaser's first visit he found a typical pattern of buck passing. When
he talked to the department heads, each of them placed the blame
elsewhere.

Glaser recommended to the corporation president that the name
of the game be changed from "surviving by not admitting any mistakes"
to frankly admitting problems and solving them or perishing. In
executive conference, goals were established regarding the percentage
of the market this division should expect to capture if design, price,
quality, and service were first-rate. Then department heads were told
that unless they could capture the desired share of the market the
company would stop making that product and lay off the 60 or so
hourly workers involved.

Once it became clear that they would be held accountable for
specific results, the supervisors shifted, with the help of the consultant,
to a problem-solving approach. Three months after the change in
approach, productivity had risen 32%, and rejections had dropped from
12 to 9%. In less than three years after intervention productivity was

190% greater than in the beginning, and rejects had dropped to 3.2%.

There are many devices to establish accountability—performance reviews, audits, inspection reports, and the like. Executives need to be careful what they measure, especially if measurement is coupled with pay and advancement. When a school principal established attendance at meetings as one of his criteria for teacher performance, teachers made it a point to attend meetings. Unfortunately this activity had virtually no correlation with their major objective, which was to be effective classroom teachers. In most cases measurement of an activity will cause an increase in people's productivity, even though the measurement is not related to pay or promotion.

When accountability is used in a positive manner to establish the basis for approval, recognition, achievement, and promotion, then results tend to be positive. When management uses statistical information in a critical and destructive way, the employees react accordingly. Now they may conceal their errors and even falsify records.

Peter Drucker gives two examples showing the difference between positive and negative accountability, which he says "will inflict incalculable harm by demoralizing management, and by seriously lowering the effectiveness of managers." He cites General Electric as an example for the positive approach.

> General Electric has a special control service—the traveling auditors. The auditors study every one of the managerial units of the company thoroughly at least once a year. But their report goes to the manager of the unit studied. There can be little doubt that the feeling of confidence and trust in the company, which even casual contact with General Electric managers reveals, is directly traceable to this practice of using information for self-control rather than for control from above.

> But the General Electric practice is by no means common or generally understood. Typical management thinking is much closer to the practice exemplified by a large chemicals company.

> In this company a control section audits every one of the managerial units of the company. Results of the audits do not go, however, to the managers audited. They go only to the president, who then calls in the managers to confront them with the audit of their operations. What this has done to morale is shown in the nickname the company's managers have given the control section: "the president's Gestapo." Indeed, more and more managers are now running their units not to obtain the best performance but to obtain the best showing on the control-section audits.[11]

Job Enrichment

Job enrichment, or job enlargement as it is sometimes called, is receiving increasing attention from a variety of organizations. Andrew Kay, president of Non-Linear Systems, influenced by Maslow, Likert, McGregor, and Drucker, started motivational experiments in 1960. His company was the inspiration for Maslow's *Eupsychian Management.*

Non-Linear manufactures digital voltmeters in competition with 30 other companies. Kay threw out the assembly line approach and divided production workers into teams of three to nine people with a great deal of independence. "Responsibility for quality," says Andrew Kay, "is placed where we feel it should be—upon the individual making the instrument . . . we regard management as basically an affair of teaching and training, not one of directing and controlling. We control the process, not the people."

Time clocks and regular coffee breaks were abandoned. Workers took a break whenever it was convenient. The first result of the experiment was to boost morale sky high and completely disrupt production, but after three months, production began to climb. Within three years productivity per worker was up 30%, while employee turnover was down to one-fourth the national average; customer complaints had dropped more than 70%. An unexpected bonus was increased corporate flexibility. New models, which used to take eight and ten weeks to develop, were now turned out in two or three weeks.

Now Non-Linear uses job enrichment throughout the company. For example, the company formerly had several men in the purchasing department who did nothing but place orders. Today their responsibilities are much broader, including planning, buying, scheduling, stock control, and expediting. Engineers have more variety too. It is not unusual to see a top designer working at the bench with a screwdriver or soldering iron. Sometimes technicians and assembly workers are found in the engineering department discussing a design problem. Kay admits that some of the procedures might not be possible in a union shop, but his enthusiasm for job enrichment is higher today than it was in the beginning, and he considers the program essential for the maintenance of high morale, low turnover, and increased worker efficiency.

Frederick Herzberg helped AT&T install experimental job enrichment programs in 1965. One problem was low morale in a department handling correspondence with AT&T's more than three million stockholders. Herzberg's recommendation was to relax supervision and let each girl take full responsibility for writing and signing her own replies. "All we did really," says AT&T personnel executive Robert Ford, "was let them run their own jobs." As a result, turnover dropped and productivity and morale went from 33 to 90 (on a scale of 1 to 100) in six months without changes in salary classifications.

More recently the Bell System launched an ambitious program to enrich jobs at all levels. The project is called "Work Itself." Alfred Van Sinderen, president of Southern New England Telephone Company, defines the concept as: "A planned, continued effort managed from the top, on a companywide basis, to provide satisfying jobs for employees and to increase the company's effectiveness and health." A typical application is at Indiana Bell, where 16 girls were performing 21 operations in producing telephone directories for a number of small cities. Management started "green light" sessions, inviting the girls to voice their criticisms and make suggestions for improvement. Now one girl does an entire directory herself and checks for her own errors. The result is fewer errors, reduced turnover, and significantly higher production.

American Airlines uses job enrichment at its huge maintenance base at Tulsa. In place of assembly line techniques a small team of aircraft mechanics are given a full responsibility for a jet engine. They take it apart, inspect it, and rebuild it. The result is greater pride in the job and a return to craftsmanship.

Job enlargement can be either horizontal or vertical. Horizontal enlargement involves the worker in a greater variety of operations on the assembly line or in the work situation. Vertical enlargement involves the employee in the functions previously reserved for supervision—planning, organizing, leading, and controlling.

Shigeru Kobayashi describes horizontal job enlargement at Sony, calling it the "one-man production method." He tells how it is used to enable one man to assemble a whole television unit.

A table which looks like the lazy-Susan in a Chinese restaurant is placed in front of a worker. Around this table is placed one lot of 20 chassis, and on both sides of the worker there is an array of parts. For his first process, he takes up one part and attaches it to each of the 20 chassis, turning the table as he does so. Next, for the second process, he picks up another part and adds it to all the chassis. Then he proceeds to the third process—and so on. In this way he does a complete job on the product. . . .

One-man production admittedly does require time for training, but the higher intelligence level of workingmen nowadays makes it easy for us to implement the method. Also, workers are better motivated to work. One-man production creates a strong sense of responsibility in a man because of the identification of his workmanship with a final product such as a television set. However, nothing like this sense of responsibility would ever exist under the conveyer-belt system. . . .

We applied this one-man production method to jobs that used to be meaninglessly segmented, and we achieved excellent performance in these work areas. In fact, phenomenal improvements in quality and efficiency resulted.[12]

Financial Incentives

Douglas McGregor concentrated attention on nonfinancial objectives. Some observers believe that the pendulum has swung too far. In discussing money, for example, Du Pont personnel man James Sears says, "Just take it away and see what happens."

Mitchell Fein has been particularly critical of what he considers the behavioral scientists' overemphasis on nonfinancial motivation. He has assembled an impressive array of statistical data in support of his contention that financial incentives are still of prime importance. He points to a Conference Board survey of the pay practices of salesmen revealing that in the past decade the use of incentives, in addition to salary, increased from approximately 53 to 86%.

And in another Conference Board survey of compensation for top executives, the conclusion was that approximately 63% of the top three officers in manufacturing companies are paid on an incentive basis, with the median bonus equal to 37% of their base wages. If financial incentives are necessary to motivate executives and sales personnel, asks Fein, why should we expect them to be less important for production workers? He says that an estimated 60% of the Soviet Russian workforce is on wage incentives, compared to about 27% in the United States.[13]

The Cuban government, in spite of Castro's personal antipathy to material incentives or rewards of any kind, has been forced into the use of incentives because of the need to stimulate production. In July 1971 Castro announced that the best sugarcane cutters would receive cash bonuses in addition to their regular wages. These bonus payments are equivalent in American dollars to some $50 to $110 a month. Similar incentive devices are now being extended into industry too.

During World War II, D. B. Milliken Company utilized a variety of individual and group incentive procedures. One group bonus plan was spectacularly successful, enabling us to achieve production records which in the beginning we would have considered impossible. The job involved a subassembly for a five-inch rocket, and consisted of such tasks as cutting, soldering, staking, assembling, grinding, inserting, and testing—22 operations in all.

The work was performed by ten girls on each shift; thus each girl had to perform, on the average, about two operations. The parts moved from station to station on roller conveyers, and the line included a variety of standard and special machines, tools, and fixtures. At the end of each shift we totaled the number of units produced. Customer rejects were deducted from the daily total on the day they were returned and each rejected part was counted as if it were two. The assemblers were paid a cash bonus in addition to their regular hourly wage, and the bonus was based on units produced per worker hour. Our estimated time per unit—our breakeven plus reasonable profit time—was 30 minutes. In the beginning it took 40 minutes a unit, but by the time we had produced a hundred thousand units the production time was approaching 8 minutes.

After we had been in production for about six months the government sought to establish a second source for five-inch rockets. The new manufacturer planned to do most of the operations in his own plant, including the subassembly we were making. His engineers, under disclosure procedures in our manufacturing contract, studied our setup carefully and went back and devised one twice as good (mechanically, that is). But two months later their purchasing agent came to us and asked if we could increase our production to furnish the subassembly to them. It seemed that in their bid they had assumed that they could equal or exceed our production rates since their equipment was much better. But the purchasing agent admitted that at the end of two months of operation their assemblers were spending more than twice as long per assembly as our girls. They had observed our mechanical layout very carefully but ignored our incentive system.

Lincoln Electric Company, manufacturer of welding supplies and equipment, has used cash incentives since 1934. The 1969 bonus, distributed to 1,926 workers, was $16.4 million. In recent years the annual bonus has frequently exceeded the employee's regular pay. Lincoln Electric believes that integrity, trust, and worker security are essential to the success of its plan. After two years of employment, employees are guaranteed 52 pay checks for at least 30 hours of pay each week. With some of the highest paid industrial workers in the world, Lincoln also reports higher earnings than its competitors.

In 1959 the Profit Sharing Research Foundation made a study of 14 department store chains, 7 with and 7 without profit sharing, and 16 food store chains, 11 with and 5 without profit sharing. In each case the profit-sharing organizations showed significantly better growth and profits than those without.

In 1970 the Foundation completed a follow-up on the department store study to see whether the earlier trends had continued through the sixties.[14] The researchers found that performance trends set in the fifties had continued and accelerated during the sixties. None of the profit-sharing companies discontinued their programs and some of them broadened their programs. And three of the non-profit-sharing companies established profit-sharing plans. The comparison of the profit-sharing stores with the non-profit-sharing group, 1952 to 1969, shows the following.

1952–1969	*Profit-Sharing Companies*	*Non-Profit-Sharing Companies*
Net income as a % of net worth	12.78%	8.00%
Net income as a % of sales	3.62%	2.70%
Growth of invested dollars	$9.89	$5.61
Increase in people employed	103.70%	75.50%

The conclusion of the study is that stockholders, employees, and customers all benefit from profit-sharing plans when properly administered.

The Team Approach

In Chapter 4 we discussed the organizational advantages of the coordinated team approach: how it provides continuous communication and coordination throughout the organization. With skillful leadership it also taps several powerful motivational forces. One is the need to belong —to be an accepted member of a group—as identified by Maslow. A second and probably more powerful force is the desire for approval from a group of one's peers.

Peer-group pressure is the secret of success of Synanon and other similar self-help programs for drug addicts. Synanon succeeds where federal and state institutions with all their psychiatrists and expensive methods of therapy generally fail. They do it by putting each person in a "family," whose approval can only be gained by staying 100% free of drugs.

Peer-group pressure can either increase or decrease production. When the group is in sympathy with company objectives, the result is increased productivity. When they are not (usually because of negative motivational factors in the company), the group will discourage its members from doing any more than is necessary.

Justice

Says outspoken Robert Townsend:

> Fairness, justice, or whatever you call it—it's essential and most companies don't have it. Everybody must be judged on his performance, not on his looks or his manners or his personality or who he knows or is related to. . . .
>
> Rewarding outstanding performance is important. Much more neglected is the equally important need to make sure that the under-achievers *don't* get rewarded. This is more painful, so it doesn't get done very often. . . .
>
> The absolute dollars people get paid are not nearly as important as the pay in relation to someone else. . . . Wilbur worries a lot about the relative fairness of the pay check.[15]

Workers are more perceptive than most managers realize. Whether their formal education is high or low, workers quickly see through managers who try to exploit and deceive them. It is essential that people within an organization receive fair treatment. When justice prevails, it is important that workers know it. Jackson Martindell, head of the distinguished American Institute of Management, says, "Two very important purposes of management are to maintain justice and to maintain authority. Justice comes first, to uphold morale."

Mitchell Fein concurs, stating:

> The secret of how to unloose the motivation genie lies with workers; only they have the power to rub the magic lamp. Workers will want to do this only when relations between management and labor are such that workers see identification with management and increased productivity as in their best interest. Unfortunately, . . . the opposite now prevails: relations between employee and employer are such that if employees cooperate in raising productivity, some employees' interests are damaged. Most managing strategies do not adequately respond to this contradiction and so it is not surprising that practically all plant managers encounter resistance in some form when they move to increase production.[16]

Hand in hand with the need for justice is the need for a climate of trust. Unless this exists, all motivational attempts will fall far short of their full potential. It is not unusual to see an incentive program work exceedingly well in one organization and fail in another because a climate of trust is lacking.

Herb Otto says, "The element of trust is the basic rule in human relations. When we distrust people, they usually sense our attitude and reciprocate in kind." But it is not true, as some psychologists have implied, that trusting everybody will make them trustworthy. People who are habitually dishonest won't reform just because they are trusted. The one thing an executive can control is his own behavior. If he is reliable people will trust him and unless they are habitually dishonest, will respond in kind.

Organizational policies, to be most successful, need to be mutually advantageous to management, labor, customers, and stockholders. The same obtains for universities, schools, government agencies, and churches.

Freedom and Responsibility

Frederick Herzberg maintains that responsibility is a motivator—give workers more responsibility and they will work harder. M. Scott Myers believes that motivational research at Texas Instruments confirms Herzberg's position. Yet observation from many quarters indicates that people generally attempt to minimize effort.

If responsibility is a motivator, then it should be listed as one of man's basic needs. It seems more consistent with the known facts to believe that it is not responsibility that workers seek, but the benefits— greater freedom, the feeling of achievement, and possible financial rewards—that stem from it.

Suggestion Systems

One executive, who prefers to remain anonymous, developed a highly ingenious method to solicit employee suggestions. His past experience with traditional suggestion systems had been less than satisfactory. Workers had been asked to submit suggestions to an appraisal commit- tee, which determined what the suggestion was worth to the company, if anything. Then employees were paid 25% of the first-year value to the company, a policy which was producing a lot of ill will because employees always seem to think their ideas were worth more than the evaluation committee thought they were. It was even worse when the committee turned the idea down entirely.

His new system was an annual idea contest. It sought to encourage the submission of cost reduction ideas from all levels in the organization, which already had a companywide profit-sharing program. The contest lasted for several months each year. Each month while the contest was on, a series of prizes were distributed. The prizes had no relation to the value of the suggestions to the company. They were awarded to the employees whose ideas were rated highest in a 1, 2, 3 order. Only suggestions which offered tangible savings to the organization were eligible.

When suggestions were adopted, the employee was notified in writing and complimented on his idea. When suggestions were not adopted, the employee was also notified in writing, with an explanation of why his idea was not used. Only the three best ideas each month won a prize. In addition to his prize, the first-place winner had his picture taken, receiving the prize from the president of the company, and the framed picture was presented to the winner. This contest system created a lot of interest and many excellent ideas, and it avoided the ill will which the previous system had generated.

Other Motivators

We have listed some important techniques of motivation. Actually the division between these various techniques is not clear-cut. Goals, recognition, accountability, opportunity, participation, job enrichment, the team approach, and similar concepts are intermingled in practice. There are other motivational devices that we have not discussed—achievement dinners, company parties, in-plant newsletters, and other useful ideas to increase employee morale and productivity as well.

What to Do About Motivation

There is probably not an organization in America, large or small, profit or nonprofit, which cannot improve its motivational climate. A truly successful motivational program starts at the top with the chief executive. He must be personally interested, involved, and informed. He may seek the interest and participation of executives and workers, but he cannot avoid personal involvement.

A motivational program starts with the decision to do something, to establish on a continuing basis a systematic approach to motivation. The procedure should be the same as that for any other aspect of management. Establish measurable goals, devise plans, assign responsibilities, allocate resources, get the facts, learn from the experience of others, and utilize outside consultants who have a record of success. Frederick R. Kappel said it rather well:

> Leadership is stirring people so that they are moved from inside themselves. It is stating goals that excite them and lift their sights. It is setting the personal example, putting enthusiasm into the operation, communicating both ways (listening as well as talking). It is rewarding merit and penalizing demerit, honestly and fairly. It is the right combination of these so that people will do the work that makes a business successful *because they want to.*[17]

12

Leadership by Participation

Involvement of people in the planning and controlling, as well as the doing, of their work must be understood not as an act of good "human relations" nor as a means of exploitation, but, rather, as a sound business practice that benefits both the organization and its members.[1]

Mark Shepard, President, Texas Instruments

PARTICIPATIVE leadership offers exciting possibilities for executives seeking to increase organizational effectiveness. There are also unexpected pitfalls when improperly used. Participative leadership involves workers at all levels in the decision-making processes. Management consultant Louis Allen says simply, "Motivation to accomplish results tends to increase as people are given an opportunity to participate in the decisions affecting these results." And Warren Bennis says, "people tend to work more efficiently and with more commitment when they have a part in determining their own fates and have a stake in problem solving."

The Harwood-Weldon demonstration described in a previous chapter offers an excellent model for other organizations. With the late Kurt Lewin as consultant, Harwood's first experiments with worker participation go back to 1939. In the late 1940s the corporation made a number of changes in equipment and methods that required workers to be transferred to new tasks and sometimes to a different department. Workers did not welcome the changes and expressed their resistance by complaints about piecework rates, resignations, low output, and poor morale.[2]

Management set up three experimental groups. The first group followed traditional management practices. The workers were called together and told about the company's situation, and the new methods and procedures were explained to them. The workers were given the opportunity to ask questions about what they were to do.

Group 2 also met with management to hear about the changes. Management stressed the importance of greater efficiency in order to remain competitive in the industry and protect the workers' jobs. This group was asked to choose worker representatives to work with management and help determine the new methods and procedures, explain them to the other workers in the group, and return with the group's ideas and suggestions.

In Group 3, all the workers were invited to participate with management in deciding on new methods and procedures. Although there was no formal vote, there was an attempt to reach decisions based on consensus. Here are the production results.

For Group 1 production dropped 35% after the changes were made and did not improve for a month. Morale was poor and 9% of the group quit within two weeks. A number of others filed grievances about pay rates.

Group 2 adapted to the changes very rapidly and morale was high. Fourteen days after the changeover the group members achieved standard rates of production; by the end of the month productivity was higher than before the changes. The same manager who was being criticized by Group 1 was receiving cooperation from Group 2, and none of the workers quit.

Group 3 performed significantly better than the other two groups. The workers reached their former level of production on the second day, and production continued to increase until it was 14% higher than ever before. Morale was high and none of the workers quit. This experience, says Marrow, "demonstrates that the success of a modern enterprise depends upon motivating the people in the enterprise to accept responsibility, to work together, and thus to maximize their performance and their well-being."

These experiments and others like them enabled Harwood Manufacturing to take over and change leadership practices at Weldon Manufacturing with such great success. When the Weldon executives changed their style of leadership, workers recognized the difference and responded with enthusiasm. "What a welcome change," said one; "this is something Weldon never did before. You have a chance to tell them what you think and you feel you're a part of the company. In the past they told you what to do and you did it."

Another worker's reaction was, "This is a real switch—to get a chance to express ourselves. Before, if you had a problem and told them about it, they'd just pass it off and forget about it." [3]

The Autonetics Division of North American Aviation tested participative leadership in the late sixties. The first 12-month study tested two approaches to participation. In the first test the entire group was involved with their supervisors, but in the second case the employee worked individually with his supervisor. This study indicated that group participation was more effective than individual worker–supervisor participation.

In a second test, nine supervisors were trained in participative procedures. The supervisors were rotated between work groups to observe the differences in their performance. The conclusion was that participative management was highly effective, but not all supervisors were equally successful in obtaining worker participation. Success seemed to be related to the workers' confidence in their supervisors. One of the supervisors discouraged participation by his defensiveness and apparent lack of interest in workers' suggestions. The performance of this group quickly improved when another supervisor took over.

In 1970, like most aerospace companies, TRW had to reduce staff and budgets substantially. One major department had to go through five or six major budget reductions within ten months. Sixteen managers worked on the problem as a team. First they appointed a smaller task force to investigate alternative ways to reduce the budget. Their proposals and recommendations were discussed by the total group, and in many cases a consensus was reached. When it was not, the top-ranking executive made the decision. Sheldon Davis reports that because there was group involvement in the decision-making process, the top man had not only access to more data but also the feelings and opinions of the group to assist him in reaching decisions. And because of group participation, he had their active support in implementing the decisions reached. "This is a very different approach," says Davis, "to the top man pulling way back and making most of the decisions by himself or as a result of a series of individual meetings with his subordinates." [4]

Rensis Likert reports the success of participative leadership in a nonprofit organization. He made a study of 104 representative chapters selected from more than 1,000 chapters of the League of Women Voters. Chapter effectiveness was measured by size compared to the community, rate of growth, success with projects, and successful fundraising campaigns. The poorest results came from those Leagues which Likert described as having "laissez faire" management—a lack of leadership, vague goals, and objectives, and where there was little pressure to participate from any source. At the other extreme were the chapters where the pressure for member participation was very strong but came primarily from the top. These groups were also less effective than in the cases where the pressure came from other sources.

Likert concluded:

> If pressure to participate is to be productive and to lead to greater member activity and greater League effectiveness, the pressure must come from an "acceptable" source [such as] . . . one's own commitments, values, and internalized goals [or] . . . from the goals and objectives established by the face-to-face group of which the person is a regular member. These goals and objectives, established through participation by the group, become powerful sources of pressure. Each member of the group expects each other member to carry her fair share of the task required to realize the goals which the group has established.[5]

Participation is essential in establishing meaningful organizational goals. M. Scott Myers is emphatic about this.

> If the man at the top defines his goals with the genuine involvement of the people below him, his goals are also their goals. But if goal setting is a "top management" function to be "sold" downward through the use of persuasion, authority, bribery, and manipulation, his people respond with words and actions that say, "Those are not my goals, they are management's goals." If "management" is seen as his enemy, the individual fights back in subtle or overt ways, often ingeniously, sometimes unconsciously, to thwart management goals; if management is perceived as benevolent and friendly, he may curb his inner frustrations, turn out a fair day's work, and appreciate their well-intended praise and rewards. But most of the time he thinks and talks about his own goals—which he finds off the job.[6]

Texas Instruments pulls blue-collar people off the line for conferences with executives and engineers. TI President Mark Shepard says, "We've got to get all of our people involved. The girls on the production line may not understand solid-state physics, but they sure as hell do understand the problems of nailing that radar together."

At one time the company was losing money on the production of radar units. The problem and all the pertinent facts were presented to the assemblers involved. Their supervisor asked their help in establishing new procedures to lower man-hours below the 100-hour-per-unit breakeven point. After a two-hour meeting and careful examination of the problem, the group set a standard of 86 hours per unit. Within a short time they had achieved this goal and were producing assemblies in 75 hours. In following meetings, in which the original group increased its effectiveness by calling in engineers, inspectors, and assemblers from other lines, they improved the method still more to achieve a 41-hour level of performance.[7]

Participation does not always work. When supervisors are themselves defensive and insecure, their ability to achieve worker participation will be greatly restricted. Other failures occur when management does not understand how to achieve genuine participation. Mitchell Fein tells about World War II efforts at participation.

In 1942, as a result of the efforts of the War Production Board, approximately 5,000 labor–management committees were established. These committees had the support of government, management, and most of the unions and, yet, according to Fein, the effort was futile. "Despite the tremendous efforts put behind labor–management committees and the all-out publicity, the committees failed in their major goal to involve workers in production and to raise productivity through participation." Fein also cites an international study conducted by Haire, Ghiselle, and Porter, covering 3,600 managers in 14 countries, including West Germany, Japan, and the United States. The study revealed a strange paradox: "These managers felt that participative, group-centered methods of leadership are more effective than traditional directive methods." The survey also revealed: "In each country, in each group of countries, in all the countries taken together, there is a relatively low opinion of the capabilities of the average person." [8]

Fein's conclusion was that the supervisors surveyed believed in participative management because they had been told again and again that it was a good thing, but they did not practice it because, at a deeper level, they did not have sufficient respect for their workers' capabilities.

Fein's interpretation is that a high percentage of workers do not wish to become involved in functions previously reserved for managers. My interpretation is that supervisors who do not believe in worker potential will not succeed until *their* attitude is changed. Supervisors who do not believe in themselves will fail, too.

Participation should not be confused with "democracy"—the idea that everyone should have an equal say in every decision. Participative management is decentralized, but not at the expense of coordination. Likert says, "Although group decision making strives for consensus, not every member has an equal influence on every decision nor do decisions reflect the point of view of the least competent member. . . . Effective group decision making enables every person to be heard, but the weight of each in the decision-making process is influenced appreciably by his demonstrated competence." [9]

Successful participative management might be described as hierarchical participation. Who participates, and the amount of his participation, is still controlled through normal lines of authority. Marrow says:

> [Worker participation] must be consistent with what is feasible and must be realistic in terms of the work to be done. They are not asked to "decide" on anything unless the decision is really up to them. If it is not, they may be asked for their counsel, but not their consent. The distinction is clearly made, in discussing problems with them, between "we'd like your opinion" and "the final decision is going to be up to you." [10]

Texas Instruments does not let workers become involved in the decision-making process until they have had sufficient job experience. TI executive Earl Gomersall says, "It takes three to five months to train an employee to a skill level where he can meaningfully participate in a work improvement program."

Participation is not easy. To succeed, it must be done right. But when it is done right, the results are more than enough to repay the effort involved. Successful participative management not only brings significant increases in production but improves quality and worker morale as well.

13

The Leader Himself

It is generally believed that we need enlightened and responsible leaders—at every level and in every phase of our national life. Everyone says so. But the nature of leadership in our society is very imperfectly understood, and many of the public statements about it are utter nonsense.

John Gardner

IT is the leader himself, as we have previously emphasized, who determines to a large degree the success or failure of the organization. We have discussed his need for three general categories of knowledge and ability—technical, organizational, and psychological. We have found that the leader's need is not for great technical skill, but for broad general knowledge of all technical aspects of his organization. In preceding chapters we have discussed various essential organizational functions such as organizing, goal seeking, staffing, training, communication, research, and motivation. What remains is the need to examine the leader himself—his personality, attitudes, style, and understanding of self and others—the *psychological* aspect of leadership.

Dozens of studies involving many thousands of executives at all levels have sought to discover what determines excellence—those personal characteristics that make some leaders outstanding. Some authorities consider the job hopeless. Koontz and O'Donnell state, "After many years of effort to prove that certain specific qualities should be possessed by managers, the task has been virtually abandoned." And Peter Drucker maintains there is no single "effective personality." His observation of outstanding executives is that they differ widely in their temperaments and abilities, and "all they have in common is the ability to get the right things done." This is a little like saying that among professional football players there are some who are big and some relatively small, some fast, some slow, some strong, some agile, some who are brilliant strategists and others who are not. But would anyone question the idea that the ideal player would be one who is big, fast, agile, strong, and a brilliant strategist?

Since 1942 Sears, Roebuck and Company has conducted research into the characteristics of leadership. Their studies have measured the characteristics and traced the careers of thousands of employees over a period of years. The research results were recently summarized by UCLA professor Theodore Guyton.[1] The tests revealed significant differences between successful executives and random samples of all Sears employees. Guyton says that the Sears study "lends strong support to the hypothesis . . . that there are differences in personal character- istics of more and less successful executives, that the differences can be identified, and that the characteristics associated with executive effective- ness can be measured early in an individual's career."

Guyton says of the excellent leaders, "[Their] outlook is largely involved with setting up and maintaining long-range career expectations . . . they demonstrate a basic involvement with long-term results of efforts, rather than a concern for the specific aspects of the 'here and now.' "

In our seminars we have found it a valuable exercise to identify and describe some of the important characteristics contributing to leadership effectiveness. This information is useful to supervisors at all levels in their self-development efforts and also in their efforts to identify, train, and develop other supervisors.

Here are some of the qualities that contribute to excellent leadership.

Ambition

"A man can succeed," said Charles Schwab, "at almost anything for which he has unlimited enthusiasm." Whether we call it drive, energy, enthusiasm, motivation, ambition, or need for achievement, it is an essential. Almost by definition a leader is a self-starter. People who are unable to motivate themselves must be content to be followers. The popular assumption is that ambition is something you either have or you don't. Yet the literature of personal growth and success says otherwise. Ambition is an attitude, and attitudes, even adult attitudes, can change, sometimes dramatically.

Of course, excessive ambition can be self-defeating, both in achievement of organizational goals and in the life of the executive himself. A few years ago the president of a young but fast-growing corporation managed to take six weeks for a vacation in Europe. Both he and his wife enjoyed the experience so much he decided he would return to his job with renewed vigor and work night and day until he had made enough money to retire so that he and his wife would be free to travel. His colleagues report that from the day of his return he was a changed person. At his insistence the sales department began shading their bids and seeking large orders, which strained production facilities. Soon the company was deep in a program to expand their personnel, plant, and equipment. The rapid expansion with untrained personnel drove costs up and profit margins down. Soon the corporation had reached its credit limit at the bank, and a team of bank auditors came to investigate. Their report showed the previously thriving corporation was now in serious trouble. A week later, in perfect health, the president shot himself. He was not yet 45.

Persistence

Napoleon Hill spent most of his adult years studying the lives of outstanding individuals. He studied more than 500 of the most successful men in America and got to know many of them personally. He found that the one indispensable ingredient, the common element in the success stories of them all, was persistence. These men kept trying even after repeated failure. He found that great success, it almost seemed, was only won by people who overcame incredible obstacles and great discouragement.

Hill states, "I had the happy privilege of analyzing both Mr. Edison and Mr. Ford, year by year, over a long period of years, and therefore the opportunity to study them at close range, so I speak from actual knowledge when I say that I found no quality save persistence, in either one of them, that even remotely suggested the major source of their stupendous achievements." [2]

Courage

Closely related to the quality of persistence is that of courage. If there is a distinction it is perhaps that courage is the willingness to start and persistence is the willingness to continue. Maxwell Maltz quotes two men of an earlier era. " 'No man ever became great or good except through many and great mistakes,' said Gladstone. 'I have learned more out of my mistakes than from my success,' said Sir Humphry Davy."

Arthur Mortell, who makes his living by teaching salesmen how to sell, considers the fear of making mistakes the most frequent cause of low sales performance. He teaches his students how to recognize this tendency in themselves and what to do to overcome it. Their failure constitutes an attitude, usually the result of unfortunate childhood experience—perhaps a reprimand or deep embarrassment over a childish error. This past experience, lodged deep in their unconscious, continues to affect their adult behavior and may continue to do so until death unless recognized and corrected.

Elbert Hubbard once said, "The greatest mistake a man can make is to be afraid of making one." And Theodore Roosevelt, who spoke from personal experience, said, "Far better it is to dare mighty things, to win glorious triumphs, even though checkered with failure, than to take rank with those poor spirits who neither enjoy much nor suffer much because they live in the great twilight that knows neither victory nor defeat."

Faith

Closely related to ambition is faith. Andrew Carnegie said the secret of his success was "Faith in myself, faith in others, and faith in my business." Faith is the key to sustained effort whether the original inspiration be self-confidence, belief in an idea, belief in the laws of success, of nature, or a supreme being.

Bob Richards, former Olympic pole-vaulter, studied the success of hundreds of athletes. Richards found that 90% of the world's finest athletes are under five feet ten inches tall and weigh less than 185 pounds. The secret of their success, he says, is not great size or strength but determination and absolute belief in themselves.

Integrity

Joe Batten, advocate of tough-minded management, believes that we must "blast the fallacy that you must compromise integrity to run a truly profitable business or home—this is an absolute lie and an inexcusable fallacy." I made a similar remark to a professor of management at one of the nation's leading graduate schools of business. His retort was, "I doubt if many of our graduate students will buy that." The prevalent concept for many Americans, including many executives who should know better, is: Be successful or be honest.

No one can deny that there are many successful people, at least financially, who are not very honest. And yet, the study of excellent leadership reveals that *integrity is an essential quality. It is exceedingly difficult to achieve success in handling people, over the long span, without it.* Arthur Gordon, writing for the *Reader's Digest*, says,

> Year after year businessmen study college records, screen applicants, and offer special inducement to proven people. What are they after, really? Brains? Energy? Know-how? These things are desirable, sure. But they will carry a man so far. If he is to move to the top and be entrusted with command decisions, there must be a plus factor, something that takes mere ability and doubles or trebles its effectiveness. To describe this magic characteristic there is only one word: *integrity.*[3]

In 1930, Herbert J. Taylor was vice president of Jewel Tea, in line for the presidency and receiving the then princely salary of $33,000 a year. A group of bankers asked Jewel Tea to lend Taylor to them for a few months to see if he could save Club Aluminum Products from bankruptcy. It was the bottom of the Great Depression. Millions of men were out of work, and many companies and banks were failing. Taylor found Club Aluminum $400,000 in debt and losing more each month. Any three creditors were in a position to throw the company into bankruptcy.

Taylor made a daring decision to leave his secure, well-paid job with Jewel Tea, borrow $6,100, and take over the presidency of Club Aluminum. His starting salary was $6,000 a year. One of his first moves was to devise some guiding principles for the company. He called them "The Four-Way Test" and years later assigned the copyright to Rotary International, which still uses it around the world. These are the four principles:

1. Is it the truth?

2. Is it fair to all concerned?

3. Will it build goodwill and better friendships?

4. Will it be beneficial to all concerned?

© 1946 Rotary International

Taylor's associates agreed to abide by the test, and everyone in the company was told about it and encouraged to use it in all their dealings.

The advertising department had been billing Club Aluminum ware as "The greatest cookware in the world." Under the new policy these superlatives were eliminated, and advertising sought to tell only the facts about the product. The company's sales strategy had been to try to load dealers with as big an inventory as possible on the theory that this would force them to push the product harder. Now salesmen were taught to consider the best interests of the dealers. On one occasion the company turned down a desperately needed order for 50,000 aluminum utensils because the buyer wanted to sell them at a cut price which would not be fair to other dealers. The result was that Club Aluminum won the confidence and respect of all its dealers, and this feeling was passed on to customers. Sales climbed steadily. At a time when many other companies were failing Club Aluminum was able to pay back its $400,000 debt in 5 years with interest, and during the next 15 years went on to distribute over one million dollars in stock dividends.[4]

Norman Jaspan, head of a firm specializing in detection and prevention of white-collar crime, says, "Dishonesty starts from the top and works downward. Show me a half-dozen honest key supervisors who know their business, and I'll show you a thousand honest employees. Show me a couple of executives who are dishonest, disinterested, and disloyal, and I will show you a thousand dishonest employees." [5]

Creativity

Creativity and its importance were discussed in Chapter 3. Lloyd Marquis, when president of the American Institute of Management, analyzed the behavior of thousands of excellent managers. He concluded that one of the most important characteristics was what he called "creative dissatisfaction." In other words, it was more than creativity, it was the constant desire to do better. Incidentally, the other characteristics Marquis found were:

> More of them have a clear understanding of the nature and function of entrepreneurship and the need for continuity in it.
>
> More of them have a clear, inclusive, and fundamental concept of what management is.
>
> More of them have a deep and realistic understanding of human nature and motives.
>
> More of them have a clear view of the full range of their moral responsibilities, and the need for maintaining a balance among them.[6]

Sense of Justice

People, regardless of rank or level of education, are very quick to detect unfair treatment. It is almost impossible to develop a positive motivational climate without justice.

Dr. Likert warns, "The members of the organization and the persons related to it must feel that the reward system of the organization—salaries, wages, bonuses, dividends, interest payments—yields them equitable compensation for their efforts and contributions." Justice must start at the top in the organization; chances are very poor for its existence at lower levels if not stressed at the top.

Objectivity

Excellent leaders have the ability to see things realistically. They are not easily deceived by others, nor do they practice self-deception. Maslow found this one of the most important characteristics of psychological health, saying:

> One of the most striking superiorities reported of self-actualizing people is their exceptional perceptiveness. They can perceive truth and reality far more efficiently than the average run of people. . . . Our subjects see human nature as it *is* and not as they would prefer it to be. . . . The first form in which this capacity was noticed was as an unusual ability to detect the spurious, the fake, and the dishonest in personality, and in general to judge people correctly and efficiently.[7]

In his work with Georgia criminals Dan MacDougald found that faulty perception was one of the criminal's most basic problems. And, perhaps more important, MacDougald discovered how to quickly change criminal perception as an important step to dramatic changes in attitudes and behavior.

Flexibility

L. S. Kubie wrote:

> The measure of health is flexibility, the freedom to learn through experience, the freedom to change with changing internal and external circumstances, to be influenced by reasonable argument, admonitions, exhortations, and appeal to emotions; the freedom to respond appropriately to the stimulus of reward and punishment,

and especially the freedom to cease when sated. The essence of
illness is the freezing of behavior into unalterable and insatiable
patterns.[8]

There is a tendency to think of flexibility as external, but the basis
is actually internal and psychological. Objectivity is the ability to see
things as they are. Flexibility is the ability to make the necessary
changes.

Self-discipline

Many centuries ago the great Chinese sage Confucius pointed out
that followers seldom display virtues not first present in their leaders.
A leader who is lazy, poorly organized, and undisciplined can scarcely
expect more of his employees. "The man who cannot control himself,"
says Napoleon Hill, "can never control others. Self-control sets a mighty
example for one's followers, which the more intelligent will emulate."

Decisiveness

It seems obvious that a man who vacillates and procrastinates is
poorly qualified for leadership. Perhaps less obvious is the fact that
decisiveness is the result of clearly defined objectives and policies. The
leadership of others begins with the leadership of self. Only individuals
who have established goals can lead others decisively.

Joe Batten says that top executives often are frustrated because their
subordinates fail to respond. Such executives, says Batten, "have not
taken an objective and penetrating inventory of their own personal
goals, desires, strengths, and weaknesses; and it is fundamental in
attempting to motivate subordinates that the superior must at all times
know what he, himself, actually wants."

Other Characteristics

Napoleon Hill lists 11 important factors of leadership: unwavering
courage, self-control, a keen sense of justice, definiteness of decision,
definiteness of plans, the habit of doing more than paid for, a pleasing
personality, sympathy and understanding, mastery of detail, willingness
to assume full responsibility, and cooperation.

Thomas Edison placed great importance on memory: "The first
thing an executive must have is a fine memory. Of course it does not
follow that the man with a fine memory is necessarily a fine executive.

But if he has the memory, he has the first qualification. And if he has not the memory, nothing else matters."

Among other frequently mentioned characteristics are health, ability to handle money, generosity, and patience. But the one characteristic which stands high on virtually every list is undoubtedly the single most important skill an executive can have—the ability to get along with people.

Skill with People

J. P. Morgan, who knew the value of a dollar better than most, once said, "I will pay more for the ability of a man to lead others than for any other asset." What is it that makes some people so successful in their human relations while others just as intelligent fail? Isn't it precisely the qualities described above—ambition, persistence, courage, faith, integrity, sense of justice, objectivity, flexibility, self-discipline, decisiveness? Isn't it a series of related attitudes one holds toward others? Consideration, cooperation, humility, and loyalty? Isn't it, as we discussed in Chapter 6, the ability to communicate? But isn't it also something more basic than all of these things—self-respect and self-confidence?

The two fundamental attitudes which affect nearly all our human relations are respect for self and respect for others. When one is low, so is the other. Increase either one and the other seems to increase, too. Maxwell Maltz said:

> The person who feels that people are not very important, cannot have very much deep-down self-respect and self-regard—for he himself is "people" and with what judgment he considers others, he himself is unwittingly judged in his own mind.
>
> One of the best known methods of getting over a feeling of guilt is to stop condemning other people in your own mind—stop judging them—stop blaming them and hating them for their mistakes. You will develop a better and more adequate self-image when you begin to feel that other people are more worthy. Practice treating *other* people as if they had some value—and surprisingly enough your own self-esteem will go up.[9]

People who lack self-respect, although they may do a tremendous job of bluffing, lack self-confidence and never achieve the kind of success with people which good leadership requires.

Albert Dunn, advocate of "high-level wellness," which he defines as "maximizing the potential of which the individual is capable," maintains: "You cannot be on good terms with your fellow man, with your wife, with your children, unless you are on good terms with yourself. This is an absolute necessity, in the human relationships between people."

Emotional Maturity

The leadership qualities we have listed on the preceding pages and the qualities Dr. Maslow found in his self-actualized people are remarkably similar. Maslow's case histories came from a variety of disciplines, but not many of them were business executives. His list included, among others, Abraham Lincoln, Thomas Jefferson, Albert Einstein, Eleanor Roosevelt, Jane Addams, William James, Spinoza, Albert Schweitzer, Aldous Huxley, G. W. Carver, Eugene V. Debs, Fritz Kreisler, Goethe, Martin Buber, Adlai Stevenson, Ralph Waldo Emerson, Benjamin Franklin, John Muir, and Walt Whitman. The common characteristics he found were that these people were purposeful, realistic, creative, humble, considerate, ethical, spontaneous, courageous, self-disciplined, self-confident, and integrated (see Chapter 10).

In *Eupsychian Management* Maslow wrote specifically about the mental health of excellent managers: "The best managers under the American research conditions seem to be psychologically healthier people than the poor managers in the same researches. This is easily enough supported by the data from Likert."

The Sears study of excellent supervisors found these individuals to be superior in such characteristics as purpose, social composure, self-confidence, emotional strength, objectivity about self and others, optimism, tolerance of others, and flexibility.

Emotional maturity does not guarantee that a man will be an excellent manager, but the individual who is mature can sometimes shift to an effective style of leadership quite easily. He can use effective methods of motivation, communication, and leadership without any major change in personality. Executives who lack emotional maturity, and quite a few of them do, can read all the books, attend all the seminars, and try very hard, but they simply will not achieve excellence. In other words, it is relatively easy for already highly mature individuals to learn effective management, but it is almost impossible for immature people to do so until their self-image, attitude, philosophy—their whole personality—change.

A. A. Imberman, Chicago management consultant, has discovered that about 70% of foremen respond to training in communication and motivation but 30% do not respond to the training. He says:

> Three out of ten foremen regard any criticism of anything in their departments as criticism of the foreman himself and his leadership qualities. *They take everything personally.* These men are more or less neurotic and emotionally insecure, and are often the source of trouble in their departments. Once identified in foreman training courses, the recommendation is to move these men sideways (away from people) and into planning, or paperwork, or out. They cannot motivate men for any company benefit; they do nothing but create trouble in a department and plant.[10]

To attain leadership excellence, one must develop psychological maturity. But unfortunately, the development of maturity is missing in the vast majority of executive training programs.

Leaders should familiarize themselves with the characteristics of psychological maturity. It is the key to self-improvement and to the selection and training of other supervisors at all levels. The list of characteristics on page 136 may be helpful. Of course, no one is perfect, and most of us have some of the characteristics listed in the left column.

Leadership Style

Studies involving thousands of supervisors at all levels have demonstrated rather conclusively that supervisory style is a major determinant of employee productivity. In several cases merely changing supervisors, while all other conditions remained constant, produced substantial changes in worker behavior. When the American Management Association Learning Center at Hamilton, New York, was dedicated several years ago, Edwin R. Henry described effective managers as "the ones who have set high standards of performance for their organizational units and for individuals in those units. They have performed outstandingly themselves, and they have demanded that kind of performance of their organizations. Also, the more effective managers of today gave evidence of being more mature—and independent—than most people of their age." [11]

It was Douglas McGregor who opened Pandora's box with his Theory X and Y concepts of management. He quite correctly pointed out that leadership styles are related to the leader's frequently unrecognized assumptions about the nature of man.

INDICATIONS OF PSYCHOLOGICAL MATURITY

Immature	*Mature*
Has poor self-image	Has good self-image
Sensitive to real or implied criticism	Not sensitive to criticism
Critical of others	Tolerant of others
Can't admit own mistakes	Admits mistakes
Can't see other people's ideas	Accepts ideas from others
Communicates poorly	Communicates well
Lacks confidence	Confident
Does not understand self	Understands self
Does not understand others	Understands others
Needs approval of others	Less need for approval
Seldom approves of others	Can easily give approval
Slow to learn from mistakes	Learns from mistakes
Uncomfortable with people	Comfortable with people
Indecisive	Decisive
Doubts people's motives	Understands people's motives
Self-conscious	Confident
Forgets names and faces	Remembers people
Not interested in others	Interested in others
Has low energy and drive	Has high energy and drive
Works poorly on a team	Works well on a team
Often arrogant	Has humility
Subjective (self-centered)	Objective
Secretive	Candid
Negative	Positive
Has poor self-discipline	Self-disciplined
Argumentative	Persuasive
Dogmatic	Flexible
Emotional	Calm
Inconsiderate	Considerate
Defensive	Nondefensive
Tense	Relaxed
Apathetic	Goal-oriented
Often irresponsible	Responsible
Impulsive and expedient	Patient

Dr. Likert's classification system describes four management styles. System 1, the least desirable, is exploitive–authoritative, which depends on unquestioning authority and coercion and little or no regard for followers. System 2 is benevolent–authoritative. Authority is still concentrated at the top but the needs of workers are considered in a paternalistic way. System 3, consultative, maintains the organizational hierarchy authority but involves workers in the decision-making process. System 4, participative group, is Likert's ideal model. System 4 seeks to minimize authority and maximize participatory problem solving based on competence rather than organizational rank.[12]

"Supervisors with the best records of performance," says Likert, "focus their primary attention on the human aspects of subordinates' problems and on endeavoring to build effective work groups with high performance goals." He gives the following example of the attitude of an employee-centered manager:

> One way in which we accomplish a high level of production is by letting people do the job the way they want to so long as they accomplish the objectives. I believe in letting them take time out from the monotony. Make them feel that they are something special, not just run-of-the-mill. . . . If you keep employees from feeling hounded, they are apt to put out the necessary effort to get the job done in the required time. . . . If people know their jobs, I believe in letting them make decisions. I believe in delegating decision making.

In contrast, the point of view of the less successful supervisor tends to be, "This interest-in-people approach is all right, but it's a luxury. I've got to keep pressure on for production, and when I get production up, then I can afford to take time to show an interest in my employees."

"The relationship between the superior and subordinate is crucial," says Likert. "The more often the superior's behavior is ego-building rather than ego-deflating, the better will be the effect of his behavior on organizational performance." [13]

The Blake-Mouton Managerial Grid ® mentioned in Chapter 9 describes the ideal managerial style as one that combines a high concern for production with a high concern for people. As Blake and Mouton said:

> It is assumed in the 9,9 managerial style that there is no necessary and inherent conflict between organization purpose of production requirements and the needs of people. Under 9,9 effective integration of people with production is possible by involving them and their ideas in determining the conditions and strategies of work. . . .

A basic aim of 9,9 management, then, is to promote the conditions that integrate creativity, high productivity, and high morale through concerted team action.[14]

Bowers and Seashore, of the Institute for Social Research, analyzed the performance of sales offices for a large company with 100 offices scattered across the United States. Each office was independently owned, operated, and managed and ranged from 8 to 50 salesmen plus supporting staff. The study compared 20 offices with the best performance with 20 whose performances were average or below. The studies showed that the high-producing offices were those whose managers used a supportive style of leadership and set high goals. The study concluded:

> Subordinates are unlikely to set high performance goals for themselves and organize their own work well if their superiors do not have such aspirations for each salesman and for the whole office.
>
> A superior with high performance goals and excellent job organization is much more likely to have subordinates who set high goals for themselves and organize their work well when he uses group methods of supervision and applies the principle of supportive relationships effectively than when he does not.[15]

Considerable evidence indicates that if an executive must deviate from the 9,9 ideal, productivity will be higher if his deviation is toward greater consideration for productivity, rather than an overconcern for people. "Technically competent, job-centered, insensitive, and tough management can achieve relatively high productivity," says Likert. And Saul Gellerman, another authority on motivation, states, "The human relations enthusiast must somehow reconcile his theories with the fact that not only does industry as a whole continue to be run on an authoritarian basis but it even seems to be thriving on it." Maslow wrote:

> My vague feeling is that we can generalize about practically all leaders or bosses, that they *should* be able to pay attention to the objective requirements of the situation without fussing too much about the delicate sensitivity of the followers or of the employees, of the people who have to take orders. For instance, I think most leaders have to be able to withstand hostility, that is, to be unpopular, without falling apart. The kind of person who must be loved by all probably will not make a good leader.[16]

When he was a graduate student, Maslow spent a summer with a northern Blackfoot Indian tribe in Alberta, Canada. In contrast to most

American Indians, this Canadian tribe was still living much as they had for hundreds of years and were relatively independent and self-reliant. Maslow was impressed by their system of leadership. The leader for each type of activity was obviously best suited for that particular job because he knew more about it than the others. A hunting expedition would have one leader and a fishing trip another. The ability to lead was the basis of selection, rather than inherited tribal status.

Shigeru Kobayashi's experience at Sony demonstrates that the 9,9 style of management is practical. His style of leadership maximizes concern both for people and production. The result was more production than previously thought possible. Paradoxically, by treating the workers with consideration, the emphasis was shifted from people's ego-centered needs to the work itself. In other words, by minimizing the forces which tend to have people defending themselves and their egos and becoming emotional, their energy could be devoted primarily to production. Says Kobayashi:

> The ultimate right to make decisions lies in the hands of facts and situations surrounding us. . . . The worst type of manager is the one who blames his people in case of a fiasco yet who wants to exercise his power and authority by taking credit for their successes. A manager who will not allow himself to dodge any responsibility has no other course but to trust his people. This boldness of spirit, when shown by a manager, kindles a similar spirit in those people and assures their voluntary cooperation. Here we have the real basis of leadership.[17]

The style of leadership that Kobayashi describes will only succeed in a positive motivational climate, where workers perceive their interests as concurrent with those of the organization, and work with the kind of cooperation and enthusiasm generated on a good college football team.

Leadership style must be adaptable. Obviously an adult leading a group of three-year-old children needs an approach different from that required to lead a group of nuclear physicists. The style of leadership which will succeed with a highly emotional, insecure type of individual will be different from the style best suited for a self-reliant, emotionally secure individual. According to Likert:

> The subordinate's reaction to the supervisor's behavior always depends upon the relationship between the supervisory act as perceived by the subordinate and the expectations, values, and interpersonal skills of the subordinate. . . .

Supervision is, therefore, always a relative process. To be effective and to communicate as intended, a leader must always adapt his behavior to take into account the expectations, values, and interpersonal skills of those with whom he is interacting.[18]

The Executive's Time

> *Time goes, you say? Ah, no!*
> *Alas, time stays, we go.*
>   Henry Austin Dobson
>   *The Paradox of Time*

If there is one thing shared by executives, administrators, and supervisors at all levels, in both large and small organizations, it is a shortage of time. Time is inelastic and demands for it frequently exceed the available supply. "Nothing else," writes Peter Drucker, "perhaps distinguishes effective executives as much as their tender loving care of time. . . . Unless he manages himself effectively, no amount of ability, skill, experience, or knowledge will make an executive effective."

Drucker became interested in executive effectiveness during World War II, when he observed that some businessmen recruited into wartime government service were successful on their new assignments, others apparently equally capable were not. Drucker set out systematically to find out why. His conclusions were published in *The Effective Executive* in 1966: "The most important thing to report is that I have found that effectiveness can be learned—but also that it must be learned. It does not come by itself. It is a practice that must be acquired."

He lists five essential practices—five habits of mind—that executives must acquire to be effective. These five practices are:

1. Effective executives know where their time goes. They work systematically at managing the little of their time that can be brought under their control.

2. Effective executives focus on outward contribution. They gear their efforts to results rather than to work. They start out with the question, "What results are expected of me?" rather than with the work to be done, let alone . . . its techniques and tools.

3. Effective executives build on strength—their own strengths, the strengths of their superiors, colleagues, and subordinates, and on the strengths of the situation, that is, on what they can do. They do not build on weaknesses. They do not start out with the things they cannot do.

4. Effective executives concentrate on the few major areas where superior performance will produce outstanding results. They force themselves to set priorities and stay with their priority decisions. They know that they have no choice but to do first things first— and second things not at all. The alternative is to get nothing done.

5. Effective executives, finally, make effective decisions. They know that this is, above all, a matter of system—of the right steps in the right sequence. They know that an effective decision is always a judgment based on "dissenting opinions" rather than on "consensus on the facts." And they know that to make many decisions fast means to make the wrong decisions. What is needed are few, but fundamental, decisions. What is needed is the right strategy rather than razzle-dazzle tactics.[19]

What can leaders do to improve their utilization of time? Once more, the answer is to establish goals, priorities, and plans. To be truly effective you must convince yourself that planning is an important activity and that *an hour of planning will save hours in execution.* Then act accordingly. Alec Mackenzie, in his special study of time management among top corporate executives, reports that the president of one midwestern manufacturing company actually proved this principle to his skeptical executives, who asked, "When you are swamped with more to do than you can get done, how do you find time to plan?" They were asked to compare the total time of accomplishment between projects completed with minimum initial planning and similar projects where planning time was almost doubled. The test demonstrated that the increased planning time produced a significant reduction in the total time for project accomplishment.[20]

The Schwab story has been told and retold, but it is still relevant. Years ago Charles Schwab, then president of Bethlehem Steel Company, asked efficiency expert Ivy Lee how he could better handle his time. Lee gave him the following advice.

Write down the six most important tasks you have to do tomorrow and number them in order of their importance. Now, put this paper in your pocket and the first thing tomorrow morning look at Item 1 and start working on it till it's finished. Then tackle Item 2 in the same way, then Item 3, and so on. Do this until quitting time. Don't be concerned if you have only finished one or two. You'll be working on the most important ones. The others can wait. If you can't finish them all with this method, you couldn't have by any other either; and without some system, you would probably not even have decided which was the most important.

Do this every working day. After you've convinced yourself of the value of this system, have your men try it. Try it as long as you wish, and then send me a check for what you think it is worth.[21]

Weeks later Schwab sent Lee a check for $25,000. And years later he said that this was one of the most important lessons he ever learned.

In leadership seminars we recommend that executives write projects on 3 x 5 cards—one project to a card. This is not for the small, piddling detail type of thing you must do anyway, but for more important projects that take time. Each task can be assigned a tentative cost in hours and dollars, and a tentative value to the organization. This bank of cards then serves as a reference in preparing daily, weekly, and monthly time schedules.

You must continually ask yourself, "What are the most important and profitable things I can do with my time?" As we've seen, one problem is that the important things are seldom urgent. General Eisenhower tried to arrange his affairs so that only the truly important and urgent matters came to his attention. But he discovered that the two seldom went together. Really important matters were not often urgent, and the most urgent matters were often unimportant. The trick is to identify these important-but-not-urgent tasks and assign them time.

Important projects are frequently sidetracked because they seem too tough to handle. The solution is to break these large, frightening projects down into manageable bits. The longest journey, it is said, starts with a step. The 3 x 5 cards help because they assist you to identify important projects and constantly remind you of them. One of our seminar participants owned and managed an office equipment store. He also wrote books, but as his business grew he found less and less time to write. The solution for him was to "take time off the top." He formed the habit of coming in half an hour before opening and reserving that time specifically for writing.

A few years ago Michigan Millers Insurance Company instituted a plan to have all their people take an hour off the top. Their policy was to have underwriters, adjusters, actuaries, and clerical employees spend the first hour each morning—8:00 to 9:00 A.M.—with a minimum of interruption. Employees were encouraged to use this hour for thinking and planning; there were no outgoing phone calls, interoffice visits, paging, or the like.

Delegation

Efficient leaders must learn what and how to delegate. Delegation is easy to describe but most executives find it difficult in practice. Perhaps the best way to find out what you really can delegate when you have to is to examine what you do the last few days before your long-anticipated annual vacation. Mackenzie says that failure to delegate is probably the single most serious failure of chief executives, as it is of managers at every level. He quotes a comment by Charles Percy at the time he was president of Bell & Howell: "I was so busy doing things I should have delegated that I didn't have time to manage." The failure to delegate may have several reasons; three of the most common of these are (1) failure to analyze your job and identify elements that can be delegated, (2) lack of assistants sufficiently qualified to help you, (3) personal insecurity—the fear of failure.

The first of these problems is the easiest to deal with. If delegation is important, then take time to analyze your activities and identify those aspects of your job that should be delegated. The second item can usually be traced to a previous failure in staffing or training. *Your inability to delegate today probably reflects a failure to identify a need, and hire and train for it a year ago. And unless you start planning ahead now, your situation probably will be even worse a year from today.* It is difficult to delegate work to an individual unless you have confidence in his competence and integrity. And confidence, even under the best conditions, usually takes time to establish. William Oncken says, "How much authority will you, yourself, delegate to a man for whose character you do not have complete respect, or with whose personality you do not have complete rapport, or in whose competence you do not have complete confidence?" If your problem is personal insecurity, determine to overcome it. Or, if you are unwilling to make that effort, decide to curtail your ambitions as a leader. If the problem is with one of your subordinates, seek to increase his self-confidence, or you will be compelled to limit his advancement.

David S. Brown, professor of public administration at George Washington University, warns:

> Delegation involves risk. Those most willing to accept it are often those with the most self-confidence. When failure looms, they are the ones who have sufficient confidence in self and others to look to ways of overcoming it. Their willingness to risk—to support subordinates—speaks loudly where others, both superiors and subordinates, will surely hear.[22]

Investing Time to Save Time

Have you ever stopped to estimate what an hour of your time is worth? If not, you should. Treat time exactly as if it were money. In a sense, it is. Effective leaders constantly seek ways to "invest" their time in ways that will pay handsomely in the future. Merely putting out fires seldom does this. The profitable activities are goal-seeking and growth activities—that is, activities which increase your effectiveness and that of your organization. An example is the improvement of your work area. Perhaps you need a larger desk, a bookcase, or a better system to keep and quickly find telephone numbers. Perhaps you need an improvement in the way you handle dictation. Dictating equipment today is almost standard practice among executives. Executive secretaries who take dictation are occasionally very useful, but as a general rule the most efficient way to create letters, memos and reports is through the use of a dictating machine. Time spent improving personal procedures is the type of investment which pays excellent dividends.

Many executives take speed reading courses. Such courses can be tough and time-consuming but are frequently a good investment. I know an attorney who took a reading course. He summed it up for me very quickly. "As an attorney," he said, "I already knew how to read quite rapidly. What I gained from the course was quite different. It was a new attitude toward printed material. I realized in taking the course that I was reading a lot of material which really wasn't important. The thing to do was to glance at it and throw it away without wasting time. In other cases I was reading material word for word when all I needed to do was read the summary and then file the material away." His conclusion was that for him the gain was not so much in learning to read faster, but in learning to be more efficient and selective in handling written material.

Obstacles to Efficient Use of Time

Procrastination is a problem for many of us. If our analysis shows that a job needs to be done, the thing to do is give it a priority and make a commitment to get started. If the procrastination is because the job is too large, break it down into manageable bits. Sometimes it's good to start with the easiest part of the job first. Sometimes our procrastination is due to indecision. Is the job important? How do we handle it? Frequently the best approach to such a decision is to get more facts. Sometimes the answer is to seek the advice of others whose experience qualifies them to give a helpful answer. If indecision is habitual with you, it is probably a matter of self-confidence. Overcome your problem of self-confidence and you will overcome your problem of indecision.

William Oncken warns executives to avoid the "retreat to the familiar." He says that executives tend to do the jobs easiest and familiar to them, and avoid tasks and problems which are new and threatening.

If you spend enough time in time planning and identifying important jobs, you will be helped to overcome your unconscious tendency to avoid them.

Resistance to planning—goal-seeking activities—is a major cause for the inefficient use of time. "Thinking," said Henry Ford, "is the hardest work there is, which is a probable reason why so few engage in it." Leaders need to recognize people's almost universal resistance to thinking and planning, and devise creative ways to overcome it.

A common pitfall for inexperienced leaders is trying to do it all themselves rather than devoting time to directing the efforts of others. The higher one goes in supervision, and the more people under his direction, the more time must be spent in supervising. Alec Mackenzie calls it managing versus operating. He suggests that the proper ratios might be something like the following.[23]

Level of Supervision	Managing	Operating
Chief executive	90%	10%
Vice president	70%	30%
Middle management	50%	50%
First-line supervisor	30%	70%

Fear, worry, the inability to handle pressure can seriously reduce an executive's efficiency. Ralph Cordiner, former president of General Electric, wrote:

> Worry is fundamentally a form of fear. It is a realization of inadequacy, which in turn is the byproduct of lack of time to think through confidently to sound objectives and good plans. Hurry, in turn, is a parallel evidence of mismanagement of a specific and limited time available to the individual manager. It means that his work as a manager is poorly done because he is trying too many things in too few hours, and hence is doing them badly and thus is himself creating the vicious spiral of worry, and the emotional strains which can only end in physical disaster.

> So the work of the manager, in the hours which he should be able to devote to doing it while still leaving proper hours for his family, for recreation, and for rest, requires conscious selection of the tasks reserved to himself. And then it requires deliberate delegation of everything else to others in the organization within the framework of his well-designed organization pattern, no matter what wrench this may require from his working habits. Only then can he surely organize himself to reverse the destructive trend of early mortality for business executives and meet the true challenge of professional management with which he must cope.[24]

Leadership roles usually involve pressure; it is essential that leaders learn to cope with it. This one topic alone is the subject for many books. Drucker says, "The typical (that is, the more or less ineffectual) executive tries to hurry—but that only puts him further behind. Effective executives do not race. They set an easy pace, but keep going steadily."

To what extent is the pressure on you self-imposed? Are your goals unrealistically high? Are your time deadlines too short? Do you consistently fail in your planning to allow time for expected interruptions? Do you habitually procrastinate until the very last minute, and then find yourself under such pressure that you have difficulty doing a good job?

If your pressure is self-imposed, why not consider extending your deadlines and reducing your goals? Perhaps you are a compulsive overachiever who makes life less pleasant than it should be and actually achieves less than you otherwise could.

The *Executive Health Digest*, with a panel of distinguished doctors as advisers, describes the effect of excessive ambition on health:

> What is this emotional facade or behavior pattern A? Fundamentally, it consists of those feelings and their respective motor expressions displayed (even at rest) by an individual possessing an *exaggerated* drive, ambition, aggressiveness, competitiveness, and, above all, *sense of time urgency.* . . .
>
> Most persons have some or all of these attributes, but the young patient ill with ischemic heart disease possesses them to a much greater extent. *It is the extreme exaggeration of one or more of these attributes that allows him little surcease even in situations where there is no need for the application or involvement of drive, competitiveness, or sense of time urgency. He thus, even at supposed times of leisure, talks, walks, eats, indeed performs every act as if he were pacing himself with the second hand of a stopwatch.* . . .
>
> *If a man's ambition and drive are unbridled, no matter how efficient he becomes, he will increasingly shatter himself against the obdurate panels of the inelastic factor, time.* . . . In contrast, the "Pattern B" man is more relaxed . . . more inclined to use a calendar than a stopwatch.[25]

The report describes a California study of 3,182 men in eleven corporations which showed that most of the chief executives were relaxed Pattern B rather than hard-driving "A" men. "Apparently," says the report, "*quality* of work spells success . . . and quality is destroyed if you are always pressing."

If your pressure is the result of unreasonable demands by your superiors, do something about it. Frequently, a frank discussion with your boss will solve the problem. Perhaps all that is needed is the agreement to extend a time deadline.

How do you find time to do the things that save time? There are dozens of tricks to save time if you work at it. One device which is extremely helpful is the "backward calendar." When you get a new assignment, perhaps a speech or a report which must be prepared, start right away by making a list of the necessary steps to get the job done. Assign an estimated time, in days, to each step and then work backward from the due date. This is a simple way to avoid the realization five days before the job is due that the job simply can't be done in five days. Many consultants recommend concentrating on one job at a time. Concentration has its advantages, but so does changing jobs for variety. Sometimes such a change will give you renewed vigor.

Have you ever considered changing your work schedule? One highly successful corporation president found that he could get more done in a week if he spent one day working at home. Some executives work an hour at home before breakfast. One attorney told me that he made his entire day easy by reaching his office two hours before his secretary. He spent the two hours in dictation and then took time for breakfast. This method of operation took the pressure off and with the hard work out of the way the rest of the day was easy.

This idea made such sense to me that I tried it myself. My former practice was to get up early, eat a hurried breakfast, and rush to the office, which is only a four-minute drive from my home. Now I get up early and go immediately to the office. When my secretary arrives at 8:30 I have done some of the tough work for the day. I then go home for a leisurely breakfast. This procedure breaks up the day. I am able to work hard for an hour and a half because I know that it is only an hour and a half. My wife likes the procedure because it gives her more time, too. One of our seminar participants said he would often go to a nearby library and work for several hours in quiet. Another made it a practice to always carry a small tape recorder with him in his car, which he dictated into while waiting in traffic.

These are only a few suggestions to stimulate your imagination. You can increase your effectiveness by better utilization of time, and you can encourage your subordinates to do the same. Apply creative goal-seeking procedures to the problem of time utilization in the same manner you do to other aspects of leadership. It's worth taking time to save time.

14

Personal Potential and How to Develop It

Compared with what we ought to be, we are only half awake. Our fires are damped, our drafts are checked. We are making use of only a small part of our possible mental and physical resources.
William James

VERY early in the twentieth century William James, one of America's most distinguished psychologist-philosophers, concluded that the average individual was using only a small part of his full potential—perhaps only 10%. James considered this one of his most important discoveries. He said:

> Most people live, whether physically, intellectually, or morally, in a very restricted circle of their potential being. They make use of a very small portion of their possible consciousness, and of their soul's resources in general, much like a man who, out of his whole bodily organism, should get into a habit of using and moving only his little finger. Great emergencies and crises show us how much greater our vital resources are than we had supposed.[1]

Energy, creativity, memory, judgment, perception, ability to communicate, psychological maturity, physical strength, and other human attributes can all be greatly increased when the right techniques are used. But somehow, incredibly, after the death of William James the idea of undeveloped personal potential lost favor among American behavioral scientists, and with it their enthusiasm for the Horatio Alger success stories. Herbert Otto, one of the exceptions, said in 1967, when he established the National Center for the Exploration of Human Potential, "The topic of *human potential* has, for the last 50 years, been almost totally ignored as a focus of research activities by workers in the social and behavioral sciences. . . . All that one finds are individual pioneers conducting limited studies under extremely difficult conditions."

Studies of potential and methods to develop it have gone on almost entirely outside our universities. Among the leading proponents have been such men as Claude Bristol, Dale Carnegie, Napoleon Hill, Clement Stone, Earl Nightingale, John Boyle, James Newman, Maxwell Maltz, and Paul Meyer. Meyer, founder of the Success Motivation Institute, says, "I've learned from men whom I've never met that the only real limitations I shall ever encounter are those which I place on myself."

The theoretical work of Abraham Maslow has provided new impetus to the personal potential movement. Herbert Doan, much impressed by Maslow's work, says, "We in industry are discovering how new management ideas and philosophy and, of course, good leadership can be used to produce growth and self-actualization of the individual as well as growth and development of the company."

It is frequently said that most workers only produce about 50% of what they could. No one knows what the exact figure is; estimates vary from 10 to 70%. The motivational techniques described in the previous chapters are designed to capture this unused energy. Efforts to develop human potential go beyond this. In other words, motivation, as the term is generally used, refers to achieving more effective utilization of existing talent. The development of potential refers to the development of new or improved talent. We have found that most executives are not aware of this distinction. The possibilities for developing and utilizing personal potential in organizations of all types are far greater than most leaders ever imagine. Edison said, "If we all did the things we are capable of doing, we would literally astound ourselves."

Intelligence tests, we are now realizing, do not measure potential, only that portion of the potential that has been developed. In an experiment at the Institute for Behavioral Research in Silver Springs, Maryland, some 40 "uneducable" boys, age 13 to 18, were offered incentives for learning: small amounts of cash to begin with; later, the opportunity to study subjects they liked. Eighty percent responded favorably and in one year the average Wechsler Intelligence Test score increased for the group by 16 points, an achievement in one year of what normally takes two to three years. Psychologist Harold Cohan, director of the Institute, believes that a teenager's IQ can be influenced upward by as much as 20 points.

A study conducted by the National Institute for Mental Health in cooperation with Catholic University showed that the IQ of infants could be greatly increased. Sixty-four 15-month-old boys from Washington, D.C., were divided into two equal groups. One group received an hour of tutoring each weekday; the other group did not. After 21 months the tutored group had an average intelligence quotient of 106, the untutored group an average of 89.

Even more dramatic results have been obtained by a group led by Professor Rick Heber at the University of Wisconsin. A *Washington Post* reporter said:

> Heber's experimental program, now in its fifth year, has taken young children of poor and illiterate parents living in the city's worst slums —children who, on the basis of everything that we know, could be predicted to show a progressive decline in intelligence as they grow older—and produced results that are a little short of startling. For example, IQ scores have jumped by more than 50%, some of them reaching as high as 135.[2]

Actually men like Earl Nightingale who have made it their business to study the success and failure of people have found little correlation between IQ and successful living. This conclusion is supported by the testimony of great men themselves. Walter Russell said, "Mediocrity is self-inflicted and genius is self-bestowed." Buckminster Fuller adds, "There is no such thing as genius. Some children are less damaged than others." Jerome Bruner, Harvard psychologist, states, "We know from a variety of studies that most of the variance in human intelligence is accounted for during the preschool years." And according to Otto, "Dr. W. Ross Adey and his associates of the Space Biology Laboratory of the Brain Research Institute of UCLA have reached the conclusion that 'the ultimate creative capacity of the brain may be, for all practical purposes, infinite.' "

Russian scientists are apparently years ahead of their American counterparts in the recognition of and attempt to develop human potential. According to Ivan Yefremov, prominent Soviet scholar:

> Man, under average conditions of work and life, uses only a small part of his thinking equipment. . . . If we were able to force our brain to work at only half its capacity, we could, without any difficulty whatever, learn 40 languages, memorize the large Soviet encyclopedia from cover to cover, and complete the required courses of dozens of colleges.

Self-image Psychology

The majority of psychologists are not aware of this specialized area of study. Maxwell Maltz, a foremost authority on the subject, called it "the most important psychological discovery of this century." [3] Of an earlier proponent, Prescott Lecky, Maltz wrote: "He conceived of the personality as a 'system of ideas,' all of which must seem to be consistent with each other. Ideas which are inconsistent with the system are rejected, 'not believed,' and not acted upon. Ideas which seem to be consistent with this system are accepted."

Lecky found that students had trouble with certain subjects because succeeding in these areas was inconsistent with the image they held of themselves. When Lecky succeeded in changing a student's self-image, his learning ability changed, sometimes dramatically. In one case a student whose spelling tests were only 45% accurate and who was flunking most subjects made an average of 91 the following year and became outstanding in spelling. A second boy who dropped out of one college because of his poor performance became a straight A student at Columbia. A girl who failed Latin four times achieved a grade of 84, with proper coaching. Anyone not familiar with Maxwell Maltz' *Psycho-Cybernetics* —a book that has sold over 500,000 copies—should certainly read it. Maltz is a plastic surgeon, not a professional psychologist. As he remarked, plastic surgeons also need to be psychologists. Over the years Maltz discovered that plastic surgery sometimes changed far more than people's physical appearance; sometimes their personalities were changed, too. Twenty years before he wrote *Psycho-Cybernetics* Dr. Maltz published a collection of case histories telling about remarkable changes in people's personalities. But some patients showed no change in personality after plastic surgery at all.

"In some cases," wrote Dr. Maltz, "the patient continued to feel inadequate and experienced feelings of inferiority. In short, these 'failures' continued to feel, act, and behave just as if they still had an ugly face." Maltz puzzled over this phenomenon for many years and finally found the answer in the work of physicists and mathematicians and the concept of cybernetics. He developed the idea of "self-image."

"Once I began to explore this area," Maltz wrote, "I found more and more phenomena which confirmed the fact that the 'self-image,' the individual's mental and spiritual concept, or 'picture,' of himself, was the real key to personality and behavior." He concluded that man was a goal-striving organism. Most people are convinced that personality is formed early in life and seldom changes thereafter.

Sigmund Freud, who, for the most part, studied emotionally disturbed people, was one of the influential proponents of this point of view. Freud believed that personality was well formed by the age of five to seven, that it could be changed, but that the process was a long and costly one. And psychoanalysis is the only way to do it. He failed to recognize that personality frozen at an early age is an indication of emotional disturbance. The healthy individual, as Maslow discovered, continued to grow and change and become more mature year after year.

Clinton T. Duffy, former warden at San Quentin Prison, said that anyone, even a hardened criminal, could change his pattern of behavior. His skillful persuasion reclaimed the lives of a number of tough convicts. But Duffy's ideas weren't too popular. A radio announcer said to him, "You should know that leopards don't change their spots!" Duffy snapped back, "You should know I don't work with leopards. I work with men, and men change every day!"

Advocates of self-image psychology stress the importance of holding proper goals and images in the mind. Maltz says that the subconscious mind cannot distinguish "between an 'actual' experience and an experience imagined vividly and in detail."

One recommended process to improve self-image is affirmation and visualization. Alfred Montapert, another success expert, describes the positive affirmation as "a written, positive statement describing the goals you are going to attain. . . . Affirmations mean to affirm in the affirmative. That is to state, confidently, in a positive statement, that you already possess your goal. Example: I am very successful in all that I do. Success comes easily to me." [4] After the affirmation is written the subject must visualize himself in the situation his affirmation describes. Repeated use of affirmation and visualization changes the self-image. Maltz says it takes at least 21 days to change a self-image. "Numerous case histories have shown that one is never too young or too old to change his self-image, and thereby start to live a new life. . . . The 'self-image' is the key to human personality and human behavior. Change the self-image and you've changed the personality and behavior." [5]

Similar advice may be found in the writings of philosophers throughout the centuries. Harry Emerson Fosdick said, "Hold a picture of yourself long and steadily enough in your mind's eye and you will be drawn toward it. Picture yourself vividly as defeated and that alone will make victory impossible. Picture yourself vividly as winning and that alone will contribute immeasurably to your success." And thousands of years before that, Aristotle, another believer in personal potential, said, "Whoever sees the picture and holds it before his mind so clearly that all external things which favor it are chosen for its sake, and all proposed actions which would hinder it are remorselessly rejected in its holy name and by its mighty power—he rises to the level of personality, and his personality is that of a clear, strong, joyous, compelling, conquering, triumphant sort which alone is worthy of the name."

The Thomas Jefferson Research Center has examined hundreds of case histories and has found that people do change, sometimes quite dramatically. But there is no one, guaranteed formula that works for everyone. Some people respond to one approach, some to another, and perhaps some don't respond at all.

Studying the literature of success is an excellent starting point.

W. Clement Stone, president of Combined Insurance Company of America, used Napoleon Hill's *Think and Grow Rich* as his personal success manual. Now he uses it for training employees. "Ordinary salesmen," he says, "are motivated to become supersalesmen through *Think and Grow Rich*."

Success Motivation Institute recommends repetitive listening. Their records and tape cassettes are sold throughout the country.

Founder Paul Meyer says the average individual can increase his effectiveness ten times. Nightingale-Conant Corporation is another source of records and tapes designed for executives and sales people.

Seminars have proved the secret of success for many thousands of Americans. The granddaddy of them all is the Dale Carnegie Courses. Dale Carnegie was himself an outstanding example of a young man who turned poverty, failure, and discouragement into fantastic success. He began educational courses for business and professional people in New York City in 1912. At first he taught public speaking, but gradually realized that these adults needed more than that; they needed training in the art of getting along with people. He estimated that even for engineers, about 15% of their financial success was due to technical knowledge, and the remaining 85%, due to their skills with people. His famous *How to Win Friends and Influence People* is still a classic. Carnegie said he searched for years to find a practical working handbook on human relations and there was none. To write the book, he read everything he could on the subject and then hired a research assistant to spend a year and a half reading everything he had missed and studying the biographies of the great men of all ages. Carnegie claimed to have established the first laboratory of human relations for adults in existence.

I knew an outstandingly successful sales manager who attributed his success to the Dale Carnegie seminars. He once said to me, "When my son completes college I'll have him take the Dale Carnegie course. He needs the degree to get a job but he will probably learn more from the Carnegie course than from his four years of college."

John Boyle, West Coast consultant, has taught thousands of executives and their wives how to develop their latent potentials. Calling it the Executive Power Seminar, he describes the philosophy as, "total personal responsibility." [6] Boyle quotes William James, "Man alone, of all the creatures of earth, can change his own pattern; man alone is architect of his own destiny." "Change and growth," he writes, "are the natural state of man. They are absolutely necessary for a satisfying, healthy, and mature life. . . . Thousands of success stories among seminar class members testify to the simplicity and speed with which it is now possible to reprogram oneself to move toward realization of the hidden potential."

When his course was started in 1957, Boyle intended to teach success to social failures. He soon discovered that although his fees were reasonable, these men were not interested. Instead, the men who did seek his advice were already successful, but wanted to improve. The program is based on extensive research and John Boyle's personal discovery that man can change. He says of his early life, "I was a failure in nearly every possible way." In a desperate attempt to create a new way of life, he studied the work of William James, Jung, Emerson, Pavlov, Assagioli, Gardner Murphy, and many others. He then spent months interviewing hundreds of successful businessmen to discover the common denominator of success and personal effectiveness. These ideas and the influence of his wife, Helen, a trained psychotherapist, changed his life from failure to success.

Boyle encourages wives to take the course with their husbands because the principles he teaches are universal and apply equally well to home or business. Most graduates find the course improves their relationships with others, especially with their mates and children. The benefit most frequently mentioned is "self-assurance with growth toward maturity."

J. W. Newman, a former associate of John Boyle, formed his own organization (the J. W. Newman Corporation) in 1961. The corporation, which has offices in six major cities across the nation, offers a seminar called PACE (Personal And Company Effectiveness). PACE teaches that most adults have a distorted perception of themselves and others—an inaccurate image of REALITY—usually acquired in their childhood. Fortunately, this problem is not irrevocable. Thousands of adults, mostly business executives and their wives, have discovered that they have the ability to change their habits and personalities. Newman calls the philosophy "a concept of goal-directed responsibility . . . as a man thinks in his heart, he is." [7] Newman and Boyle both advocate the use of the positive affirmation.

Arthur Mortell, founder and president of Systematic Achievement

Corporation, directs his Personal Potential Development seminars to sales people. Mortell says that recent breakthroughs in the behavioral sciences (he mentions Maslow specifically) have provided new methods to unlock personal potential.

Anyone who wants to increase his interpersonal effectiveness and psychological maturity should review Joe Batten's *Tough-Minded Management* and Blake and Mouton's Managerial Grid,® and look into the variety of programs classified under the general description of organization development (OD).

Sensitivity training, developed in the late forties by the National Training Laboratories, originally headquartered in Bethel, Maine, is one approach to psychological development. The success or failure of sensitivity (T-group) training is still controversial. Experienced observers agree that results depend to a large degree on the skill of the training facilitator. For some individuals sensitivity training has been highly productive. For others, the experience has been unproductive, tending to diminish rather than increase self-confidence. At the time Richard Farson was director of the Western Behavioral Sciences Institute of La Jolla, he shocked a professional audience with his statement that there was no hard evidence that sensitivity training was increasing managerial effectiveness.

A large manufacturing company, which prefers to remain anonymous, conducted a study of the reactions of a typical cross section of their executives who had experienced sensitivity training. Questionnaires were sent to 300 former participants in company-sponsored training programs modeled after NTL sensitivity training. The majority of the executives reported that their experience had been positive and had increased their understanding of self and others. However, there was uncertainty about the contribution of the training to their understanding of group morale, productivity, and increased leadership skills. When asked whether they believed such programs were useful in developing dynamic management with decision-making skills, 44% said yes, 38% were uncertain, and 18% said that sensitivity training did not contribute.

Dr. Otto is critical of the negative aspects of sensitivity training. He has developed more than 100 different techniques to increase individual effectiveness. All his techniques stress the need to emphasize strength as the best means to overcome weaknesses.[8]

Self-analysis is an essential step for the executive who is determined to improve his psychological skills. Self-examination based on the theoretical ideas described in Chapter 10 offers real possibilities. As you become more familiar with your own goals and psychological needs, you learn to understand other people, too. The techniques, seminars, books, etc., mentioned above are by no means a complete list.

Personal development—dealing with attitudes, personality, and style —is the key to excellent leadership. It has been the most neglected aspect of leadership training, but now all that is changing. Leaders and those who aspire to leadership will find the development of potential one of the most promising ways to increase personal and organizational effectiveness.

15

Policies and Procedures

I firmly believe that any organization (private, government, or religious), in order to survive and achieve success, must have a sound set of beliefs on which it premises all its policies and actions.
Thomas J. Watson, Jr.

POLICIES and procedures are valuable tools for all types and sizes of organizations. "All companies have policies," writes Koontz and O'Donnell, "whether they are written or unwritten, sound or unsound, followed or not followed, understood or not understood, complete or incomplete. It is virtually impossible to delegate authority without the existence of policies, since a subordinate manager cannot make decisions without some kind of guidelines." [1]

Goals and objectives refer to *what* is to be accomplished while policies provide guidelines for *how* it is to be achieved. George Terry defines a policy as "a verbal, written, or implied overall guide setting up boundaries that supply the general limits and direction in which managerial action will take place." Others have defined policy as standing decisions that apply to repetitive questions, or as settled courses of action.

A procedure is a more specific discussion of how something is to be done. An organization's policy, for example, might be to lock all external doors at the end of the normal working day. A statement of procedure might list the doors, specifically, establish the times they are to be closed, and assign responsibility to specific individuals. Still more specific are rules such as NO SMOKING, NO PARKING, MAXIMUM SPEED LIMIT 15 MILES, and the like.

Other terms related to policies and procedures, which sometimes replace them, include "purpose," "philosophy," "belief," "creed," "strategy," "bylaws," and "directives." Various organizations use and define these terms to suit their own purposes. There is no standard terminology.

During the sixties the American Management Association made an extensive investigation of what business organizations did about policies.[2] The study revealed that while most executives agreed that policies are important management tools, there was a diversity of opinion about the details of their use. Many organizations were reluctant to reveal the specific details of their organizational policies, considering them one of the more confidential aspects of their business. Perhaps this is the reason that policy making has received relatively little attention from management researchers and writers. This AMA conclusion confirmed the earlier observations of Koontz and O'Donnell, who said, "It is surprising that so many companies neglect this powerful tool of management. Many companies do not have policy manuals, and of the increasing number of companies that do, many manuals are not kept up to date and the majority of them contain a mixture of policies, rules, and procedures." [3]

A discussion of policies and procedures highlights some of the same conditions existing in other areas of leadership. There is, for example, the same confusion in terminology, which exists throughout management literature and impedes communication among managers, not only of different companies, but within the same company. This is even more true when communication is among leaders in industry, education, government, hospitals, and churches. There are the same pro-and-con arguments about policy that we found in our discussion of organizational structure; the conflict between the need for system, order, and efficiency and the need for freedom, creativity, and flexibility.

A common finding is the contrast between new and small organizations which have failed to establish consistent policies, and large, mature organizations which have so many policies that individual judgment and flexibility are severely limited.

In the establishment of policies there is the same need to achieve maximum involvement (participation) in their development and constant reevaluation.

And there is a need to recognize that no policy or procedure, no matter how well conceived, is really valuable unless sufficient attention is paid to its implementation.

The Chase Manhattan Bank listed the following advantages for creation and use of policy.

- It secures consistency of action throughout the undertaking.
- It acts as a basis for future actions and decisions.
- It insures coordination of plans.
- It requires control of performance in terms of the corresponding plan.
- It provides a means by which authority can be delegated, thus contributing directly to one of the most important principles of organization.
- It preserves morale of employees when they know the declared policy of the undertaking, particularly if the policy is ethically sound and strictly followed.
- It stimulates the staff to greater effort and sustains loyalty in difficult times, with beneficial effect on labor turnover.
- It maintains sound relations with customers and agents.
- It enhances prestige and reputation in the eyes of the public.[4]

Critics of written policies see them as threats to flexibility and creativity and as crutches which inhibit the growth of executives. Some organizations seek to overcome this problem by placing the emphasis on objectives. Dow Chemical, for example, in their statement of corporate objectives, states, "We will let ethical ends triumph over means and prefer substance over form; we will seek the goals we set rather than be preoccupied with the methods or techniques or procedures for reaching them."

Robert Townsend sums up some of the faults of policies and policy manuals:

Don't bother. If they're general, they're useless. If they're specific, they're how-to manuals—expensive to prepare and revise.

The only people who read policy manuals are goldbricks and martinets. The goldbricks memorize them so they can say, "That's not in this department," or, "It's against company policy." The martinets use policy manuals to confine, frustrate, punish, and eventually drive out of the organization every imaginative, creative, adventuresome man and woman.

If you *have* to have a policy manual, publish the *Ten Commandments*.[5]

Probably the best (or worst) example of what Townsend is talking about is the U.S. Post Office manual. Every post office in the nation has one and it is more than nine inches thick. The postal manual tells post office employees at every level the policies, procedures, methods, and rules they are to follow. Very little is left to individual discretion, and postal employees are rarely asked how the manual could be improved. Every change in policy and procedure involves printing and mailing many thousands of the revised page or pages to each post office and their insertion. This alone discourages changes and improvements.

When organizations follow professional goal-seeking procedures, including feedback and evaluation, policies are worthwhile, saving time because they eliminate the need to constantly remake decisions regarding many routine and repetitive types of problems. "Policies, if they're well thought out, don't change every time the wind shifts," says J. W. Keener, B. F. Goodrich executive. Leaders must constantly seek a balance between the needs for order and consistency, and the needs for growth, improvement, and change. The problem is the same for policies as it is for goals and for organizational structure. Too many behavioral scientists, emphasizing freedom at the expense of order, seek to throw out the baby with the bath water.

The place to start is with a policy about policies. To be effective, policies should be created in the same participative manner as are goals and objectives. This is an important break with tradition, which has seen policy making as highly centralized and nonparticipative. Strangely enough, even organizations that have accepted the idea that objectives should be formulated at various levels in the organization have not always followed the same procedure with policies. Objectives and policies should be considered together, as they form the what and how of accomplishment. Policies connected to overall corporate objectives should be established at the corporate level. Other objectives and their policies should be established at divisional and departmental levels. Policy manuals need, as their first page, a statement that policies are guidelines and should never be used as an excuse to take action not in the best interest of the organization. In other words, the "policy about policy" should permit exceptions and deviations.

One consumer goods corporation uses the following statement in the foreword to its policy manual.

PROVISIONS FOR EXCEPTION

It is possible that unusual cases may occur where the best course of action in an isolated situation differs from the actions we would take in accordance with expressed policy. This does not mean that an otherwise sound policy must be distorted to accommodate the exceptional case, nor should the value of our policies be eroded by ignoring the inconsistencies. Rather, we must critically weigh the problem of the moment and have the courage to make an exceptional decision where unusual circumstances prevail, but with full awareness of its exceptional nature and of the serious ramifications of our actions.[6]

Such provisions for exception usually include a requirement that, time permitting, the exception should be cleared with the person who formulated the policy before proceeding.

Other policies about policy should specify such procedural details as who is to formulate them, what form is to be used, how and to whom will they be distributed, and the procedure for revision. Policy manuals should always be loose-leaf binders to provide for easy addition and revision.

Policies are useful in every area of organizational activity. The area most frequently neglected is policies regarding human relations and motivation. Organizations wishing to improve their performance will find this one way to start: Establish objectives, goals, policies, and procedures in each motivational area discussed in previous chapters. The same may be said for such frequently neglected activities as communications and creativity.

Companies stressing creativity seek to establish an environment which tolerates mistakes. "The Maytag Company," states Joe Batten, "which is consistently regarded as one of the nation's best run businesses, has laid down a basic managerial philosophy which allows for mistakes in a calculated invitation to innovation and improvement." And Kobayashi says, "We at Sony take the attitude that we can expect our workers to grow only if they know they will not be punished unduly for making mistakes."

Some policies and procedures are mandatory, imposed by government, unions, or even by trade associations. Most organizations require strict adherence to them. Growth, diversification, decisions to make or buy, and promotion from within are examples of important concepts affecting a wide variety of organizations and requiring policy determinations.

Authorities agree almost unanimously that growth is essential to organizational health. Only growing organizations provide their members with pride in achievement, job security, and opportunity for promotion. One way to achieve it is to establish written objectives, policies, and goals concerning growth.

Policy making involves important long-range decisions affecting the success of organizations. Again, important, but never urgent, policy making is easily neglected. Excellent leaders must make a continued

effort to overcome this tendency. A written policy does not guarantee
its use, but generally speaking, people are more apt to follow a policy
if it is written. In-plant orientation and training programs, especially
for supervisors, should include a systematic effort to teach and discuss
organization policies.

The following expressions of company policy from the Chase
Manhattan Bank and Westinghouse Electric Corporation (see Exhibits
8 and 9) are included as good examples of policy.

Exhibit 8. Organization and policy guide (The Chase Manhattan Bank).

SECTION: Management Policies	SECTION NUMBER
SUBJECT: CUSTOMER RELATIONS – –	II-D-3
CONFIDENTIAL NATURE OF CUSTOMER RELATIONS	DATE 4-7-71
SUPERSEDES: Same Section, Page 1 of 1, dated 2-10-65	PAGE 1 OF 1

All customers can be expected to regard the Bank as a unified organization
which is sensitive to their known interests.
In view of this, the following specific points deserve renewed emphasis:

1. Every aspect of the customer relationship is strictly confidential.

2. Unfavorable information in particular may be given only in the context
   of a relationship of trust. This is to say it may be given only to a
   person of unquestioned discretion when to withhold it would cause
   harm which we have an obligation to help prevent. Such information
   should be expressed in specific terms which minimize the chances
   of misinterpretation.

3. The affairs of the Bank and its customers should never be discussed
   in public. The greatest care should be exercised at all times in
   elevators, public hallways, dining rooms, and public transportation.
   Even though the subject matter might be innocent, persons overhearing
   it might form an impression of indiscretion that could reflect un-
   favorably on the Bank.

Rev. No. 396

ISSUED BY:	APPROVED BY:
Chairman of the Board and the President	

THE CHASE MANHATTAN BANK, N. A.

**Exhibit 9. Company purchases for employes
(Westinghouse Electric Corporation).**

PROBLEM

Legislation in numerous states prohibits employers from making purchases for employes, on the basis that such purchases constitute an unlawful trade practice that can have a serious effect on regularly established channels of distribution. Even in those states where legislation has *not* been passed prohibiting such personal purchases, it is in the best interest of the Company to make this policy consistent.

To permit the Company to make purchases for employes is definitely unfair to the suppliers with whom we do business. Moreover, the practice can become extremely time-consuming and can adversely affect the efficiency of our Purchasing Departments.

POLICY

Members of the Purchasing Department and other agents of the Company are not permitted to make purchases for employes. This policy is to be interpreted broadly enough to apply to any situation where a buyer, purchasing agent, or other agent of the Company might negotiate the purchase — even though the employe himself actually consummated the purchase.

The laws that have been passed and this Westinghouse policy do not apply to selling products of the Company's own manufacture, nor do they apply to other products that the Company sells in its regular course of business. Nor do they apply to such things as meals, candy, beverages, cigarettes, cigars, safety equipment, gloves, tools or equipment for the conduct of business, or to the disposition of surplus. In substance, the laws are designed to prevent a company's buying power from being used to make personal purchases for employes.

COMMUNICATION OF POLICY

It is the responsibility of Elected Officers, Divisions and Division General Managers, Presidents of subsidiary companies and members of Purchasing management to make this policy known to appropriate executives and employes in their organizations, and to administer the execution of this policy.

16

Nonprofit Organizations

All organizations are profoundly similar.
Sheldon Davis, Vice President, TRW Systems

CAN the knowledge of leadership developed and tested primarily in industry be utilized effectively by schools, universities, churches, cities, hospitals, government, and other nonprofit organizations? When I first suggested this in an article published in 1964, the editor in chief of a major magazine took me to task, stating that he "saw no reason to believe that business methods could or should be applied to government." A great many people seem to share this editor's skepticism, their image of industry being one of cold, mechanical, selfish organizations that are autocratic and inconsiderate of people. Unfortunately, these negative conceptions are frequently true. The type of leadership and organization described in this book by no means represents the typical industrial concern today. I have not described the average but rather the excellent, the professional.

Do the principles of professional leadership apply to *all* types of organizations? It is my emphatic conviction that they do.

This is not to minimize some profound differences between profit and nonprofit organizations. Not only are the objectives and goals of these organizations very different, but the goals of most nonprofits are far more difficult to define in measurable terms. The overall objective of business organizations is profit. This objective may be defined in a variety of ways, but whatever the definition, it is not hard to make it specific, concrete, and measurable. Nonprofit organizations must meet different legal requirements. Obviously, procedures for selecting the president of a company are vastly different from selecting the president of a country. Schools, colleges, and government have to deal with tenure requirements, which business would find exceedingly difficult to cope with. If business organizations are more efficiently managed on the average than their nonprofit counterparts, businessmen can't take too much of the credit. In business, accountability is built in; executives can hardly avoid it because they are directly responsible to customers and stockholders (and frequently their bank). The government requires them to keep sufficient records to report a year-end profit or loss, whether they want to or not. And when business leadership is grossly inefficient, the organization merely becomes another statistic in the Dun & Bradstreet record of business failures. Nonprofit organizations, especially schools and government, rarely fail if they are inefficient. Such institutions, instead of seeking greater efficiency, tend to increase their budgets.

Regardless of their nature, all organizations deal with people. Is it reasonable to believe that motivational techniques that work exceedingly well in one organization have no significance in another? Can anyone who is familiar with the literature regarding planning and goal seeking doubt that these techniques apply to all kinds of organizations? Is creativity something that business needs, but schools and churches can disregard? Is there any reason to believe that the problems of communication in profit organizations are radically different from those in other organizations? Is the selection of the right person for the right task only important in industry? Is research, especially procedural research, something that nonprofit organizations can't possibly use? Is there any reason to believe that leadership, repeatedly demonstrated as the difference between success and failure in business, is any less important for the elementary school, university, police department, or the like? Absolutely not. Concepts of professional leadership are universal; they apply to all types of organizations, and they apply, for the most part, at every organizational level.

Only a few years ago Lloyd Marquis, when president of the American Institute of Management, estimated that probably only 5 to 10% of business executives had really kept abreast of the exploding knowledge about leadership. If this is true in organizations where competition demands that leaders keep on top of this kind of thing, it must be even more true of organizations lacking the challenge of survival. Qualified observers have repeatedly remarked that hospitals, schools, colleges, etc., continue to choose leaders for their "technical skills" rather than their skills in organizing and leading people.

A tremendous gap exists between what we know about excellent leadership and what is practiced in the majority of our nonprofit institutions. Professional leaders and leadership consultants have failed to close this gap—failed to sell their ideas to these organizations so essential to our society. Leadership training and development efforts have tended to be greater in the business sector because, generally speaking, this is a more lucrative field for consultants. The disturbing lag in the application of leadership concepts in nonprofit organizations suggests, I am convinced, that most business executives do not have a sufficiently clear understanding of these concepts themselves. An examination of boards of directors, or trustees of nonprofit organizations, confirms the fact that business executives are well represented. But they seem not to have been very successful in improving the leadership performance of these organizations.

For anyone who might remain skeptical about the application of professional management principles to nonprofit organizations, or that a gap presently exists between knowledge and application, here are representative opinions of a variety of qualified observers.

> The studies of voluntary organizations not only revealed the same basic principles of organization and leadership as were found in industry and in government, but one of these studies, . . . the League of Women Voters of the United States, added important new dimensions and gave new insights into organizational processes.[1]—*Rensis Likert, University of Michigan, Institute for Social Research*

> All agree that college presidents have tough jobs. Yet qualified observers give a low rating to most presidential administrative performances. Arthur S. Flemming, illustrious president of the University of Oregon, has been in industry, government, colleges, and universities. He, as is usual, awards industry first in administrative effectiveness, but he puts government in second position and higher education last.

> The assumption that almost any distinguished scholar can be an effective president, that oratorical excellence is an essential, that a minister is ideal is not supported by fact. The requirements are integrity, courage, administrative ability, training, and experience. Also enthusiasm, physique, personality, and a strong belief in the venture's worthiness. . . . College bungling usually originates in a fuzzy focus, a diffused concept, of college objectives.[2]—*Paul H. Davis, former vice president, Columbia University*

> The Managerial Grid . . . has been applied in widely different organizational settings in the United States, Canada, Europe, and Asia. Included are industrial facilities of manufacturing, sales, R&D,

and union organizations, as well as military, governmental, professional and welfare settings such as community agencies.[3]—*Robert Blake and Jane Mouton*

Let us say a word about private nonprofit activities in general—cultural, civic, social service, religious, scientific, and charitable organizations. Some of the worst known examples of organizational decay are in this category. And one of the gravest agents of decay is a sense of moral superiority that afflicts such institutions. Sad to say, people who believe that they are doing a noble thing are rarely good critics of their own efforts.[4]—*John Gardner*

The problem with government is not, by and large, the people in government . . . no, the major cause of the ineffectiveness of government is *not a matter of men or money*. It is principally a matter of machinery. It will do us little good to change personnel or to provide more resource unless we are willing to undertake a critical review of government's overall design. . . . The diffusion of responsibility makes it extremely difficult to launch a coordinated attack on complex problems. It is as if the various units of an attacking army were operating under a variety of highly independent commands.[5]—*Richard M. Nixon*

In education, faculties of great universities, jealous of academic freedom and distrustful of managerial power, traditionally circumscribe the power of presidents and deans with a myriad of committees. In one large university, more than 300 standing committees share in administration or advice on policy, ranging from the academic senate and the budget committees to committees on committees, coordinating committees, and committees on alumni records, university welfare, and maintenance of order during examinations.[6]—*Harold Koontz and Cyril O'Donnell*

It is an ironic fact that so much research has been done with the industrial situation (because of the money available and the money involved probably) and so little of the same kind of research has been done in the educational system. . . . The trouble with education today, as with so many other American institutions, is that nobody is quite sure of what the goals and the ultimate ends of education are.[7]—*Abraham Maslow*

We have tried to apply traditional methods of academic governments, which worked very well in small private institutions of the nineteenth century, to massive institutions of the twentieth century and it hasn't worked. . . . Somebody has to be able to act fast and decisively, and educational administration as presently constituted, doesn't provide that opportunity.[8]—*Glenn S. Dumke, Chancellor, California State College System*

The U.S. Chamber of Commerce recently published the results of a detailed national analysis of the U.S. system of justice—police, courts, and correction agencies. The report, based on a great deal of factual evidence, concluded that major organizational changes are needed—and fast. In the words of a former top Justice Department official, "There is no system yet. What we have is a set of nonsystems. The criminal justice system is ludicrous when compared to that of a business organization." [9]

Public schools in California have been undergoing critical appraisal by state officials concerned by continually mounting costs. California legislative analyst A. Allen Post has been particularly critical. Post says the California school system lacks measurable goals and, without them, the system cannot determine objectively whether a particular teaching technique or program is working or not. Post sent a five-man team of analysts to 39 representative school districts to seek answers to legislators' questions about cost effectiveness in the school system. The conclusion was that the legislators' requests could not be met because "the pervasive lack of standards and accounting procedures makes comparisons and evaluations impossible. . . . When we compared levels of expenditures to rates of achievement, there were no significant correlations." [10]

Fortunately, the situation is beginning to change. Nonprofit organizations are beginning to realize that leadership concepts developed and tested by industry will work for them as well. The knowledge transfer is still only a trickle, but it is a beginning and it is increasing.

Leadership for Schools

The change in La Canada Unified School District (Los Angeles County) began in the mid-sixties. School District Superintendent Donald Ziehl became interested in some of the ideas that business executives were talking about, such as goal seeking, performance standards and the like. Dr. Ziehl began reading management literature, starting with Peter Drucker and then going on to Likert, Odiorne, Bennis, Gardner, McGregor, Argyris, and Herzberg. Then he attended several management seminars sponsored by local universities. Excited by what he heard and read, Ziehl held several meetings with his administrators as the beginning of a plan to move toward management by measurable objectives.

Beginning in the fall of 1968, administrators were asked to prepare measurable objectives for their personal performance. "Very deliberately," says Dr. Ziehl, "this activity was left unstructured because our administrators were at varying levels of sophistication, and the purpose of the activity was to strengthen them and improve their performance as administrators. This activity established success patterns that resulted in monthly reviews with each principal and improved communications within the organization."

The La Canada Unified School District established as its overall objective: "To provide a Model of Professionalism, thus providing a vitalized and more efficient and effective educational program."

Education was defined as "a process to provide the society with persons capable of perpetuating it, and as a process to provide each student with the opportunity to develop his personal life style. It is not a case of one or the other, but of both."

Dr. Ziehl and his staff established eight major categories for performance objectives:

Community relations	Monitoring
Instruction	Administration
Self-renewal	Evaluation of personnel
Pupil personnel service	Staff relations

Each administrator, including the superintendent, prepares a list of performance objectives in August for the following year. The first drafts are reviewed by the administrators' peers, staff, and superiors before they are finalized.

All administrators in the district used the same eight major categories but chose their own measurable goals under each category. One elementary school principal, for example, chose as her community relations goal: "Submit five newspaper articles featuring some aspect of the school program during the school year." And: "Conduct four parent-education meetings in the month of January and involve the PTA chairman in the planning." Under "Evaluation of Personnel" the same principal listed these goals: "Each Friday block out time for a minimum of four classroom visits the following week." And "for at least half of the visits preplan with the teachers so the observation will be of a specific lesson with prestated objectives."

An important aspect of the goal-seeking procedure is the superintendent's monthly meeting with the individual administrators to evaluate results and revise objectives if necessary.

Superintendent Ziehl's own objectives include many concepts from industry such as, "decentralized decision making . . . each level in the organization will be given the professional autonomy to make decisions appropriate for that level," "job enlargement," "accountability," "cost effectiveness."

"Management by objectives," states Ziehl, "has become the prevailing mode for performance, planning, and position evaluation within the La Canada Unified School District. The process continues because the staff supports it and the management by objectives activity has expanded to include department chairmen and total grade levels in various schools. Communications within the organization have improved, administrators know where they stand with their peers and their superiors, and the superintendent knows where he stands with the board."

He says that it is still difficult to provide statistical proof of the success of the program, although those involved are convinced that student instructional gains are significant. California state procedures for testing school performance are still very new—since 1968—and undergoing constant change. Existing statewide performance evaluations do not fully take into consideration the quality of students entering the system. It can be stated that during the four-year period that the La Canada School District has used measurable objectives, the district has consistently rated among the top 10% of all California school districts. Fall 1971 reports from Sacramento reveal that La Canada students rank in the top 5% of California unified school districts.

Here are the reactions of some of the administrators in the La Canada System. Principal Jeanne Maus writes:

> The technique of the principal's writing specific performance objectives under the eight categories is proving to be an excellent way of insuring efficiency, variety, and accountability in our service to children, teachers, parents, and the community. . . . I feel strongly that the monthly reviews are invaluable in helping me to make steady progress toward achieving my objectives and letting the superintendent know that I am. I also find that I do more than I intended to do because I am directed by written objectives from my own professional decisions.

Lawrence Kemper, also a principal, says:

> I am a great enthusiast for the concept.
>
> I feel that it is a step which all school districts should be taking. Prior to its inception I felt difficulty in conveying to the superintendent our problems and successes. The yearly evaluation pro-

cedure was a meaningless and unpleasant experience calculated only to driving the superintendent and me apart. . . . However, there is an inherent weakness in evaluation-by-objectives concepts. It requires a superintendent who is willing to look at your set of objectives and encourage you to make them a bit more challenging when needed. With a superintendent who cares less, it would be a useless exercise calculated to make his life a little easier each year as evaluation rolled around. . . . I have expanded the concept to involve the teachers at the school in much the same type of procedures.

And Frank J. Abbott, formerly from La Canada, states:

Performance objectives have assisted me in more clearly defining my priorities. As a high school principal I was confronted with a variety of tasks in such areas as instruction, budget, plant management, community relations, staff relations, and student problems. Quite frankly, it was virtually impossible to cover all areas; therefore, priorities had to be identified. The establishment of performance objectives in selected areas enabled me to more specifically define the tasks I had to achieve. The objectives also assisted me in more clearly defining the job descriptions of my assistant principals. These assistant principals were also responsible for the development of performance objectives in their identified priority areas. . . . After the performance objectives were cooperatively developed, Dr. Ziehl would meet with me on a monthly basis to examine the progress that was being made on the stated objectives. Without these regularly scheduled meetings it would have been quite easy to stray from my stated tasks and become caught up in the day-to-day activities of the job. . . .

In my present position as Assistant Superintendent—Instruction in the Oceanside Unified School District my primary responsibility is working with the principals of our 17 schools in the area of instruction. . . . By December 15, 1971, all building principals and curriculum coordinators had established at least five performance objectives for evaluation. A calendar for monthly reviews had also been established. . . .

I have witnessed individuals accomplish tasks that appear to be beyond their grasp or capability because they had established specific directions and they knew whether or not they were on course and if they had arrived.

Henry K. Swenerton, an executive with Southern California Edison Company and president of the La Canada School Board, states:

Today we are becoming aware that there is a *universality about management policy—that management (or administration) is an activity in itself and that it is unlike any other activity*. It requires people of specific qualifications and preparations. When they act in their managerial capacity, superintendents of school districts, college presidents, bishops of churches, heads of governmental agencies, or chief executives in business are all performing essentially the same function.

The manager and administrator should be the dynamic life-giving element. He should lead, guide, and direct the organization toward the accomplishment of *objectives*. . . . The late Douglas McGregor has pointed out, however, the sterility of setting objectives for somebody else. He has emphasized the great value of participating with that person in establishing his own objectives and standards. "Free men must set their own goals and be their own difficult taskmasters," says McGregor. And in order to feel success, the individual has to have "feedback" to know how well he has done. . . .

We on the board have been working closely with the administration of the district to establish and apply the principles of accountability and management by objectives. We are gratified with the results. However, we have a long way to go. We recognize that it is more difficult to measure results . . . in the education field than in a business that is producing a tangible product.

Gary, Indiana, is the first city to turn an entire school over to a private corporation—Behavioral Research Laboratories (BRL) of Palo Alto, California—on a guaranteed-performance basis. Banneker Elementary School, with approximately 800 students, began operation under its new management in September 1970. BRL was responsible for all aspects of management, including staffing and training. Utilizing the total systems approach, they set out to create a new educational environment in which all children could learn and enjoy learning. Their contract guaranteed that the cost per student would be less than that of the previous system.

An important aspect of the program is its emphasis on preservice and in-service training for administrators, teachers, and paraprofessionals. The staff is taught to create a positive motivational environment by making the program student-oriented. Children actually participate in devising their own schedules. Traditional grade levels were abolished and replaced with learning levels. In other words, children were no longer grouped by age, but instead by ability. With the BRL system, each child proceeds at his own speed, using individualized programmed instruction materials. Banneker's instruction program was divided into five curriculum areas: language, mathematics, social studies, science, and enrichment (arts and crafts, music, drama, and physical education).

Continuous community involvement accomplished through parent-community meetings and constant interaction between parents and school staff is an important part of the strategy. Paraprofessionals, called "Learning Supervisors," are selected from the community—most of them parents with children at the school. Parents are also given teaching materials to use at home, and taught how to encourage their children. Children take tests before starting a unit of study, enabling the staff to tailor the instruction program to the needs of each student.

The use of programmed instruction materials gives teachers time for individual diagnosis and for greater individual attention to each child. Children learn at their own speed, and their progress is monitored through tests. There are precise educational objectives in each subject, and students cannot proceed until they have met the specified criteria for that particular lesson unit.

The Behavioral Research Laboratories have a three-year contract at Banneker Elementary. At the end of the first year, 73% of the 850 students at the school met or exceeded national norms in reading and/or mathematics. In the previous year, 75% of the pupils scored below national norms. The first-year cost was $850 per pupil, which was $74 less than the average cost for all Gary's schools. And 87% of parents want BRL to continue the program. Alphonso D. Holliday, II, school board president, said, "This contract was negotiated because of the gross underachievement of our children. The parents of the children attending Banneker feel that the contract curriculum-centered concept will insure that every one of our children will have the opportunity to learn."

Leadership for Churches

The Northwest Yearly Meeting of Friends Churches coordinates the activities of 60 Friends Churches in Oregon, Washington, and Idaho. The organization recently completed a study of growth patterns of the churches to determine why a few of the churches were growing dynamically, while most of the others were static or declining.

The committee responsible for the church study gathered statistics and charted the attendance, age profile, and income for each of the 60 churches. Questionnaires probing the thinking, concerns, and attitudes of pastors and church members were completed by hundreds of members representing all but two of the churches. The committee also visited a number of churches all over the country which were noted for their growth ability. In addition the committee members conferred with church growth specialists in seminaries and studied literature on the subject.

The study revealed significant differences in leadership styles and techniques between the churches that were static and those that were growing. The pastors of the growing churches were described by such words as "enthusiastic," "cheerful," "confident," "positive," "has we-can-do-it attitude," "is interested in all ages," "is alert," "keeps up in reading," "always encouraging others," "involving people who haven't been involved," "leads the congregation rather than tagging along," "one who inspires others to enjoy their service," "ability to bring about and maintain unity." [10] Survey respondents were more reluctant to list leadership qualities which seemed to hinder church growth. Heading the list for those who did respond was "inability to delegate work or trust others." Another negative trait mentioned was "too domineering and inflexible."

The study revealed that churches that failed to grow had policies that seemed to lack imagination and vision. "Goal setting," the committee states, "without exception, is a vital factor in each of the growing churches studied." One church reported, "Goal setting has helped our church every year we have done it; decline has followed each year we failed to set goals."

The church growth committee made a number of specific recommendations to improve the effectiveness of their churches. In addition to the need to establish clear and positive goals and objectives, the recommendations included the need to reevaluate methods, the need to develop leaders, and constant evaluation of results. According to the report:

> Goal setting is useless unless we realistically scrutinize our success in reaching the goal. We may miss the mark we have set to attain, fall short of it, or go beyond it. But we need to honestly face up to the facts of either our failure or our success. The facts will not go away simply because we avoid looking at them or systematically observing the results of our effort. Realistic evaluation will enable us to know exactly what the facts are and enable us to plan and project for the future.[11]

Reverend Norval Hadley, present general superintendent of the Northwest Yearly Meeting of Friends Churches, says of the study:

Partly as a result of this work, our churches had their largest numerical membership increase in history during 1970 and 1971. But I am convinced that our real growth is just beginning. Our Board of Evangelism has now suggested "Breakthrough" goals for each church. These are measurable goals. Each church is to obtain an average attendance for six months in excess of its breakthrough goal by the end of 1973. We need to work a little harder on implementation and periodic evaluation, but results show that we are started in the right direction.

Leadership for Government

Can the management techniques of industry be applied to government? The Economic Development Council of New York City, Inc. offers impressive evidence that they can. EDC was established in late 1965 as an independent, nonprofit organization of businessmen to help bring the resources of the business community to bear on vital urban problems. George Champion, former chairman of the board of Chase Manhattan Bank, is full-time president of EDC. The Council's directors are presidents or chairmen of the boards of 28 corporations with New York offices, with such names as General Electric, Standard Oil (New Jersey), New York Life Insurance, F. W. Woolworth, New York Telephone, New York Stock Exchange, The Continental Corporation, Irving Trust Company, R. H. Macy & Company, American Airlines, Equitable Life Assurance, Metropolitan Life Insurance, Consolidated Edison Company, Union Carbide Corporation, and other distinguished organizations.

On May 3, 1971, members and friends of the Economic Development Council met at the New York University Club to hear the fifth annual progress report.[12] What follows are direct quotations from the men who spoke that day, starting with the comments made by George Champion.

The time has come, I believe, to say a good word for business. It is competitive enterprise which has achieved our unrivaled standard of living and generated the wealth which supports our huge and complex system of government. And one of the foremost problems of today is to harness the capabilities of business and government together in the service of the public before the business structure is overwhelmed by the size and cost of government. . . .

Does anyone seriously suppose that a modern corporation can operate in splendid isolation without regard to the conditions which surround it? Can any business build for the future without taking full account of the factors which affect the future?

Let us remember that the growth of our national economy is based on the strength of our cities and their efficiency as centers of commerce, industry, finance, and transportation. The future of our economy will depend on the continued efficiency of the cities and their ability to compete in the fast-changing national and world markets of today and tomorrow.

When we look at the components of the "urban crisis," therefore, we see a series of interrelated problems—problems in employment, education, housing, public safety, welfare, transportation, and all the rest. . . .

If municipal costs skyrocket beyond control while municipal services actually deteriorate, both in quality and availability, then the cities—and, indeed, the nation—are in trouble.

That is precisely the problem in New York City, and it traces back to an urgent and growing need for more efficient and effective government organization and management. . . .

Ten years ago the city of New York had 253,000 employees with a total payroll of $1.2 billion and an expense budget of $2.4 billion. Today it has 412,000 employees with a total payroll of $3.4 billion and an expense budget of $7.7 billion. . . . Has the total population of the city doubled or tripled meanwhile? No, it is just about where it was ten years ago—7.87 million in the 1970 census as against 7.78 million 1960.

Ten years ago, the New York City Board of Education employed about 56,000 teachers and other employees with a budget of $601 million. Today we have 105,000 teachers and other employees, and a projected school budget of $1.8 billion—the highest cost per pupil in the country. Has the total number of pupils in the New York public schools doubled or tripled meanwhile? No, it has increased by about 15%.

In the same ten-year period, the police department has increased from 27,000 to 39,000 employees, the fire department from 13,000 to 15,700, and the sanitation department from 13,000 to 16,000— and so it goes in other city departments and agencies. Yet we hear on every hand that the taxpayers are paying more for less and less— while business is finding it increasingly difficult to operate efficiently in an inefficient city. . . .

Clearly, the real key to the crisis lies in the application of business methods, systems, organization, and management to the delivery of the City's services. The need is for clear lines of authority and

responsibility, work measurement, planned program budgeting, and
personnel policies which encourage initiative and enable people to
grow in their jobs. Can this be done? As recently as two years ago I
could not have answered that question with the certainty with
which today I say: "Yes, it can be done." In fact, it is being done—
now.

Mr. Champion goes on to explain how Joseph A. Grazier, former
board chairman of American-Standard, proceeded to work with the
New York system of justice.

After a comprehensive study of all the possibilities, Mr. Grazier
saw a great opportunity to apply business concepts to the organization and management of the criminal courts—an area of vital need.
He then set about creating a task force composed of ten skilled
specialists drawn from the staff of three insurance companies which
are members of EDC.

These ten men, "on loan" from their companies, went to work on
a full-scale basis last July, making detailed studies of court operations and, until very recently, they have been on the job ever since.
In conjunction with their work, the EDC "Organization Study of
the New York City Criminal Court" was released early this year—
and has since been in great demand throughout the country.

At all times, the EDC Task Force has had the full cooperation of
the presiding justices and other court administrators. This bears out
a point I have often emphasized: The vast majority of our public
employees are wonderful, dedicated people who want to do the best
possible job and will welcome all the help they can get in the application of modern business systems and methods to their operations.

Thus we are witnessing a bold new venture into the realm of cooperative urban action which has brought the best thinking and experience of government and business together in the solution of a
major public problem. The big question then arises: Is this just one
more "study" doomed to gather dust, unheeded in the pigeonholes
of government? Or will its recommendations be implemented ener-
getically and transformed into real action?

The implementation of the Task Force Report, I am glad to say, is
going forward strongly on a daily basis. Concrete results are already
becoming apparent. But I am not going to ask you to take my word
for that.

George Champion then introduced Justice Harold A. Stevens, Presiding Justice, Appellate Division, New York State Supreme Court.
What follows are excerpts from Mr. Stevens' report.

The study by your group under the leadership and with the strong support of your president, Mr. Champion, and the dedicated efforts of Mr. Grazier, Mr. Coyne, and the management specialists was unique. It demonstrated a concern by private industry with the judicial process and the further commitment to the goal of making this city a better place for all residents. It is a landmark in pointing out to the entire nation how the private and public sectors can work together for the common good and join in seeking reform in the Court. . . .

The report, as presented and later issued to the public, highlighted administrative problems in the Court and offered specific recommendations for improved organization, management, and efficiency. It is magnificent! Many of its recommendations have been implemented, in fact a restructuring and reorganization of the Criminal Court is well under way. . . .

If we are to handle with dignity, fairness, and efficiency the huge caseloads with which the courts are daily confronted, we must introduce and utilize successful business and management techniques. Your study has proved invaluable in finding the sore spots and pointing out how and which tools should be utilized to obtain maximum efficiency with the resources presently available. . . .

The end product of our interests and of our operations is different. Because that is so, there is necessarily a point of departure. When you [businessmen] encounter individual inefficiency in your operations, you discharge the person. When we encounter inefficiency, it is usually blanketed in the system with Civil Service protection. When you call a conference of department heads and involved personnel, your operations continue. When we call such a conference, it must be in odd or after hours; otherwise, because of the shortage of personnel, our operations cease. . . .

While the courts belong to, and serve, the people, there is little interest in or support for their activities by the people or by the media unless some unfortunate or tragic incident occurs. . . .

Your generosity made possible a study which should have been undertaken long ago. Your continued assistance and advice is enabling us to improve the total system. For this I thank you.

The Economic Development Council's School Partnership Program is described by J. Henry Smith, president of the Equitable Life Assurance Society. What follows are portions of the report by Mr. Smith.

We are not adequately developing the city's most important asset —its potentially productive manpower. This fact was brought home by a survey which EDC conducted last year. . . .

The survey revealed a shortage, amounting at the time to about 50,000, of applicants suitably qualified for clerical employment even at the entry level. This shortage tracks back to the high schools, where some 30,000 students drop out annually while another 16,000 receive general diplomas, which, all too often, signify very little in terms of actual education.

Clearly, then, the Economic Development Council School Partnership Program is directed to the right address. In essence, this program seeks to motivate young people towards education and employment. . . .

Business is truly involved in this program. Today, in all four schools, you will find young businessmen and women on loan from EDC member companies, working as motivators on a full-time basis. . . .

The spirit of these school partnerships is one of constant exploration and innovation. At Brandeis, for example, tests of the new Gattegno Approach showed gains in reading skills of 2.9 years per year of study—as against only .5 heretofore. The same approach can also be applied to the teaching of mathematics and of English as a second language. . . .

At James Monroe, a promising pilot tutorial program is well under way. Each Monday evening, an average of 80 volunteer "tutors," employees of EDC member companies, go by bus to the school to help youngsters with remedial reading and mathematics, English as a second language, and business subjects. . . .

At Bushwick High, students are learning to relate the classroom to employment opportunity—which many find hard to visualize. Ninth-grade pupils are enrolled in a new Job Readiness Program, receiving class credit for a course in Careers in Business. Here they get practical instruction in such matters as how to fill out job application forms, what to wear, what to say in interviews, and how to act in business. . . .

The drug problem has been tackled head-on at Monroe by a student group called The Brotherhood Establishment. They have literally driven the pushers out. . . .

George Washington Prep opened its doors just last February in a church near the school. It is staffed by faculty volunteers eager to show that potential dropouts can be motivated and educated if given more personal attention. Some 200 youngsters applied for admission and 42 were accepted. With a teacher-student ratio of one to 18, "Prep's" pupils are rapidly gaining academic ground no matter how far behind they were when they started. . . .

Contributing manpower as well as funds, business has unleashed a
powerful new force in the schools. Young executives with ideas and
enthusiasm are finding a ready and dynamic response among dedicated teachers and administrators. . . . Scores and hundreds of
youngsters are being turned toward lives of employment, achievement, and self-reliance.

What Should Be Done About Nonprofit Organizations?

Our nonprofit organizations are important to all of us. They have
a great deal to do with the quality of our society. Obviously, it is in
everyone's best interests to improve the quality of these organizations.
How? Narrow the gap between their present practice and the best
examples of professional leadership. Demonstration projects are needed
in schools, colleges, churches, hospitals, police departments, city governments, etc., where, with the help of outstanding practitioners of and
consultants in professional leadership, what is possible can be actively
demonstrated.

Business executives should familiarize themselves with the problems
of nonprofit organizations and become more active in helping them
achieve greater efficiency.

Everyone in our society needs greater awareness of the importance
of professional leadership. We must learn how to recognize and encourage it. We need leadership appreciation courses in our schools and
colleges. If we can teach music appreciation to students who never
become musicians, it seems reasonable to believe that we can teach
leadership appreciation to people who will never become leaders. There
is need to develop leadership training programs specifically tailored to
every type of nonprofit institution. Of course, nonprofit administrators
can benefit from some of the generalized types of leadership training
programs which exist today. But they could benefit far more from
programs designed and conducted by men who are thoroughly familiar
with their particular and unique organizational problems.

The benefits to our entire society from these types of activities can
be far greater than most people realize. If well-run business organizations
can greatly increase their efficiency, isn't it reasonable to assume that
nonprofit institutions can benefit at least as much?

17

What the Leader
Should Do Now

*Every worthwhile accomplishment has a price tag
on it: How much are you willing to pay in hard
work and sacrifice, in patience, faith, and endur-
ance to obtain it?* Harold Sherman, *How To Turn
Failure into Success*

AVERAGE golfers envy the pro who steps up to the tee and drives
the ball 250 yards down the center of the fairway. It seems so effortless.
But professional excellence in golf, as in any sport, is the result of
training and effort. So too with leadership, professional excellence is
the result of persistent effort. Executives who achieve the most are those
who consider long-range objectives.

The problem with many executives is that they are simply too busy
to think. They are so eager to succeed that they charge ahead blindly,
not taking sufficient time to determine where they wish to go or how
best to get there. The solution is not merely to work harder, it is to
work smarter. Many of the activities which contribute most to the
overall success of leaders take time to bear fruit. Expediency seldom
pays, even in the short run.

I have sought to establish a model for professional leaders—a model
of excellence. To some these standards may seem discouragingly high.
Fortunately, the greater the gap between present performance and
professional performance, the greater the possibilities for rapid improvement. Leaders who study and adopt the methods and techniques of
excellent leaders can achieve excellence too. The rewards, financial and
nonfinancial, make the effort worthwhile.

Professional leaders apply creative goal-seeking procedures to the basic functions essential to organizational success—planning, organizing, staffing, communication, training, research (including procedural research), and motivation. They constantly strive for a proper balance between what is urgent and what is important, and between creative flexibility and disciplined order.

Psychological factors are of central importance. Psychological fitness (emotional maturity) is as essential to the leader as physical fitness is to the athlete. Emotional maturity is not the only requisite of professional leadership, but to the extent it is lacking, nothing else helps. Because of the important new knowledge of psychology, advances in this vital area of leadership can be rapid and dramatic.

In previous chapters I have discussed some of the ways in which executives can improve various aspects of their performance. The possibilities include study of the literature, audio and visual materials, seminars, and consultants.

Many executives approach golf, tennis or skiing with more intelligence than they approach their task as leaders. Neophytes to these sports generally seek someone who obviously knows a great deal about the subject, and ask him to show them what to do. True, it's much easier to identify a competent golf instructor than a competent management consultant, but competent consultants do exist and can be identified if one goes at it systematically. Everyone finds it difficult to perform new tasks the first time around. It is much easier to do something new with the assistance of someone who knows exactly how. Management consultants are, however, seldom equally skilled in all areas of leadership. One may be an expert on communication, another on management by objectives, and a third on financial incentives.

People seldom change in any profound way by reading a book or hearing a lecture. These activities may identify problems and describe proper solutions, but *to achieve results, ideas must be used. Action is required.*

Do you want to improve your ability to lead? Do you want to seek professional excellence? If so, the way to proceed is to decide on the first step and take it. Centuries ago Confucius correctly said: "The thousand-mile journey starts with one step." Here are some of the steps you might take:

———— I will reserve the following dates and times for an improvement program.

———————————————————————————————————

———————————————————————————————————

———————————————————————————————————

_____ I want my associates to read this book and then we will develop an action program. The ones to involve are:

_____

_____

_____

_____ I will use the Organization Checklist (see Chapter 18) as the basis to establish priorities for an action program.

_____

_____ I will schedule a meeting with my staff to plan an organizational improvement program. Who? When? Where?

_____

_____

_____

_____ I will start holding regular meetings with my staff as the first step toward adopting the coordinated team approach at all levels under my jurisdiction. Who? When? Where?

_____

_____

_____

_____ I will attend some seminars. Which seminars? When?

_____

_____

_____

_____ I will start reading leadership literature. What? When?

_____

_____

_____

_____ I will start a leadership library. How? When? Where?

_____

_____

_____

_____ I will obtain and display some signs to remind me and my associates to do things in a professional way.

_____

_____ I will analyze my own use of time. This is how I will proceed:

_____

_____

_____

———— I will seek a qualified consultant to help improve personal and organizational effectiveness. Who? When?

_____

_____

_____

———— The area which shows the greatest possibility for improvement is

_____

I will start there. What? How? When?

_____

_____

_____

———— I will do the following:

_____

_____

_____

18

The Organization Checklist

THE checklist offers a way to evaluate organizations and their leadership. It may be used as a tool to identify areas requiring attention and offering opportunities for improvement.

Not every item applies to every type of organization. New organizations in particular must concentrate on activities essential to survival. Gradually, as organizations grow, they should adopt the procedures of mature organizations—the methods of professional leadership.

The Organization Checklist

DIRECTORS OR TRUSTEES

The number is correct. (We recommend 9 as optimum.)	
If the board must be more than 15 there is a smaller executive committee.	
There is a system to maintain proper age balance.	
There is a system to maintain sufficient diversity of experience related to the organization's activities.	
There is a system for rotation without losing the continuity of experience.	
There is provision for a proper insider–outsider ratio. (We recommend over 50% outsiders.)	
The board members are qualified for their task.	
The board has a strong, well-qualified chairman.	
The board participates in the establishment of major objectives and policies.	
The board avoids involvement in the details of daily operation.	
The board receives regular outside financial audits of the organization.	
The board supervises salary determinations at the highest levels.	
The board members are active and regular in attendance.	
Board members receive systematic training to maintain and improve their effectiveness.	
The board is kept systematically informed about the major events of the organization and its field of endeavor.	
The board provides for both the excellence and the continuity of active leadership.	

© 1972 by Thomas Jefferson Research Center

LEADERSHIP

The leader has a good general knowledge of the organization and its activities.	
The leader has systematic procedures to keep abreast, in a general way, of technical developments in the organization's field of endeavor.	
The leader understands and takes a personal part in such major organizational functions as Organizing Goal seeking Policies and procedures Staffing Communication Training and development Research Worker motivation	
The leader is a mature person with Personal goals Ambition Persistence Courage Faith Integrity Creativity Sense of justice Objectivity Flexibility Self-discipline Decisiveness Skill with people Self-respect Respect for others Ability to communicate Patience	
The leader knows what and when to delegate.	
The leader's style is one that stresses both people and tasks.	
The leader gets others to participate.	

The leader achieves a balance between needs for flexibility and creativity and order and discipline.	
The leader is well organized.	
The leader personally understands and uses positive motivation.	
The leader plans his own time on a daily, weekly, and monthly basis.	
The leader achieves a proper balance between urgent and important tasks.	
The leader invests some time in activities that will improve future efficiency.	
The leader does not procrastinate.	
The leader achieves a proper balance between working and supervising the work of others.	
The leader avoids undue pressure by avoiding unreasonable goals and deadlines.	
The leader creatively seeks ways to save time through changes in work schedules, use of odd times, backward calendars, etc.	

The leader seeks to develop his own potential
 	
Through:
    Reading
    Seminars
    Consultants
In such areas as:
    Creativity
    Communication
    Motivation
    Reading skills
    Public speaking	

GOAL SEEKING

Supervisors at all levels are trained in the use of goal-seeking procedures.	
Leadership at the top uses goal-seeking procedures on a regular basis.	
Specific time is allocated for goal-seeking activities at the top.	
Supervisors at all levels use goal-seeking procedures regularly and willingly.	
Time is allocated for goal seeking at all levels of supervision.	
Employees are trained to use goal-seeking procedures.	
Goal-seeking activities are used for nonproduction as well as production workers.	
Goals are specific and measurable. (Long-range objectives are less so.)	
Goal seeking is seen as a way to give recognition rather than a way to criticize.	
People participate in the establishment of the goals they are to achieve.	
Individual goals are established by mutual agreement between each individual and his superior.	
Goals and progress towards them are reviewed regularly.	
Goals are considered more important than the means to achieve them. Ends determine the means.	
Organizational planning includes long-range as well as short-range goals.	
Organizational goals are all related to some overall objective.	
Short-range goals are coordinated with long-range goals.	
Control—feedback and a system for constant evaluation and modification—is recognized as an essential part of the goal-seeking process.	

CREATIVITY

Creativity is taught and encouraged in the organization.	
A specific attempt is made to increase creativity by increasing the amount of time spent in thinking (goal seeking) at all levels.	
A specific attempt is made to maintain a creative climate in the organization. Mistakes are tolerated. Brainstorming is encouraged. Killer phrases are discouraged. Fresh viewpoints are encouraged. People at all levels are encouraged to think. Creative decisions are not hurried. Pressure is kept at a reasonable minimum. Differences of opinion are encouraged. A positive motivational climate is maintained.	
Fact gathering is seen as an essential aspect of creative problem solving.	

ORGANIZATION

There is a continuing program of organization planning, with personnel projections at least three years ahead.	
There are well-defined lines of responsibility and authority.	
When a person is given responsibility, he is also given sufficient authority to do the job.	
There is an organization chart (or charts) and it is kept current.	
The organizational structure is a "flat pyramid" shape. Span of authority is maximized at each level. There is a minimum of levels of supervision.	
When size requires it (around 500), there is decentralization into divisions.	
Leadership considers the use of project teams and special task forces when appropriate.	
Staff functions are held to a minimum and line functions are emphasized.	

The organization is viewed and managed as a system.	
Overlapping teams are used to provide creativity, participation, and coordination throughout the organization.	
The teams meet at regular intervals without interruptions.	

STAFFING

Staffing is recognized as a major organizational function, receiving continuous attention at the very top.	
The organization approaches staffing in a creative and systematic way.	
Sufficient time is spent to do a good job.	
New people must complete a period of probation (90 days). It is the responsibility of their supervisor to decide during this period if their performance is adequate.	
Hiring strategy seeks to move rapidly yet carefully—the procedure is not drawn out.	
All sources of applicants are considered.	
Promotion from within is an organizational policy.	
There are procedures to make present employees aware of opportunities for promotion from within.	
Hiring is seen as primarily a line rather than a staff function.	
Applicants receive preliminary screening to eliminate the obviously unqualified.	
Application forms ask enough questions—and the right questions.	
The applicant's previous work record is carefully checked.	
Manual skills are tested.	
Supervisors are trained in interview techniques designed to appraise the applicant's character and personality.	
Written tests are carefully evaluated to determine their validity.	

Performance appraisals occur regularly at all levels in the organization.	
Supervisors at all levels are trained in the use of *positive* evaluation techniques.	

COMMUNICATION

Communication receives top-level attention.	
Supervisors at all levels are taught how to communicate.	
Emotional factors are recognized as a major block to effective communication, and leaders are taught how to handle them.	
Listening is recognized as a vital aspect of communication.	
Feedback is always sought and by all methods—verbal, written, and so on.	
People's *real* reasons are sought.	
Persuasion by involvement is utilized.	
Communication stresses the other person's point of view (the "you" approach)—stressing benefits rather than product.	
Direct criticism is usually avoided.	
Supervisors are taught to understand perception and its effect on people's ability to communicate.	
The organization and its executives have written communication objectives and policies.	

TRAINING AND DEVELOPMENT

Training and development receive top-level attention.	
Supervisors at all levels are taught to be teachers.	

Training activities cover all major areas of organizational activity:
 	
    New person orientation
    Job skills
    Leadership development	

Creativity Goal seeking Communication Motivation Teaching others Staffing Organization policies Personal potential	
There are written training objectives, goals, policies, and procedures.	
Responsibilities for training activities are clearly assigned.	
All levels of people are involved as students in suitable training programs.	
Directors or trustees receive training too.	
Line supervisors are held responsible as trainers.	
Both in-plant and outside locations are used.	
Both in-plant and outside trainers are used.	
Training is carried through to on-the-job do it.	
All types of instruction are used: Lecture Discussion Role playing Strip film Records Tape cassettes Film Television Charts Programmed learning	
Training programs are carefully evaluated for cost effectiveness.	
People are encouraged to take personal responsibility for self-improvement.	
Team problem solving is used as a training device.	

Job rotation is used as a training device.	
Organization development (OD) is considered as a leadership training device.	
Leadership development efforts pay particular attention to psychological aspects—personality, positive attitudes, understanding of self and others, and leadership style.	
Leadership development covers theory as well as practice.	
Various training programs are followed up at regular intervals by review sessions.	

RESEARCH

Research is seen as an important organizational function.	
Research activities receive continuous top-level attention.	
Research is allocated an adequate portion of the annual budget.	
Research includes products, services, and procedures.	
There is a proper balance between basic and applied research.	
The research director is trained as a supervisor.	
A creative climate exists especially in research areas.	
Multidisciplinary teams are used when appropriate (systems approach).	
Research activities are coordinated with other activities, especially marketing.	
Computers are used when suitable.	
Research activities are subject to cost evaluation.	

All sources of innovation are considered:
    In-house
    Independent inventors
    Outside research labs
    Technology transfer
    All employees	

Research activities include such areas as organization, communication, production, systems, marketing, and executive development.	
Methods improvement is taught and utilized at all levels in the organization.	

MOTIVATION

Motivational activities receive top-level attention.	
Executives from the top down receive training in motivational theory and practice.	
Organizational policies and procedures reflect positive motivational techniques.	

The organization systematically uses such motivational devices as:
 	
    Challenging goals
    Recognition and approval
    Opportunity and security
    Achievement
    Accountability
    Job enrichment
    Financial incentives
    Justice
    Freedom with responsibility
    Suggestion systems
    Participation	

The effectiveness of motivational activities is evaluated by measuring turnover, absenteeism, tardiness, worker morale, scrap loss, etc.	

POLICIES AND PROCEDURES

The organization has written policies and procedures in areas where goals are established.	
There are policies about policies—who is to establish them, and how, etc.	
Policy allows for deviation where the circumstances warrant it.	

Policies and procedures are developed at various levels in the organization.	
The people who will use them participate in the formulation of policies.	
Policies and procedures are systematically reviewed and revised.	
Each supervisor has a loose-leaf binder containing the policies and procedures that pertain to his job.	
Written policies should cover such frequently neglected areas as creativity, communications, and motivation.	

Appendix

Hewlett-Packard Statement of Corporate Objectives

THE achievements of an organization are the result of the combined efforts of each individual in the organization working toward common objectives. These objectives should be realistic, should be clearly understood by everyone in the organization, and should reflect the organization's basic character and personality.

If the organization is to fulfill its objectives, it should strive to meet certain other fundamental requirements:

FIRST, the most capable people available should be selected for each assignment within the organization. Moreover, these people should have the opportunity—through continuing programs of training and education—to upgrade their skills and capabilities. This is especially important in a technical business where the rate of progress is rapid. Techniques that are good today will be outdated in the future and each person in the organization should continually be looking for new and better ways to do his work.

SECOND, enthusiasm should exist at all levels: People in important management positions should not only be enthusiastic themselves, they should be selected for their ability to engender enthusiasm among their associates. There can be no place, especially among the people charged with management responsibility, for half-hearted interest or half-hearted effort.

THIRD, even though an organization is made up of people fully meeting the first two requirements, all levels should work in unison toward common objectives and avoid working at cross purposes if the ultimate in efficiency and achievement is to be obtained.

It has been our policy at Hewlett-Packard not to have a tight military-type organization, but rather, to have overall objectives which are clearly stated and agreed to, and to give people the freedom to work toward those goals in ways they determine best for their own areas of responsibility.

Our Hewlett-Packard objectives were initially published in 1957. Since then they have been modified from time to time, reflecting the changing nature of our business and social environment. This booklet represents the latest updating of our objectives. We hope you find them informative and useful.

William P. Hewlett

October, 1969   *President*

1. PROFIT

OBJECTIVE: *To generate the highest level of profit consistent with our other objectives.*

In our economic system, profit is essential to corporate survival and is the best single measure of corporate performance. It is not, however, the sole measure. Responsibility to our society, to our customers, to our employees—all are important factors against which the consideration of profit must be balanced. But without profit these other factors lose their meaning; a company that is bankrupt can meet none of its other responsibilities. Profit provides the money for growth, it is essential to the achievement of our other objectives, and it makes our company an attractive investment for our employees and for outside shareholders.

Profit is the difference between two large quantities—the price that is appropriate for our products on the one hand, and the total cost of providing them on the other. Small increases in cost can cause significant decreases in profit. Our success depends upon doing a myriad of jobs correctly and efficiently. The day-to-day performance of each individual adds—or subtracts—from our profit. Profit is the responsibility of all.

2. CUSTOMERS

OBJECTIVE: *To provide products and services of the greatest possible value to our customers.*

In the last analysis, it is the customer whom we seek to serve—through application of advanced technology, efficient manufacturing, and imaginative marketing. We will stand or fall on the basis of whether the products and services we provide excel in the marketplace.

If we can anticipate the customer's needs, if we can provide products that will enable him to operate more efficiently, if we can offer him the kind of service and reliability that will merit his highest confidence, if we can do all this at a reasonable price, then we are truly meeting our responsibilities to our customer.

3. FIELDS OF INTEREST

> OBJECTIVE: *To enter new fields when the ideas we have, together with our technical, manufacturing, and marketing skills, assure that we can make a needed and profitable contribution to the field.*

The original Hewlett-Packard products were electronic measuring instruments. Today our product line has expanded to include instruments for chemical and biomedical measurement and analysis, computers to automate measurement and to process the data, as well as electronic calculators and complete computer systems. Thus our growth has led to a continuing expansion of our fields of interest. To a large extent, diversification has come from applying our resources and skills to fields technically related to our traditional ones.

The key to HP's prospective involvement in new fields is *contribution.* This means providing the customer with something new and needed, not just another brand of something he can already buy. To meet this objective we must continually generate new ideas for better kinds of products. It is essential that before final decision is made to enter a new field, full consideration be given to the associated problems of manufacturing and marketing these products.

4. GROWTH

> OBJECTIVE: *To let our growth be limited only by our ability to develop and produce technical products that satisfy real customer needs.*

How large should a company become? Some people feel that when it has reached a certain size there is no point in letting it grow further. Others feel that bigness is an objective in itself. We do not believe that large size is important for its own sake; however, for at least two basic reasons, continuous growth is essential for us to achieve our other objectives.

In the first place, we serve a rapidly growing and expanding segment of our technological society. To remain static would be to lose ground. We cannot maintain a position of strength and leadership in our field without growth.

In the second place, growth is important in order to attract and hold high-caliber people. These individuals will align their future only with a company that offers them considerable opportunity for personal progress. Such progress is more rapid and challenging in a growing company.

5. OUR PEOPLE

> OBJECTIVE: *To help HP people share in the company's success, which they make possible; to provide job security based on their performance; to recognize their individual achievements; and to insure the personal satisfaction that comes from a sense of accomplishment in their work.*

We are proud of the people we have in our organization, their performance, and their attitude toward their jobs and toward the company. The company has been built around the individual, his personal dignity, and the recognition of his achievements.

We feel that general policies and the attitude of managers toward their people are more important than specific details of the personnel program. Personnel relations will be good only if people have faith in the motives and integrity of their supervisors and of the company. Personnel relations will be poor if they do not.

The opportunity to share in the success of the company is evidenced by our above-average wage and salary level, our profit-sharing and stock purchase plans, and by other company benefits.

The objective of job security is illustrated by our policy of avoiding large ups and downs in our production schedules, which would require hiring people for short periods of time and laying them off later. We are interested that each employee carry his full load and be eager to remain with and grow with the company. This does not mean we are committed to an absolute tenure status, nor do we recognize seniority except where other factors are reasonably comparable.

In a growing company there are apt to be more opportunities for advancement than there are qualified people to fill them. This is true at Hewlett-Packard; opportunities are plentiful and it is up to the individual, through his personal growth and development, to take advantage of them.

We want people to enjoy their work at HP, and to be proud of their accomplishments. This means we must make sure that each person receives the recognition he needs and deserves. In the final analysis, our human resources are our most valuable asset.

6. MANAGEMENT

OBJECTIVE: *To foster initiative and creativity by allowing the individual great freedom of action in attaining well-defined objectives.*

In discussing HP operating policies, we often refer to the concept of "management by objectives." By this we mean that insofar as possible each individual at each level in the organization should make his own plans to achieve company objectives and goals. After receiving approval of his plans from his supervisor, he should be given a wide degree of freedom to work within the limitations imposed by these plans, and by our general corporate policies. Finally, his performance should be judged on the basis of how well he achieves the goals he helped establish.

The successful practice of "management by objective" is a two-way street. Management must be sure that each individual understands the immediate objectives, as well as corporate goals and policies. Thus a primary HP management responsibility is communication and mutual understanding. Conversely every employee must take sufficient interest in his work to want to plan it, to propose new solutions to old problems, to stick his neck out when he has something to contribute. "Management by objective," as opposed to management by directive, offers opportunity for individual freedom and contribution; it also imposes an obligation for everyone to exercise initiative and enthusiasm.

7. CITIZENSHIP

OBJECTIVE: *To honor our obligations to society by being an economic, intellectual, and social asset to each nation and each community in which we operate.*

All of us should strive to improve the environment in which we live. As a corporation operating in many different communities throughout the world, we must assure ourselves that each of these communities is better for our presence. This means building plants and offices that are attractive and in harmony with the community; it means solving instead of contributing to the problems of traffic and pollution; it means contributing both money and time to community projects.

Each community has its particular set of social problems. Our company must help to solve these problems. As a major step in this direction, we must strive to provide worthwhile employment opportunities for people of widely different backgrounds. Among other things, this requires positive action to seek out, train, and employ members of underprivileged groups.

As citizens of their community, there is much that HP people can and should do to improve it—either working as individuals or through such groups as churches, schools, civic, or charitable organizations. At a national level, it is essential that the company be a good corporate citizen of each country in which it operates. Moreover, our employees, as individuals, should be encouraged to contribute their support to the solution of national problems.

The betterment of our society is not a job to be left to a few; it is a responsibility to be shared by all.

References

Chapter 1
1. "A Report on Key Factors Influencing Printing Profits," Harris-Intertype Corporation Report to the 77th Annual Convention of the Printing Industry of America, Los Angeles, Calif., September 10, 1963, pp. 13–20.
2. "Syria: Warming Toward U.S.," *U.S. News & World Report*, December 6, 1971, p. 43.
3. Stanley E. Seashore and David G. Bowers, "Durability of Organizational Change," *American Psychologist*, March 1970.
4. Alfred J. Marrow, David G. Bowers, and Stanley E. Seashore, *Management by Participation*, Harper & Row, New York, 1967, p. 248.

Chapter 2
1. Paul C. Fisher, "Road to Freedom," Fisher Pen Co., Forest Park, Ill., 1960, p. 5.
2. Frank Bettger, *How I Raised Myself from Failure to Success in Selling*, Prentice-Hall, Inc., Englewood Cliffs, N.J., 1949, pp. 23–24.
3. Ernest C. Miller, *Objectives and Standards: An Approach to Planning and Control*, Research Study 74, AMA, 1966.
4. Robert Townsend, *Up the Organization*, Alfred A. Knopf, New York, 1970, p. 129.
5. Ernest C. Miller, op. cit., p. 35.
6. Harold Koontz and Cyril O'Donnell, *Principles of Management*, McGraw-Hill, New York, 1955, Rev. 1964, p. 35.
7. "Long-Range Profit Planning," NAA Research Reports No. 42, National Association of Accountants, New York, December 1, 1964, pp. 7–9.

Chapter 3
1. Ernest C. Miller, *Objectives and Standards: An Approach to Planning and Control*, Research Study 74, AMA, 1966, p. 35.

2. Earl Nightingale and Whitt N. Schultz, "Creative Thinking—How to Win with Ideas" (record), Nightingale-Conant Corporation, Chicago, 1965.
3. Shigeru Kobayashi, *Creative Management*, AMA, 1971, p. 70.
4. L. C. Repucci, *Increasing Creative Performance*, Hawkins Publishing Company, Midland, Mich., 1965, pp. 1–2.
5. Charles Clark, *Brainstorming*, Doubleday & Company, Inc., Garden City, N.Y., 1958, p. 55.
6. Myron S. Allen, *Psycho-Dynamic Synthesis*, Parker Publishing Company, West Nyack, N.Y., 1966, pp. 192–193.
7. William J. J. Gordon, *Synectics*, Harper & Row, New York, 1961.
8. H. Wolf, "The Great G.M. Mystery," *Harvard Business Review*, September–October, 1965, p. 176.
9. Maxwell Maltz, *Psycho-Cybernetics*, Wilshire Book Company, Hollywood, Calif., 1960, 1964, p. 75.
10. Bertrand Russell, *The Conquest of Happiness*, Liveright Publishing Corporation, New York, 1930.
11. L. C. Repucci, op. cit., p. 7.
12. "Corporate Objectives," The Dow Chemical Company, Midland, Mich.
13. Edwin H. Land, "The Second Great Product of Industry: The Rewarding Life," *Science and Human Progress* (address presented at the 30th Anniversary of the Mellon Institute, May 22–26, 1963).

Chapter 4
1. John W. Gardner, "The Antileadership Vaccine," annual report, Carnegie Corporation, 1965, pp. 5, 9.
2. Grant A. Dove, "Objectives, Strategies, and Tactics" (address), Texas Instruments, Inc., January 19, 1970, p. 3.
3. Harold Koontz and Cyril O'Donnell, *Principles of Management*, McGraw-Hill, New York, 1955, 3d ed., 1964, p. 228.
4. Sheldon A. Davis (from Chapter 2 of a currently untitled book planned as part of the Addison-Wesley Series on Organization Development), Addison-Wesley Publishing Company, Reading, Mass.
5. Robert Townsend, *Up the Organization*, Alfred A. Knopf, New York, 1970, pp. 23, 24.
6. Shigeru Kobayashi, *Creative Management*, AMA, 1971, pp. 44, 45.
7. Stafford Beer, *Cybernetics and Management*, John Wiley & Sons, Inc., New York, 1959, p. 9.
8. Rensis Likert, *New Patterns of Management*, McGraw-Hill, New York, 1960, pp. 105–113.

Chapter 5
1. A. A. Hendrix, "Interviewing Techniques," *Industrial Medicine and Surgery*, 1950.
2. Saul W. Gellerman, *Motivation and Productivity*, AMA, 1963, p. 236.
3. M. Scott Myers, *Every Employee a Manager*, McGraw-Hill, New York, 1970, pp. 154–155.

4. Stanley R. Novack, "Developing an Effective Application Blank," *Personnel Journal*, May 1970, p. 419.
5. C. B. Buchanan, *How to Get the Right Job in Selling and Marketing*, Doubleday & Company, Inc., Garden City, N.Y., 1951, 1965.
6. Jack H. McQuaig, *How to Pick Men*, Frederick Fell, Inc., New York, 1963, pp. 4, 6, 7.
7. E. F. Wonderlic, *Wonderlic Tests*, Northfield, Ill.
8. Human Engineering Laboratories, Inc., Boston, Mass.
9. Chris Argyris, *Integrating the Individual and the Organization*, John Wiley & Sons, New York, 1964.
10. J. D. Batten, *Tough-Minded Management*, AMA, 1963, Rev. 1969.

Chapter 6
1. Frank Bettger, *How I Raised Myself from Failure to Success in Selling*, Prentice-Hall, Inc., Englewood Cliffs, N.J., 1949, pp. 87–95.
2. Alfred J. Marrow, David G. Bowers, and Stanley E. Seashore, *Management by Participation*, Harper & Row, New York, 1967, p. 25.
3. Leland Brown, *Communicating Facts and Ideas in Business*, Prentice-Hall, Inc., Englewood Cliffs, N.J., 1961, p. 199.

Chapter 7
1. Earl R. Gomersall and M. Scott Myers, "Breakthrough in On-the-Job Training," *Harvard Business Review*, July–August 1966, pp. 67–72.
2. Eugene J. Benge, "The Top Management Problems—How to Solve Them," Personnel Journal, Inc., Swarthmore, Pa., 1967, pp. 13–14.
3. Peter F. Drucker, "What We Can Learn from Japanese Management," *U.S./Japan Outlook*, Fall 1971, p. 7.
4. Frank Doeringer, *Developing Top Executives*, PA Special Report 41, The Presidents Association, Inc., January–February 1970, p. 6.
5. Robert Townsend, *Up the Organization*, Alfred A. Knopf, New York, 1970, p. 71.
6. Doeringer, op. cit., p. 12.
7. William Oncken, Jr., "A New Approach to Corporate Organization Planning and Development," Circular No. 32, California Institute of Technology, Pasadena, Calif., December 1964, p. 2.
8. Frieda Libaw, "And Now, the Creative Corporation," *Innovation*, Technology Communication, Inc., New York, March 1971, pp. 2–12.
9. Warren Bennis, *Organization Development: Its Nature, Origin, and Prospect*, Addison-Wesley Publishing Company, Reading, Mass., 1969, pp. 2–12.
10. Sheldon A. Davis, "Building More Effective Teams," *Innovation*, Technology Communication, Inc., New York, November 15, 1970, p. 33.
11. Ibid., p. 34.

Chapter 8
1. "Research and Development in State Government Agencies, Fiscal Years 1967 and 1968, Survey of Science Resources Series," National

Science Foundation, NSF 70-22, U.S. Government Printing Office, Washington, D.C., May 1970, p. 27.

2. Herbert D. Bissell, "Research and Marketing—Rivals or Partners?" *Research Management*, May 1971, pp. 66, 72.

3. H. Stephen Jenks, "Introduction to the Social Technology of Organization Development, Part 2, The Building for Organizational Effectiveness," Dow Chemical Company, p. 18.

4. Robert Vichnevetsky, "Simulation in Research and Development," Management Bulletin 25, AMA, 1969.

5. Donald A. Schon, *Technology and Change*, a Seymour Lawrence book, Delacorte Press, New York, 1967.

6. Ibid., p. 171.

7. Ibid., pp. 160–161.

8. Thomas J. Watson, Jr., *A Business and Its Beliefs: The Ideas That Helped Build IBM*, McGraw-Hill, New York, 1963, p. 5.

Chapter 9

1. J. C. Penney, "What an Executive Should Know About Himself," The Dartnell Corporation, Chicago and London, 1964, p. 6.

2. J. D. Batten, *Tough-Minded Management*, Rev. ed., AMA, 1969, p. 73.

3. Douglas McGregor, *The Human Side of Enterprise*, McGraw-Hill, New York, 1960, p. 33.

4. Saul W. Gellerman, *Motivation and Productivity*, AMA, 1963, p. 21.

5. Rensis Likert, *New Patterns of Management*, McGraw-Hill, New York, 1961, p. 6.

6. Douglas McGregor, op. cit., p. 49.

7. Chris Argyris, *Integrating the Individual and the Organization*, John Wiley & Sons, New York, 1964, pp. 6, 36.

8. T. George Harris, "To Know Why Men Do What They Do: A Conversation with David C. McClelland," *Psychology Today*, January 1971, p. 39.

9. Ibid., p. 36.

10. Frederick Herzberg, *Work and the Nature of Man*, The World Publishing Company, Cleveland, 1966.

11. M. Scott Myers, *Every Employee a Manager*, McGraw-Hill, New York, 1970, pp. 28, 31.

12. Alfred J. Marrow, David G. Bowers, and Stanley E. Seashore, *Management by Participation*, Harper & Row, New York, 1967.

13. Stanley E. Seashore and David G. Bowers, "The Durability of Organizational Change," *American Psychology*, March 1970.

14. Robert Townsend, *Up the Organization*, Alfred A. Knopf, New York, 1970, pp. 140–141.

15. Robert R. Blake and Jane S. Mouton, *The Managerial Grid*, Gulf Publishing Company, Houston, 1964, pp. 18–56.

16. Shigeru Kobayashi, *Creative Management*, AMA, 1971, pp. 131, 167.

17. Ibid., pp. 37, 16.

18. Ibid., p. 56.
19. Ibid., pp. 146, 201.

Chapter 10

1. Frank Goble, *The Third Force*, Grossman Publishers, New York, 1970.
2. Abraham H. Maslow, *Eupsychian Management*, Richard D. Irwin, Inc., and The Dorsey Press, Homewood, Ill., 1965, pp. 42–43.
3. Ibid., p. 72.
4. Abraham H. Maslow, *Toward a Psychology of Being*, D. Van Nostrand Company, New York, 1962.
5. ———, "The Need to Know and the Fear of Knowing," *The Journal of General Psychology*, 1963, p. 68.

Chapter 11

1. Neil A. Armstrong, "The Proper Role of Technology," *U.S. News & World Report*, January 11, 1971, p. 32.
2. Maxwell Maltz, *Psycho-Cybernetics*, Wilshire Book Company, Hollywood, Calif., 1964, p. xvi.
3. Herbert A. Otto, *Group Methods to Actualize Human Potential, A Handbook*, Holistic Press, Beverly Hills, Calif., 2d ed., 1970, p. 118.
4. "How to Make Your Employees Work as Hard as You Do," *Business Management*, February, 1965.
5. William J. Crockett, "End Corporate Tyranny," *Administrative Management*, July 1971.
6. Mitchell Fein, "Motivation for Work," Monograph No. 4, American Institute of Industrial Engineers, Inc., New York, 1971, p. 1.
7. Warren J. Bowles, "The Management of Motivation: A Company-Wide Program," *Personnel*, July/August, 1966.
8. Mary Parker Follett, *Freedom and Co-ordination!* Lectures in Business Organization, Pitman Publishing Corporation, London and New York, 1949, p. 21.
9. Adam Smith, *An Inquiry into the Nature and Causes of the Wealth of Nations*, The Modern Library, Random House, Inc., New York, 1937, p. 717.
10. Edward M. Glaser, "A Noteworthy Consulting Experience," *The News Letter*, Division of Consulting Psychology, American Psychological Association, Los Angeles, Calif., Spring 1969.
11. Peter F. Drucker, *The Practice of Management*, Harper & Brothers, New York, 1954, p. 132.
12. Shigeru Kobayashi, *Creative Management*, AMA, 1971, pp. 198–199.
13. Mitchell Fein, op. cit., p. 25.
14. Bert L. Metzger, *Does Profit Sharing Pay?* Profit Sharing Research Foundation, Evanston, Ill.
15. Robert Townsend, *Up the Organization*, Alfred A. Knopf, New York, 1970, pp. 61, 12.
16. Mitchell Fein, op. cit., p. 52.

17. Frederick R. Kappel, *Business Purposes and Performance*, Duell, Sloan and Pearce, New York, 1964, p. 194. By permission of Hawthorn Books, Inc.

Chapter 12
1. M. Scott Myers, *Every Employee a Manager*, McGraw-Hill, New York, 1970, p. x.
2. Alfred J. Marrow, David G. Bowers, and Stanley E. Seashore, *Management by Participation*, Harper & Row, New York, 1967.
3. Ibid., pp. 30, 121.
4. Sheldon A. Davis (from a currently untitled book planned as part of the Addison-Wesley Series on Organization Development), Addison-Wesley Publishing Company, Reading, Mass.
5. Rensis Likert, *New Patterns of Management*, McGraw-Hill, New York, 1961, pp. 145–146.
6. M. Scott Myers, op. cit., pp. 36–37.
7. Ibid., p. 49.
8. Mitchell Fein, *Motivation for Work*, Monograph No. 4, American Institute of Industrial Engineers, New York, 1971, pp. 6, 7.
9. Rensis Likert, *The Human Organization: Its Management and Value*, McGraw-Hill, New York, 1967, pp. 58–59.
10. Alfred J. Marrow, David G. Bowers, and Stanley E. Seashore, op cit., p. 26.

Chapter 13
1. Theodore Guyton, "The Identification of Executive Potential," *Personnel Journal*, November 1969.
2. Napoleon Hill, *Think and Grow Rich*, Fawcett Publishers, Inc., Greenwich, Conn., 1958, p. 164.
3. Arthur Gordon, "A Foolproof Formula for Success," *Reader's Digest*, December 1966, p. 88.
4. Herbert John Taylor, *God Has a Plan for You*, Fleming H. Revell Company, Old Tappan, N.J., 1968.
5. Norman Jaspan, "Why Employees Steal," *U.S. News & World Report*, May 3, 1971, p. 81.
6. "What Makes Them Excellent?" *Manual of Excellent Management*, American Institute of Management, New York, 1965, 9th ed., p. 2.
7. Abraham H. Maslow, *Motivation and Personality*, Harper & Row, New York, 1954, pp. 257, 207, 203.
8. L. S. Kubie, "Neurotic Distortion of the Creative Process," *Porter Lectures*, Series 22, University of Kansas Press, Lawrence, Kan., 1958, pp. 20–21.
9. Maxwell Maltz, *Psycho-Cybernetics*, Wilshire Publishing Company, Hollywood, Calif., 1960, 1964, pp. 110, 112.
10. A. A. Imberman, "How To Train Foremen," Imberman and Deforest, Chicago, 1969.

11. *Management* 2000, The American Foundation for Management Research, AMA, 1968, p. 111.
12. Rensis Likert, *New Patterns of Management*, McGraw-Hill, New York, 1961, p. 7.
13. ———, *The Human Organization: Its Management and Value*, McGraw-Hill, New York, 1967, p. 47.
14. Robert R. Blake and Jane S. Mouton, *The Managerial Grid*, Gulf Publishing Company, Houston, 1964, p. 142.
15. Rensis Likert, *New Patterns of Management*, p. 63.
16. Abraham H. Maslow, op. cit., p. 130.
17. Shigeru Kobayashi, *Creative Management*, AMA, 1971, pp. 133, 137.
18. Rensis Likert, *New Patterns of Management*, McGraw-Hill, New York, 1961, pp. 94–95.
19. Peter F. Drucker, *The Effective Executive*, Harper & Row, New York, 1966, p. *viii*.
20. R. Alec Mackenzie, *Managing Time at the Top*, Special Study 43, The Presidents Association, Inc., 1970, pp. 8–9.
21. Michael Gore, *How to Organize Your Time*, Personal Success Program, Nelson Doubleday, Garden City, N.Y., 1959, pp. 19–20.
22. David S. Brown, *Delegating and Sharing Work*, Management Series Monograph, Leadership Resources, Inc., Washington, D.C., 1966, p. 11.
23. R. Alec Mackenzie, op. cit., p. 37.
24. Ralph J. Cordiner, *The Work of a Professional Manager*, Professional Management in General Electric, General Electric Company, 1954.
25. "What Kind of Man Are You?" *Executive Health*, Vol. VI, No. 8, Rancho Santa Fe, Calif., p. 3.

Chapter 14
1. William James, *The Letters of William James*, Kraus Reprints Company, New York, 1920 reprint edition, Vol. I, p. 253.
2. William Raspberry, "Youths' Mental Retardation Laid to Slum Environment," *Los Angeles Times*, Part 2, p. 11, July 19, 1971 (© *Washington Post*).
3. Maxwell Maltz, *Psycho-Cybernetics*, Wilshire Book Company, Hollywood, Calif., 1960, 1964, p. 2.
4. Alfred Montapert, *Success Planning Manual—Executive Methods to Increase Your Worth*, Prentice-Hall, Englewood Cliffs, N.J., 1967, p. 34.
5. Maxwell Maltz, op. cit., pp. *xi* and 3.
6. Institute for Executive Research, Glendale, Calif.
7. The J. W. Newman Corporation, Los Angeles, Calif.
8. Herbert A. Otto, *Group Methods to Actualize Human Potential*, A *Handbook*, Holistic Press, Beverly Hills, Calif., 2d ed., 1970.

Chapter 15
1. Harold Koontz and Cyril O'Donnell, *Principles of Management*, McGraw-Hill, New York, 1955, Rev. ed., 1964, p. 173.

2. M. Valliant Higginson, *Management Policies I—Their Development as Corporate Guides*, Research Study 76, and *Management Policies II— Source Book of Statements*, Research Study 78, AMA, 1966.
3. Harold Koontz and Cyril O'Donnell, op. cit., p. 173.
4. M. Valliant Higginson, op. cit., Vol. I, p. 10.
5. Robert Townsend, *Up the Organization*, Alfred A. Knopf, New York, 1970, p. 147.
6. M. Valliant Higginson, op. cit., Vol. II, p. 43.

Chapter 16
1. Rensis Likert, *New Patterns of Management*, McGraw-Hill, New York, 1961, p. 140
2. Paul H. Davis, "Formula for Significant Survival of Private Liberal Arts Colleges," an address delivered in Philadelphia, January 10, 1966, at the Eighth Annual Meeting of the *Council of Protestant Colleges and Universities*, pp. 9, 24.
3. Robert R. Blake and Jane S. Mouton, *The Managerial Grid*, Gulf Publishing Company, Houston, 1964, p. x.
4. John Gardner, "A Failure of Leadership," *Vital Speeches*, January 15, 1970, p. 218.
5. Richard M. Nixon, Message to the Congress of the United States, March 25, 1971.
6. Harold Koontz and Cyril O'Donnell, *Principles of Management*, McGraw-Hill, New York, 1955, Rev. ed., 1964, p. 341.
7. Abraham H. Maslow, *Eupsychian Management*, Richard D. Irwin, Inc., and The Dorsey Press, Homewood, Ill., 1965, pp. 64–65.
8. Glenn S. Dumke, "Dumke Says Colleges Need Strong Ruler," *Los Angeles Times*, April 27, 1970, Part 1, p. 3.
9. "Marshalling Citizen Power Against Crime," U.S. Chamber of Commerce, 1970, p. 12.
10. *Friends in the Soaring '70's: A Church Growth Era*, Oregon Yearly Meeting of Friends Churches, August 1969, Newberg, Ore., pp. 5–22.
11. Ibid., p. 121.
12. "New Dimensions in Urban Action," Fifth Annual Meeting Report, Economic Development Council of New York City, Inc., May 3, 1971.

Index

profit
  corporate objectives and, 198
  management and, 2
Profit Sharing Research Foundation,
  113–114
programmed learning, 64
promotion from within, 45
Psycho-Cybernetics (Maltz), 104,
  151
psychological factors, importance of,
  182
psychological maturity, 134–136
psychological needs, 83–84
psychology
  management and, 80–81
  as new frontier, 80–92
  self-image in, 151–156
purposelessness, 99

Ramo, Simon, 38
Randall, Clarence D., 80
Reader's Digest, 129
reality, personal potential and, 154
Reality Therapy, 56
Repucci, L. C., 23, 27
"Request for Candidates" form, 45
research, checklist for, 194–195
research and development, 72–79
  computer in, 75
  employee role in, 76
  expenditures for, 73
  leadership and, 74
  procedural research in, 78–79
responsibility, 108
  motivation and, 116
Richards, Bob, 128
Rockford Motors, 64
Roosevelt, Eleanor, 134
Roosevelt, Theodore, 128
Rotary International, 129
rules, policy and, 157–158
Russell, Bertrand, 27
Russell, Walter, 150

St. Luke's Hospital, New York, 47
school children, participation by,
  172–173

schools, leadership for, 168–172
Schultz, Whitt, 21
Schumpeter, J. A., 72
Schwab, Charles, 104, 126, 141
Schweitzer, Albert, 134
"Scientific Technique" (Fisher), 10–
  11
Sears, James, 112
Sears, Roebuck and Company, 36,
  126, 134
Seashore, Stanley E., 4, 87–88, 138
security, motivation and, 105–106
self-actualized people, 83
  characteristics of, 96–98
  motivation and, 100
self-analysis, need for, 155–156
self-confidence, 98
self-criticism, acceptance of, 105
self-discipline
  leadership and, 132
  need for, 13, 98
self-image, concept of, 151–156
self-made leaders, 5
"self-organization day," 11
sensitivity training, 155
sexual needs, 99
Shepard, Mark, 119, 122
Sherman, Harold, 181
Sloan, Alfred P., Jr., 1, 26, 35, 43
Smith, Adam, 100, 107
Smith, J. Henry, 178
Sony Corporation, 37, 90–92, 111,
  139, 161
Southern California Edison Company, 171–172
span of authority, 36
Sparkletts water dispenser, 74
specific goals, need for, 13–14
speed reading courses, 144
Spinoza, Baruch, 134
spontaneity, 98
Spring Realty Corporation, 66
staffing
  checklist for, 191
  techniques of, 43–51
  see also employee